LEFT TO THE MERCY OF A RUDE STREAM

Left to the Mercy of a Rude Stream

The Bargain That Broke Adolf Hitler and Saved My Mother

STANLEY A. GOLDMAN

Potomac Books | *An imprint of the University of Nebraska Press*

Library of Congress Cataloging-in-Publication Data
Names: Goldman, Stanley A. (Lawyer), author.
Title: Left to the mercy of a rude stream: the bargain that broke
Adolf Hitler and saved my mother / Stanley A. Goldman.
Description: Lincoln: Potomac Books, an imprint of the
University of Nebraska Press, [2018] | Includes bibliographical
references and index.
Identifiers: LCCN 2018011997
ISBN 9781640120440 (cloth: alk. paper)
ISBN 9781640121492 (epub)
ISBN 9781640121508 (mobi)
ISBN 9781640121515 (pdf)
Subjects: LCSH: World War, 1939–1945—Jews—Rescue—
Germany. | Repstein, Malka. | Jewish women in the Holocaust
—Germany. | World War, 1939–1945—Concentration camps—
Germany—Biography. | Ravensbrück (Concentration camp) |
Masur, Norbert, 1901–1971. | Goldman, Stanley A. (Lawyer)
Classification: LCC D804.6 .G65 2018 | DDC 940.53/18092 [B]—
dc23 LC record available at https://lccn.loc.gov/2018011997

Set in Arno Pro by E. Cuddy.

May Day [1945] I witnessed . . . in the liberated
concentration camp at Ebensee . . . inmates
[parading] around carrying the flags of Poland,
the Soviet Union, Czechoslovakia, and other
lands from which they had come. Only one
group, the most emaciated and tattered, marched
without a banner. When I asked some of the
other inmates, "Who are those who carry
no flag and why are they not marching with
the national groups?" I was told scornfully,
"Oh, they can't march with us. They're the Jews!"

—Benjamin B. Ferencz, *Less Than Slaves*

CONTENTS

PART 3. LIVING WITH SURVIVAL

PREFACE

I noticed blood in my mouth and discovered that a shard of glass was embedded in the hamburger I had ordered at a local coffee shop. I was thirteen, and my mother, insistent on suing, took me to the lawyer who had written my late father's will, and who knew us well enough to have attended my bar mitzvah a few months earlier. His name was Donald Sterling, and he would later become the controversial billionaire owner of a Los Angeles NBA basketball team. Though still a young man who had started his own practice just a few years earlier, he already employed several attorneys. My case was assigned to an affable, heavyset gentleman in early middle age with a slight southern accent who, in spite of his being at least fifteen to twenty years older than his employer, seemed terrified of his much younger boss.

While he and I sat alone in his office I was startled to hear how impressed he was by my mother, who, he had just learned, had lived through the Holocaust. It was only recently that this gentile had come into contact with survivors. I said nothing as he made the odd and, I thought, rather far-fetched suggestion that being a child of that community of postwar Jewish émigrés, I was in a special position to write the story of those who had outlived the Nazi plague.

I couldn't quite figure out what he expected me to know and what I could tell people. Almost all my closest early childhood playmates had been children of my mother's survivor friends. Weren't we just like anybody else? I didn't see how our lives would be of interest to anyone. Surely everybody already knew about the German's camps.[1] Besides, even if I

ix

had known something other people didn't, the thought of ever writing anything seemed pretty unlikely to my thirteen-year-old self since of all my friends I was easily the worst student. In an era before anyone had ever heard of dyslexia, I was the slow one who couldn't even read. Having already been held back one semester, I was pretty sure I was being promoted from grade to grade simply because I was the oldest kid in my class. Yet, I never did forget my lawyer's peculiar advice.

After years of remedial classes, and at just about the time they graduated me from high school, I began to read at something approaching an average level. Able to understand the textbooks and do the homework, I soon transferred out of junior college to UCLA and then continued on to law school.

Careers in social justice turn out to be particularly common among children of Holocaust survivors, and sure enough I spent my first eight years in practice as a public defender in downtown Los Angeles. Ironically, given my early academic struggles, I would spend the remainder of my professional life as, of all things, a tenured law professor teaching criminal law and evidence; although with more than a decade-long overlapping stint as a cable news network correspondent, legal analyst, and occasional TV host. I am convinced I am the only person who collects, or will ever collect, a monthly pension check from both the Los Angeles County Public Defender and the Fox News Channel.

Communicating, in one form or another, has been my life. I have appeared as counsel at every level of state and the federal court, from defending drunk drivers before local traffic commissioners to the United States Supreme Court in a landmark Confrontation Clause case. I published over eighty newspaper stories as a special correspondent and Sunday columnist for the *New York Daily News* and authored more than a dozen lengthy articles in scholarly law journals, yet as the decades passed I never wrote a word about the Shoah.

Like many survivors, my mother almost never spoke of the specifics of how she had outlived a war to give birth to me in Los Angeles. She remembered the suffering all too well, but she never learned that her life had actually been saved by a bizarrely improbable and little-known bargain struck between a single German Jew with a Swedish passport and the worst mass murderer of the Third Reich.

My own discovery process began in 2006, seven years after her death, when I traveled to Israel during summer break to visit the woman who had been my mother's best friend during the war and with whom she had survived. The woman's eldest daughter, Dvora, happened to show me a pamphlet published in Hebrew, which she had acquired from the Israeli Holocaust History Museum at Yad Vashem nearly two decades before. It was a report made to the World Jewish Congress documenting the author's late war efforts to negotiate with Heinrich Himmler, the Nazi interior minister and SS head, for the release of a group of Polish Jewish women from the death camp at Ravensbrück.

Dvora had always wondered whether the circumstances reported, which sounded much like the general description we had heard from our mothers as to where and when they had been freed, might have actually been about them. As I flipped through the twenty-something page booklet, I noticed a grainy photograph of a large group of the freed women taken in Sweden just after the war. Though the figures in the picture were tiny, at the farthest left of the very last row I noticed two seemingly familiar faces. When I pointed them out to Dvora she excitedly exclaimed, "Do you think?"

It was a picture of our mothers as young women. We had stumbled across the first thread needed to unravel the mystery of how they had been saved. After returning to the United States I found an English translation of the document on the Internet. It would take years before I finally put together the entirety of the events, and once I had, it was a story I needed to tell.

As the Battle for Berlin was raging in the last days of the war, a German Jew named Norbert Masur returned to the nation of his birth from the safety of neutral Sweden in the hope of secretly meeting with the man who headed both the ss and the Gestapo. The goal of his absurdly dangerous journey was to secure the release of Jewish women from the Ravensbrück concentration camp. As luck would have it, not only would my mother be one of those women but the consequences of the bargain freeing her would soon alter the Nazi hierarchy itself.

I knew well a little Jewish woman whose
life was spared by Heinrich Himmler,
and the saving of her led to the death
of Adolf Hitler. This is how it happened,
and this is who she was.

PART 1

Malka's War

She was always cold. Even in Los Angeles, blessed with its world-famous temperate climate, my mother would still constantly complain of being chilly. Whenever people would ask, "Mrs. Goldman, it's so warm today, why are you wearing a sweater?" she would respond, "I voz vary cold for a long time, and I never varmed up." I don't think it ever occurred to her that people might not understand exactly what she meant. She never quite appreciated that a past generation of Jewish comedians and writers had long ago programmed their American audiences to immediately associate the unique, and now vanishing, Yiddish inflection with all things funny. Hearing my mother's heavily accented answer to their query would inevitably provoke a chuckle from the questioners, who would assume that the petite lady had demonstrated an unexpectedly subtle gift for humor.

She actually did have an acid sense of humor that could put people off, especially since she relished exercising it. When I was in my midtwenties a friend of mine married a woman my mother believed to be too old for him, and she never missed an opportunity to remind me of it. Once when I mentioned that I was going to be seeing him, she sarcastically asked, "Is he bringing his mudder?"

At about the same time, when I was shopping for a car, I told her that I had found a low-mileage, late-model, used Pontiac Firebird that I liked. She asked me to describe it. I told her a Firebird looked almost identical to the old used Camaro she had bought for me as my first car when I was about to turn nineteen. I added that this one was white and had a small black stripe running along the length of both sides.

"It has a stripe?" she questioned in her sardonic tone.

"Yes, they call it a racing stripe."

"Vat is it, a Circus ca? I'm not driving in any ca vit a stripe." I never bought the Firebird.

My mother could also be quite unintentionally funny; especially when it came to the malapropisms of names that were the product of her apparent conviction that seemingly everyone was Jewish. One evening I walked into the living room to discover her watching a Spanish-language telethon. Since she didn't understand Spanish, I asked what she found so interesting. She replied, "Vel, da host is Jewish." I looked at the screen and recognized only the well-known Mexican-born American television actor Ricardo Montalban as the event's master of ceremonies. Still confused, I questioned, "You mean him?" She responded, "Yeah, you see it's Ricardo Montalbaum."

She took very few vacations, but once upon returning from a week in Hawaii she couldn't stop describing how beautiful her hotel had been. She then added enthusiastically, "and ya know, it was a Jewish place." When I quizzed her about what she meant by a "Jewish place," she responded, "ya, it was at the Mordechai." For those unschooled in the nomenclature of Hawaii, she had stayed in Molokai.

While watching television during the Olympics she witnessed a few minutes of downhill racing and commented,

"What a crazy shport! You can get killed."

Shaking her head, she added, "It's not for Jewish people."

"Mom," I asked, "what is a Jewish sport?"

She thought for a moment, then said, "I doe know, I can't think of one."

"How about tennis, mom? Sometimes you watch tennis on TV."

As her face brightened, she replied, "Oh yeah, tennish vould be aw right. Dat's a vary nice game."

After my father's passing, my mother gave up cooking except on the High Holidays, when she would serve the one dish she could and did make, which was, of course, chicken soup. She would cook an entire large chicken in a pot for hours, until it produced what some chefs would describe not as a soup but rather a reduction. It was enough for barely two small bowls, but those two bowls were, as so many Jewish sons might claim about their mother's soup, very good. The problem was that she would then proceed to serve the remnant of the now overcooked and flavorless boiled fowl as the main course that night and the next. Once, when I was already in my early twenties, for the first time I finally protested this decade-old ritual by asking why we couldn't have something else to eat on the holidays instead of chicken.

She responded by saying, "Ya don't like boiled chicken?"

"No," I adamantly answered, "I don't like boiled chicken."

To which she surprisingly replied, with a slight shrug of her shoulders, her eyebrows rising, and the skin stretching a bit tautly around her mouth and cheeks, "Who likes boiled chicken?"

"Mom, you mean you don't like boiled chicken?"

"No, it's got no taste."

"Well, why do we have it for dinner?"

To which my mother logically retorted, "Vel, you can't just dro away chicken, vat would I do with it?"

"I don't know," I fumbled. "You can add celery and mayonnaise and make chicken salad."

To which my mother responded, "Oh." And then, in a rapid, thoughtful, yet matter-of-fact tone, "Dat's a good idea."

In her mid-seventies she underwent cataract surgery and about a week later said, "Stanley, I need to go back to the doctor." When I asked her if she was having trouble seeing, she simply answered, "I don't want to talk about it. Just take me back to the doctor." Her eye surgeon entered the examination room and politely asked, "Mrs. Goldman, is anything wrong, how can I help you?" "Doctor," she said, "your surgery, it gave me wrinkles." The doctor, glancing at me out of the corner of his eye, politely responding, "Mrs. Goldman, is it possible that you had them before but you were not able to see them?" "No," she disputed, "I never had a wrinkle in my life."

With her accent and her old-world, small-town naïveté, she did so often sound like the quintessential Jewish mother of an early 1950s television comedy that it was easy to think of her as an amusing stereotype; that is, unless you knew where she had been.

CHAPTER 1

"Left to the Mercy of a Rude Stream"

August 24, 1944 / Auschwitz

On August 23, Nazi control of both Romania and Greece had been overthrown. On August 25, the German garrison in Paris would surrender. The hegemony of the Third Reich was rapidly shrinking, but Stalin had just ordered his army to halt its advance into Polish territory, where Auschwitz was located, so that German soldiers and local Polish resistance fighters could continue to kill each other, thereby diminishing both of the Soviet Union's rivals for future control of the nation.[1]

There was no one to rescue or offer hope to my mother.[2] Her name was Malka, and she was one of a thousand young Polish Jewish women who waited. They had arrived in the camp a week before on one of the Łódź Ghetto transports. Having been processed together, they were now supposed to die together.[3] Five hundred women ahead of Malka were led into a chamber and did not return.[4] Now at the front of this bewildering line, she was next. Years later, her closest friend, who sat in that line with her, described to her own daughter what it had been like: "We were shaved. We were naked. We're not crying. We didn't know what crematorium means. You don't know where you're going. So I ask a woman guard and she says—'You see the chimney with the smoke, you are going to come out there.'"[5]

These waiting women were still alive while most of their friends and loved ones had already been murdered or died from the deprivations or diseases that plagued their subjugated population. In the ghetto from which they had recently arrived, none had escaped malnutrition as they lived under the daily threat of selection for transport to unknown destinations like this camp. Interviews with the survivors of the group confirmed that, until they were actually there, they were unaware that a journey to Auschwitz was a sentence of death. Such knowledge had been successfully kept from the isolated Jews of Łódź.[6]

If it had not been for her father growing homesick in America, Malka would not have been subject to a regime whose central creed called for her execution. Just after the end of World War I, hoping to eventually send for the rest of his family, my maternal grandfather, Samuel Repstein, traveled to New York City, where his eldest son had already settled. Even with the company of his firstborn, this new life was just too different. In his Polish shtetl (small town), Biala Rawska, seemingly untouched by the passage of time, he had been a respected tailor of men's suits who knew and was known by everyone. Lonely for home, he abandoned the dream and left his adult son in America and returned back across the Atlantic. Neither in the metropolis of New York nor in the shtetl of Biala Rawska was the danger to the entirety of European Jewery obvious in those first years of the twentieth century. A quarter of a century later, my grandfather's choice cost the lives of eight of his children and all of their descendants. Other than her eldest brother in America, my mother was the lone survivor of her entire family.

WHAT THE GERMAN KNEW

As a seventeen-year-old bride, Malka, who was the ninth of ten children, moved from the village where she had grown up to the nearby city of Brzeziny, where her new husband was able to obtain work in the city's flourishing garment industry. In the late nineteenth century, Russian Jews had begun a migration to this city and its surrounding areas, making it a center for the tailoring of men's suits and coats.[7] Like the other women in her community, Malka expected her life would be lived there as homemaker and mother, and eventually grandmother.

Within a few days of their September 1, 1939, assault on Poland, the Germans bombed and invaded Brzeziny. By the beginning of 1940, the entire Jewish population was crowded into a small section of the city and then circled by barbed wire. The Germans put the Jews of this ghetto of tailors and seamstresses to work making military uniforms.[8] Useful laborers were compensated with the barest subsistence of food. It was in this ghetto that Malka, her first husband, and their young son and daughter spent the first half of the war.

The lives of the Brzeziner Jews paralleled closely those of the Jews living in the nearby and much larger Łódź Ghetto, twenty-one kilometers away. Conditions were harsh, and life was terrifying for these Jews, who could be pulled from their homes or randomly stopped on the streets by guards to be "beaten or humiliated." The occupants were forbidden, under penalty of death, from venturing outdoors unauthorized after 4:00 p.m., with soldiers patrolling daily to ensure proper order and that no one dared to attempt escape.[9]

The Germans burned the town synagogue and then blamed the fire on the congregants and their rabbi.[10] As punishment for the ghetto's alleged crimes of smuggling in food and other essentials, ten residents were selected and executed.[11] One tragic innocent, who had the misfortune of being one of the ten, announced from the gallows that he was dying for his community. He was right.

With each new atrocity perpetrated by their captors, the Jews hoped that they had experienced the worst the Germans had to offer. How much suffering were human beings capable of inflicting upon others? No matter how horrific their conduct, however, the cruelty of the Nazis never stopped growing ever more unimaginable.

In the early part of 1942, Malka was walking with her seven-year-old son Archie when a German officer stopped them. The soldier simply looked down at the handsome little boy and asked if he was a *Jude*. When my mother answered that he was, the officer put his hand on my half-brother's golden blonde hair and remarked that it was a *shande* (a shame). Only later would Malka understand that the German had likely known a truth that she and the other Jews of Brzeziny were yet to learn: the fate awaiting the youngest amongst them.

About fifteen years later, when I was seven or eight years old, my mother and I began boarding a crowded bus heading eastbound down Pico

Boulevard in Los Angeles. As I got on just ahead of her, the harried and inattentive driver closed the door between the two of us and started to drive off, leaving my mother behind. She screamed and, running frantically down the street, pounded on the glass door until the bus stopped. She dragged me off and, while crying uncontrollably, did two things, neither of which she had ever done before, nor would ever do again— She spanked me until I cried from the pain, and when she had finished hitting, she squeezed me tightly against her. I was confused why she was punishing me for the bus driver's mistake, but even then I understood she had been frightened that I would be driven away, never to be seen by her again. What I didn't know at the time was that it had happened to her before.

A few weeks after my mother's street encounter with the German officer, the Nazis came and took her children—everyone's children—all the children too young to work. Archie and his eleven-year-old sister Genya had been in bed when soldiers ordered them to prepare to leave. The young ones, they said, were being taken to a village where they would be safe. The Jews were told that the transports on which their children were to be taken were already full and would return later for the parents. The adults cried and begged, but all pleas were rebuffed.

The children of Brzeziny were packed aboard trucks and delivered to a camp centered in an unoccupied castle along the Ner River at Chelmno about thirty-five miles northwest of Łódź.[12] Established in late October or early November 1941, the Chelmno camp carried out its first gassings of Jews on December 8 of that year. The airtight cargo spaces of the trucks had been converted to gas chambers. As many as 150 human beings packed aboard at a time could be asphyxiated within five to ten minutes by simply pumping in the diesel engine's exhaust. This would soon be the fate of not only the vast majority of Brzeziny's children but also hundreds of the ghetto's adults judged by the Germans as unfit for work.[13]

Attempting to remain detached so not to feel the enormity of what she was about to say, my mother once described to me how that night my seven-year-old half-brother had "dressed himself perfectly" and was led away in the care of his only slightly older sister, Genya. It was to be the last time my mother would ever hug either. She never saw her son again.

Though Chelmno was a death camp from which no one seems to have emerged, my mother always maintained that about two and a half years later, and soon after her arrival in Auschwitz, she saw her daughter in the distance and shouted out to her. The child, hearing the name Genya, turned, looked at my mother, and called back as guards quickly forced the girl to move on. If true, this would be the last time Malka would ever see or hear her daughter. Like her younger brother, she would be lost to a Holocaust that was to take 1.5 million Jewish children.

For almost two decades after the war my mother suffered from pro-longed, debilitating, and frequently recurring headaches, which first appeared the year after the war. In a time when doctors made house calls, our family physician would arrive in the evening seemingly almost once a week to administer an injection, putting her to sleep for a few hours. I was always relieved to see him. Without the medicine, the groans could go almost unabated throughout the night, sometimes lasting two or even three days.

During those days and nights of her illness, my father would insist that I be very quiet. With the sound as low as possible, I sat right up against the television screen, which I was allowed to watch while the rest of the apartment remained in all but complete darkness because even the slightest light could exacerbate her pain. Having studied to be a doctor in the old country, my father always believed that there was some medically curable physical source of her problem that the doctors had yet to uncover.

I had learned about my mother's two lost children while eavesdrop-ping on my parents' conversations when I was a child, and by the time I was nine or ten, I was convinced that their deaths were the cause of her agony. One evening I told my father that I knew why she was getting the headaches; but when he seriously asked me what I thought, I was afraid to answer because I wasn't supposed to know anything about my lost siblings and I feared getting in trouble for listening to things I wasn't supposed to hear.

My mother was blessed or cursed with an extraordinary memory. She could unerringly recall the birth dates of my friends despite having heard me mention them years before and only once. Ironically, however, she could not remember her own. If she had ever known it, the war had wiped it from her mind. When required for official documents, she had simply selected March 20. It was not a random choice. March 23 had been the day that she had given birth to her daughter. While it would have been too painful for her to have designated that exact date, she picked the twentieth as a reminder of the child's birthday. It proved an unnecessary prompt; the twenty-third was a date she would never forget.

My mother seemed never to have lost the need to atone for having been left alive when, by any realistic estimate, she should have vanished with those whose faces haunted her.[14] Nearly half a century had passed when she admitted to me that she had never again been able to see a young child, particularly a small boy, without feeling grief. The emotion had been there even when she had looked at me. It is a dark inheritance that, for decades now, when I see a little child I often cannot stop myself from thinking of the Nazis.

While the memories of those events that make us happy too often fade away, those that break our hearts seem to unceasingly abide;[15] and so even in her later years, she never spoke of her dead children except to describe their final partings, and I always lacked the courage and the cruelty to probe. I am therefore left with very little information about either of them. For example, though I know my half-sister's given name was Genya, I only know my half-bother by my mother's nickname for him—Archie. I waited too long to ask. The stories of their lives now lie only in a grave, and I must someday there, perhaps to learn them.[16]

There was, however, one other story she did once tell me about her first son. In 1937 or 1938 my mother was journeying with three-year-old Archie to visit her sister, who had moved to Belgium earlier in the decade. Knowing that they would be traveling through German territory, she bought her little boy a red ball. As guards passed through the train compartment, she told him to look down at his new present and not look up at the men. For good reason, she was frightened even then. It was a fear that would never entirely subside. Long after the Nazis had been subdued, the threat remained.

Night terrors involving the shades of their former oppressors are common among survivors,[17] and sixty years after she boarded that train to Belgium, my mother would often awake from nightmares, calling out to her caregiver. Disoriented, with glazed eyes, in a breathless attempt to focus her gaze around the bedroom, she would ask a bit sheepishly yet unsettlingly, "Are there Gestapo?" Then, regardless of the time of day or night, she would call me.

She was calling not because she was afraid for herself, rather she was checking to make certain that I was safe. Because there was no reason for the unforeseeable horror that had taken her first two children, she could never be convinced that it could not happen again. To her, the chaos of tragedy was ever lurking. Even after I had grown into middle age, if she did not know where I was every night, she could be thrown into a panic. She once confessed to me that the only time she ever felt I was truly safe was in those months just before my birth. Only then was I always with her so that she could protect me. I would be born to a generation of loss, and it is not surprising that extraordinary and pathological overprotectiveness would come to dominate our relationship.

THE END OF BRZEZINY

What the Germans perceived as the economic justification for the continued existence of Brzeziny ended in April of 1942 when manufacturing orders ceased. In mid-May the ghetto was officially closed. Malka's first husband, Wolf Hamel, was one of a few hundred men chosen to clean the evacuated areas of Brzeziny.[18] Those selected were told that after their work was finished they would be joining their families in Łódź. A surviving eyewitness who had somehow hid from the Nazis told a different story. Once these laborers completed their assignment they were taken outside the city to a nearby village and shot.[19]

Approximately four thousand Jewish workers were moved by train and wagon to Łódź. Even though the distance was short, it was so arduous a journey my mother told me that some died en route.[20] Little more than half of Brzeziny's original Jewish population of seven thousand had survived the two-and-a-half years under Nazi rule to arrive in the larger Ghetto Łódź where, when put to work in still-active factories, they would be given the chance to live a bit longer.

CHAPTER 2

"Salvation through Labor"

Before the war, Łódź had been second only to Warsaw as the heart of Jewish life in Poland. Located in the country's northwestern Warthegau area, it was a major textile production center in which a quarter of a million Jews, a third of the city's entire population,[1] lived as an organized and distinct religious and national minority. Jews and Christians shared one city and yet lived in two different communities with their own hospitals and clinics, secular and religious schools, theaters, public libraries, and publishing houses.[2]

At the end of 1939, the conquering German army ordered the Jewish organizations disbanded and forced the Jews into less than four square kilometers of the city's dilapidated northern district.[3] When my mother spoke of life within this circumscribed ghetto it was about the incredibly overcrowded block on which she resided and where, at the peak of the ghetto's population, several thousand families lived.

Given the region's substantial prewar population of ethnic Germans, the city was officially annexed to the Reich and renamed "Litzmannstadt," after the German general who had conquered it during World War I.[4] Streets were assigned German names, and, once the more desirable Jewish neighborhoods were emptied, apartments were given to ethnic Germans arriving from territory under Soviet control.[5] All of this was consistent with the Nazi obsession with what they designated *Lebensraum* (living space)—the need to eliminate indigenous populations so that the land could be occupied by more deserving Aryans. The Nazis saw large spaces in which their own kind could move around as encouraging the fulfillment of their race's physical potential, while in contrast, congested ghettos seemed to them appropriate for Jews.[6] Some thirty-five years earlier, when Germany still ruled Namibia (known as German South West Africa at the time), the African population had been subjected to the twentieth century's first genocide as German forces attempted to "exterminate two rebellious ethnic groups (the Herero and Nama)" in an effort that included concentration camps.[7] One hundred thousand Namibians would die. No longer in control of overseas colonies, like those still ruled by Britain, France, or Belgium, the Nazis would try to create their own in Europe.

The first ghetto established in occupied Poland, Łódź was intended to be little more than a short-term point of transport from which Jews would be shipped.[8] In December 1939, one of the German officials in charge emphatically urged his superiors to swiftly "burn out this bubonic [Jewish] plague."[9] Instead, settling the Jews in a closed quarter had not only made it easy for their jailers to take the last of their valuables it also provided the Germans the opportunity to exploit them as nearly free labor.[10]

Yellow stars were affixed to the chests and the backs of the members of a populace who were routinely beaten on the streets by soldiers.[11] In May 1940, after imposing a 7:00 p.m. to 8:00 a.m. curfew, the Germans had the new Jewish area encircled with barbed wire.[12] Anyone caught crossing or approaching the boundary could be shot without warning.[13] In no other ghetto was it so completely impossible for inhabitants to exit or receive goods or even information from beyond the wire.[14] There would be no armed revolt here, as would take place in the more porous Warsaw Ghetto.

Though it is difficult to reach a universal conclusion as to what exactly inhabitants may have known about the Germans' eventual plans for them, and though some clandestinely possessed radios, living in a community so fully cut off from the outside world would explain why so many of the Jews survived for so long without understanding the true nature of the German's "Final Solution" to their "Jewish Problem."[15]

Uninterested in the details of ghetto life unless it interfered with their own plans, the Germans left the daily "administrative, peacekeeping, economic, and social affairs" to a wealthy member of the committee of Jewish Elders, Mordechai Chaim Rumkowski.[16] Held responsible for all perceived production failures, Rumkowski was beaten by the Germans on numerous occasions for a myriad of minor reasons.[17] Though to the Germans he was little more than the city's most visible Jew, the authority he was given over his people was unmatched by the Jewish head of any other ghetto and also made him an easily identifiable target for the bitterness and despair of those he was charged with organizing and controlling.[18] His leadership skills and the ruthlessness with which he imposed his policies did make him the most successful of his peers at implementing and sustaining production in ghetto factories and also made him the war's most controversial Jewish figure.

There are a few who have described him as being trapped in horrible circumstances while attempting to save as many of his people as he believed possible.[19] Certainly, among the Jewish leaders of the four hundred Polish ghettos established by the Nazis he was far from alone in accepting the false promise of "salvation through work."[20]

Yet never doubting or retreating "from his program of work and peace at any cost," and in hope of placating his overlords, Rumkowski seems to have cooperated with even the most horrible Nazi orders, including working his people to death.[21] The quotas demanded of and achieved by the Jews of Łódź, who worked long hours six or seven days a week, were often nearly twice that of the Polish workers in the city.[22] The accomplished output was even more remarkable considering the near-starvation diet and the unimaginably harsh conditions of the cramped, poorly lit, inadequately ventilated factories in which they worked as well as, for want of equipment, having to perform manually tasks that would have ordinarily required machines.[23] Local officials, the local economy, and the German government profited from what these malnourished Jews were able to produce, and influential Nazis were thus given a motive to continue to support the ghetto's existence and the survival of the productive portion of its populace.

However, the ss, which supervised the concentration and "extermination" camps as well as the slave labor plants located in or adjacent to those camps, did not control these more efficient ghetto factories.[24] Because they existed outside of SS Reichsführer Heinrich Himmler's domain, he saw them as an affront to his growing authority. Therefore, the elimination of all ghettos would quickly become one of his objectives. It was a goal that would take years to achieve.

In July 1941, a policeman in Litzmannstadt, temporarily assigned to Himmler's SS, sent a communication to the mass-murdering head of the SS's genocidal Jewish Section, Obersturmbannführer Adolf Eichmann. He reported to Eichmann that the German president of the Łódź district still did "not favor the liquidation of the Ghetto" because he was earning "a great deal of money" from its factories.[25] In support of this conclusion in a letter apparently written by the mayor of the city to a high-ranking official, there appears the seemingly proud statement that "the ghetto is no longer regarded as a labor concentration camp . . . but rather as a significant element in the economic system, kind of a vast factory."[26] Because Łódź had been transformed into one of the Reich's largest industrial centers, its productivity would permit it to survive longer than any of the other ghettos in Poland.[27] Thus, Rumkowski's strategy of survival through the unremitting labor of his people could have been seen as a partial, if temporary, success. Yet, for three years prior to its 1944 demise, and even before my mother's spring 1942 arrival from Brzeziny, Łódź had been systematically and horrifyingly bled of its Jews.

Before the war, the death rate among the city's Jewish population had been 9.6 per 1,000.[28] In 1942, it reached a staggering 159.8 deaths per 1,000 Jews.[29] They were dying from starvation, suicide, typhus, or any one of a number of other rampant diseases. Yet even this devastating statistic proved insufficient to satisfy some in the Nazi hierarchy.

In the second half of 1941 the Nazis' solution to the "Jewish problem" entered its ultimate genocidal phase. In the words of German historian and Hitler expert Eberhard Jackel: "Never before had a state . . . decided to announce that a specific human group, including its aged, women, children and infants, would be killed as quickly as possible, and then carry through this resolution using every possible means of state power."[30] "The killing of human beings at once assumed forms and dimensions unprecedented in history."[31] In just over six months, from the middle of June to the end of December 1941, German mass-murdering mobile units killed approximately one million Jews throughout Eastern Europe.[32] On July 16, 1941, Adolf Eichmann received a memorandum from the German commander of the Łódź Ghetto. It included the following ominous "humanitarian" proposal to maintain efficiency: "There is a danger of not being able to feed all the Jews this winter. Serious consideration is required on the question of whether the most humanitarian solution would be to finish off those who were unfit for work by some expedient means. In any case, that would be less unpleasant than allowing them to die from hunger."[33]

Systematic mass killing now reached the ghetto. The first of the sporadic, randomly reoccurring "transports" out of Łódź to places like Auschwitz began, and after each the suicide rate would unsurprisingly rise. In a speech given on January 17, 1942, Rumkowski delivered the Nazis' cruel cover story that those fortunate enough to be selected for passage were to be shipped to agricultural areas where they would no longer be caged behind barbed wire.[34] He may have been truly ignorant, or perhaps he suspected or even knew that awaiting those being transferred were not farms but unimaginably cruel camps, pitiless slave labor factories, or gas chambers. In May 1942, in the midst of these transports out, my mother's group of potential workers was delivered into this ghetto.

In September 1942, Łódź suffered the same fate that had befallen Brzeziny half a year earlier. Most of the sick, the elderly, and the children (amid the violent reaction of some parents) were sent from the ghetto.[35] The purge not only undermined Rumkowski's unquestioning confidence in his long-term program of "salvation through labor,"[36] his complicity forever sealed his place in history.

On September 4, 1942, he delivered the most chilling and now infamous speech uttered by any Jew during the Shoah and perhaps ever:

> The ghetto has been struck a hard blow. They demand what is most dear—children and old people. . . . I never imagined that my own hands would be forced to make this sacrifice. . . . I am forced . . . to

beg: . . . Fathers and mothers, give me your children. . . . Yesterday, in the course of the day, I was given the order to send away more than 20,000 Jews from the ghetto. . . . But as we were guided not by the thought: "how many will be lost?" But "how many can be saved?" We arrived at the conclusion—that however difficult it was going to be, we must take upon ourselves the carrying out of this decree. . . . I must cut off limbs in order to save the body! I must take away children, and if I do not, others too will be taken, God forbid.[37]

THE TAILOR'S DAUGHTER

In spite of the horrors inflicted upon them, the inhabitants were left with little choice but to continue laboring in the factories. The motto may have been "Salvation through Work," but the reality was "Starvation or Work." Every person who had not yet been rendered helpless by hunger realized that his or her life was dependent on having a job.[38] Those who worked were provided a single, life-sustaining, daily meal. Without employment, death from starvation or transfer from the ghetto was all but a certainty.

In Philip Roth's 1979 novel *The Professor of Desire*, the author's alter-ego protagonist quizzes a middle-aged Holocaust survivor, curious to learn how he had made it out alive:

But how was it they didn't send you to the ovens? How do you come here to be with us?

They couldn't kill everybody, [answered the older Jew]. There was a beginning; there has to be an ending. This is what I told myself every single morning and night. Somebody has to be left. I worked for them like it was my own. I told myself this work is what I wanted to do.[39]

A master of fiction, Roth captures the essence of the mind-set that aided some captive laborers to survive.

As the daughter of a small-town men's suit tailor, and herself an experienced seamstress with a facility for the more technical tasks, Malka was an asset at one of the ghetto's uniform factories. "I vas da last von at a table of seventeen vemen," she would tell me with unexpected pride. Other women would first attach the buttons or the lining of the coats, and "vhen they had all finished, I vas the one who vood sew on the collars and cuffs. That vas the hard part nobody else could do." It was a skill that would allow her to survive for more than two years until this ghetto's end. In his chronicle of the Łódź Ghetto, historian Lucjan Dobroszycki describes how the Jews had continued to demonstrate their value to the Reich: "Toward the end of 1943, under Rumkowski's leadership, the ghetto contained more than 90 enterprises employing over 75,000 workers. . . . Uniforms and boots, underwear and bed linen were manufactured. . . . Its workers were able to supply nearly full sets of uniforms for 5,000 soldiers in a week's time."[40]

There was, of course, one very significant member of the German hierarchy who was not pleased with Łódź's continuing success as a manufacturing enterprise. Fearing, or perhaps jealous, of the competition they represented, ss chief Heinrich Himmler continued looking for an excuse to justify ending their operations.[41] The Warsaw Ghetto's 1943 uprising had given him a sufficient pretext to soon eliminate all the eastern ghettos, with the exception of Łódź.[42]

Himmler issued order after order to transfer Łódź's residents to one of the camps under his jurisdiction, yet there remained a high level of resistance to the shuttering of this particularly productive industrial center. Thus, most of these demands by Himmler were ignored, but a few were implemented.

On June 16, 1944, Rumkowski announced a German proclamation requesting the voluntary registration of workers allegedly needed for manual labor outside the ghetto. When few volunteers registered, several thousand were taken by force.[43]

In spite of these partial successes, Himmler's plans to eradicate the last ghetto in Eastern Europe were being delayed by the intervention of the Reich governor of Warthegau, Arthur Greiser, who, along with other local authorities, was still personally profiting financially from the products of the slave labor. Himmler's most formidable opponent, however, proved to be Hitler's minister of armaments, Albert Speer.[44]

Often referred to as "Hitler's Architect" because of his original profession, Speer had once been a fair-haired boy of the Nazi movement. Hitler, however, would eventually grow disappointed with his "architect," whom he would come to describe as "an unpredictable and unworldly artist."[45] After the war, Speer would be prosecuted along with Hermann Göring and the other most prominent surviving Nazis as defendants in the first and most famous of the Nuremberg Trials. Three of the accused would be acquitted, with death pronounced on eleven others. Three more were sentenced to life imprisonment, and four were to be confined for terms of between ten and twenty years. One of those sentenced to twenty years, a surprisingly light punishment considering his position in the Reich's hierarchy, Speer served out the entire term in Spandau Prison from which he was released in 1966. Dying in 1981, he outlived by at least a third of a century Hermann Göring, his Führer, and Hitler's other most important late war advisers.

Speer's primary reason for opposing the destruction of the Łódź Ghetto appears to have been neither mercenary personal financial profit nor an altruistic desire to protect the Jewish occupants. More than a quarter of a century after the war, Speer, the author of the 1970 bestseller *Inside the Third Reich*, almost casually explained that the principal motive behind his approach to dealing with Łódź was not the hope to save Jews but rather a desire to do what was best for the German war effort:

> I certainly could've helped at times, for instance in Łódź, when [others] wanted to liquidate the ghetto. Perhaps I might even say that my considerations were not merely rational when I did a few things to enable the victims to survive. But I cannot claim that humanitarian considerations stood above the interests of a wartime economy. . . . I turned my back on the misery insofar as I perceived it. . . . For me the question of efficiency was decisive. Even if it had been possible occasionally to secure better treatment, the fact remains that those people were ruthlessly exploited. . . . We did not do what we might and could have done to keep those people alive.[46]

Speer, who would save himself from execution or even life imprisonment by claiming contrition for his wartime crimes, had not only believed that Łódź Ghetto's continuing survival was of economic value to the Reich, he also appears to have hoped that by keeping its factories running he might limit the economic expansion of the SS and with it the growing power of his political rival Heinrich Himmler. Unfortunately, since their Führer had long before "decided that the Final Solution of the Jewish question took priority over all else,"[47] it was only a matter of time before the head of the SS would be allowed to impose his will upon Łódź.

On July 20, 1944, anti-Hitler Germans exploded a one-kilogram plastic bomb in a conference room at Hitler's Wolf's Lair Rastenburg headquarters in Eastern Prussia. Twenty officers and Adolf Hitler were in the room. Three of the officers and a stenographer would die from their wounds, but Germany's Führer would survive. Himmler's Gestapo arrested seven thousand alleged conspirators and executed almost exactly five thousand of them. The attempted assassination immediately resulted in the trusted Himmler being granted new powers, and with them the leverage needed to overrule the decisions of Speer and any profit-motivated local official.[48] As Peter Longerich writes in his biography of Heinrich Himmler: "Largely uninfluenced by practical considerations about . . . shortage of laborers, or constraints on the transportation system," Łódź's time had come.[49]

On August 3, 1944, the first of the truly final transports began, and within a few days the city's Jewish factories ceased operation.[50] On August 9, armed with rifles, the city fire department entered the ghetto, surrounding one block after another. Under German orders, baton-wielding Jewish police searched the buildings and dragged out those attempting to hide.[51] By the end of August, what had once been the second-largest Jewish community in all of Europe would no longer exist; most of its occupants emptied into the crematoriums of Auschwitz. It was a fate not even the lordly Rumkowski would escape. In August 1944, possibly still unaware that death was their destination, the man whose harshest critics had labeled him a false Messiah insisted on accompanying his family to the death camp.[52]

If the Russians, having reached Warsaw that month, had not halted their Polish offensive, it is possible that more of the roughly 68,500 Jews alive at the ghetto's closure might have been saved. If there had been such a liberation, history might have had a slightly more ambiguous attitude toward the quintessential collaborator Mordechai Rumkowski.

Of course, there can be no certainty that if the Russians had arrived in August 1944 the Jews would still have been there. The German people proved capable of doing many things extremely well, and near the very top of any list of that nation's triumphs would have to be the speed and efficiency with which they could murder unarmed Jews. Yet there is some evidence that, had the Soviets continued their advance uninterrupted, more of the ghetto's occupants might have been there to be liberated.

Following an established Nazi pattern, some captives in Łódź (approximately seven hundred) were selected for the months-long duty of cleaning the emptied ghetto and were informed that, after completing their work, they would be allowed to join their families.[53] In a planned repetition of what had happened more than two years before in neighboring Brzeziny, once they finished their assignment, these workers were supposed to be taken outside the ghetto and executed.

Anyone visiting the Jewish cemetery in Łódź today can still walk just past the main gate and then, turning to the left by the wall, discover a few still open graves dug in that bygone yet not-so-ancient era. The Nazis had prepared these to be filled by those last few Jews of Łódź ordered to stay behind as the other residents were being deported.[54] The hasty flight of the Germans from the city in the face of advancing troops in January 1945, however, prevented the completion of this one particular crime.

Approximately 200,000 Jews passed through the Łódź Ghetto. Records show that in the summer of 1940 there were approximately 183,000 Jews residing there.[55] Including those who had successfully and remarkably hidden from the Nazis' forced evacuations, the liberating Soviet troops found 877 alive.[56]

CHAPTER 3

A Minor Clerical Error

Göran Rosenberg, a child of Holocaust survivors who wrote an account of his parents' wartime ordeal and their adjustment to postwar life in Sweden in *A Brief Stop on the Road from Auschwitz*, relates a short conversation he had with an elderly survivor:

> I ask where she . . . came from, and she replies "Łódź. And then from Auschwitz, of course," she adds.
> "And then?" I asked.
> "What do you mean, 'then'?" she seems to wonder. "I survived Auschwitz, what else is there to say?"[1]

On one occasion when I was complaining to my mother about something that was important to me that had gone wrong, and that I have now long forgotten, she gave me a piece of indisputable and withering wisdom: "Stanley, it's better than being in Auschwitz." The breathtaking comparison may have been intended to comfort, as well perhaps as being a bit of one-upmanship in a generational gambit of suffering, but, regardless, it was coming from one of the few who actually knew. To me it was ancestral legend, for her it was always there, precise and unalterable. How could I not expect it to be the skin of her every memory? How could it not be weighed by her in every comparison?[2]—The last time she saw her daughter—the steps to the gas chamber—the smoke rising from the chimneys of the crematorium.
It was Auschwitz.

Transported on a train that had been used for horses and cattle, Malka was among the last of the human cargo, more than 150 packed in each of the 290-square-foot cars, shipped from Łódź to the death camp. Piles of straw were the only bathrooms. Each day they would stop, the locked doors would open, and someone would shovel out the chaff and replace it. Though the trip was just over two hundred kilometers, as my mother told me had happened on the transport she had taken two years earlier from Brzeziny to Łódź, some of the already weakened passengers did not survive the suffocating conditions of the slow journey.

Elie Wiesel, in his memoir *Night*, describes how early in the war a few Jews from his village had been taken away on cattle cars. One, a synagogue shammash (beadle or sexton) named Moishe, somehow managed to escape and, returning to the community, described the horrors he had witnessed.[3] Wiesel and others in town simply called him insane. Boaz Neumann, in "The National Socialist Weltanschauung: Space, Body, Language," writes that Jews who had never been in the camps would not accept the horrible rumors that had begun to circulate: "They couldn't imagine that such a reality was possible."[4]

Malka and those sent from Łódź with her were in the same mistaken state of mind as that described by renowned psychotherapist and survivor Viktor Frankl when he too was delivered on a similar train to Auschwitz: "Nearly everyone in our transport lived under the illusion that he would be reprieved, that everything would yet be well." Frankl recalls in his classic volume, *Man's Search for Meaning*: "We did not realize the meaning behind the scene that was to follow presently."[5]

On August 17, 1944, when Malka's train disembarked at its intended destination and she could see the lifeless body of a hanged man, the terror was instantaneous. As the Jews entered the camp, the Nazis culled and sent to their deaths the oldest, the youngest, and those they thought looked unfit to work. Sorting those arriving into groups was the ss officer and medical doctor Joseph Mengele, sometimes referred to today as the "Angel of Death." Malka would be one of those Mengele—whose pristinely polished boots she would always remember—selected to live. There are estimates that fully two-thirds of the roughly 67,000 Jews in these last shipments from Łódź appeared to have been quickly dispatched to the gas chambers.

Though Himmler had originally wanted all Jews killed immediately upon arrival, the camp's mass murdering capacity had been unable to keep up with the numbers of condemned, and some new arrivals had to be kept alive a little longer than the Germans had planned.[6] In addition, as a consequence of the competing demands of military conscription, most German industry had long relied significantly on non-German workers.[7] With the decline in the Third Reich's military fortunes there came a commensurate reduction in their ability to sweep up new foreign laborers.[8] By mid-1944, calls from German companies for workers were growing more urgent.[9] By the summer, as the shortage was starting to reach critical levels, all possible sources had to be exploited.[10]

Purely as a temporary measure and not designed as "a fundamental change of a racial-ideological goal," some Jews capable of working were being kept alive in case of request by one of the many short-staffed companies.[11] Regardless of these demands for workers, however, since the Nazis had brought Jews to Auschwitz to be killed, using them for slave labor was to be permitted only in limited numbers.[12] Many of those temporarily kept alive and left to an uncertain fate were relatives or offspring of others who had just been chosen for immediate execution.[13] That the Germans had planned for these prisoners' lives to be transient could have been foretold when, of approximately 22,000 recently arrived and still surviving Jews from Łódź, only 3,000 were given registration numbers.[14] None of the women in Malka's particular group were ever to bear the tattoo so commonly associated with survivors of Auschwitz.[15] Such identification was unnecessary for anyone so unlikely to be kept alive more than a few days.

When Malka's group entered the camp, their possessions were seized, and they were given clothes recently worn by those already dead. Malka was taken to a barracks that was still referred to as the "Gypsy lager" because of this previous occupants, who had been led to the gas chamber two weeks before her arrival. Those prior inhabitants had been part of the 220,000 Roma killed by the Germans and their Axis partners, approximately 19,000 of whom would die in Auschwitz.[16]

These "quarters" were now so overcrowded that "ve vere laying, a few hundred people, one on the other," my mother said. In testimonials given years later, some of the women described how they were in such a shock that they could barely believe that it was reality and not a dream.[17] Each day they were examined by the Germans, and anyone found to be ill or even slightly infirm would be taken and never heard from again.

Less than a week after my mother's arrival, the Germans decided that it was time to kill her.[18] She and her fellow prisoners sat in line to enter a gas chamber, their bodies destined to be then carried on to the crematorium, where the evidence of their murders would be obliterated. The women waited on what was the very precipice of joining the hundreds of thousands of Jews who had already passed to their deaths in this place and in this manner.

For fiction to be believed it must normally possess at least a modicum of plausibility. Truth is not so circumscribed. A bicycle messenger appeared with a note for these prisoners' female SS guard.[19] Five hundred young women under sentence of death were led from the steps of the killing chamber and again given clothing to wear. One woman, who had been sitting at the front of the line near Malka, would tell interviewers at the Yad Vashem Holocaust Museum in Jerusalem: "Two minutes later and I wouldn't be here."[20]

One of the other women from the same group would later summarize how and where they were taken:

> [From] Auschwitz [we were] transported in a freight car to Neukölln, near Berlin. There were about 500 women in the transport [all] from Łódź ... about 100 girls in each car. The trip took three days and three nights. There was nothing to eat on the way and only little water to drink. . . . We were not allowed to leave the car. . . . At Neukölln we were taken directly to three barracks surrounded by barbed wire. . . . We were guarded by many SS women who told us that it was a Krupp company.[21]

They had been shipped to a munitions factory in the Neukölln section of Berlin owned by the legendary German armaments manufacturing family Krupp. Located on Braunauer Strasse, a street named for Hitler's birthplace, the factory sat five miles from the city's center. Today, the street, renamed Sonnenallee, is in a fashionable neighborhood with only a plaque to remind passersby of what had once stood there.

The head of the company, Alfried Krupp, believed that females were better suited than males for his technical work.[22] In order to fulfill its quota for the production of control mechanisms for bombs, his Berlin plant had requested five hundred women to supplement the company's employees and non-Jewish forced laborers.[23]

The plant had actually requested non-Jews, and had stated a preference for French women. There was a misunderstanding once the request had been received in the death camp and the infinitely improbable had taken place.[24] As a by-product of this minor clerical error, and as a surprise to those in charge of the factory, the plant now had five hundred Jews, and those Jews still had their lives.

It was not the first time, nor would it be the last, that my mother would be spared by a randomly serendipitous consequence of evil. She had previously been allowed to live in order to serve the German factories of Brzeziny and then Łódź; now her life was to be extended a bit longer thanks to the greed and dedication to National Socialism of a man named Krupp.

CHAPTER 4

A Führer of Industry

In the late nineteenth century, the long-established Krupp family of merchants and industrialists had already emerged as the primary arms provider to Bismarck's Second Reich, and would continue as the country's principal munitions supplier through World War I. During the 1930s, the head of the family, Gustav Krupp, devoted a remarkable amount of time to strengthening his Nazi ties.[1] The Third Reich's leading capitalist and armaments producer, Gustav would be named by Hitler a "Führer of German Industry."[2]

It would be a profitable connection. Even before World War II, his family was to benefit "from the elimination of Jewish competition and the availability of valuable Jewish property at bargain prices."[3] As hostilities rapidly escalated, the company's significance as well as its bottom line grew to previously unheard-of levels.[4]

By the beginning of the war, however, Gustav began to slip into a form of senility and suffered strokes in both 1941 and 1942.[5] A few years later his physical problems and the advanced nature of his dementia saved the seemingly uncomprehending and all-but-voiceless Gustav from standing trial at Nuremberg. Allied prosecutors moved to drop charges against him and attempted to substitute in his place the man who succeeded him as head of the family business: his eldest son, Alfried Felix Alwyn Krupp von Bohlen und Halbach (known as Alfried Krupp).[6]

Though the judges of the International Military Tribunal (IMT) agreed to remove Gustav from a list that would eventually include the twenty-one most prominent living Nazis (including Hermann Göring and Albert

Speer), they denied the prosecution's somewhat tardy request to add Alfried to the catalog of defendants at this particular trial. The younger Krupp would be tried two years later before one of the twelve subsequent Nuremberg Military Tribunals (NMT), where his guilt would be determined by three American judges.

With respect to the company's profits, Alfried had been the perfect successor to lead the family business into the new German war. He had provided "faithful assistance to the embattled S.S. in 1931," when at twenty-four he positioned himself "in the vanguard of the movement" as a "sponsoring member."[7] His Nazi contacts gave him the opportunity to acquire wartime slaves for his factories and then to negotiate for government contracts that could only be accomplished by a company with such a seemingly limitless and definitely cheap source of workers.[8]

Hitler had not asked Krupp to exploit the Jews of Auschwitz; it was Alfried who voluntarily set his sights on taking financial advantage of the death camps as a source of labor. "Leasing slaves at 4 marks a head," and insisting that he be allowed to return any workers who proved unsuitable, Krupp's venture into "the slave market bore rapid and abundant fruit."[9] In fact, one of Krupp's own workmen admitted, while testifying in his former employer's defense at Nuremburg that, as a devoted National Socialist in good standing, Alfried had "considered it [his] duty to make . . . Jewish girls, some of them little more than children, work under the most brutal conditions."[10]

It is not known who first uttered the phrase *Vernichtung durch Arbeit* (extermination through work), or how many influential Germans may have proposed this genocidal strategy, but historians do conclude that Alfried Krupp was at least one of those suggesting it to his Führer. He is believed to have told Hitler that there was "no reason why [Jews, foreign saboteurs, anti-Nazi Germans, Gypsies, criminals, and antisocial elements] shouldn't contribute something to the Fatherland. . . . Properly driven, each could contribute a lifetime of work in the months before he was dispatched."[11] Business profits and "extermination through work" was a convenient pairing for the Nazis, and an idea Hitler readily accepted.

While many of his files were intentionally destroyed before they could fall into Allied hands, enough of these survived to track Alfried's use of slaves.[12] The plan was to have two groups of forced laborers. One group typically included foreign civilians and prisoners of war who, though compelled to toil under harsh conditions, would be allowed to survive. The other, smaller group was even less fortunate. Comprising predominantly Jewish prisoners taken from concentration and death camps, this group existed under the threat of being murdered at any moment or literally worked to death. The dead were then to be replaced by others similarly procured and equally expendable.[13] "Jews who were selected for labor rather than immediate execution at . . . Auschwitz . . . were [usually] treated like doomed sub-humans" at their new worksites, writes Richard Breitman in *The Architect of Genocide: Himmler and the Final Solution.*[14]

One of Alfried Krupp's Nuremberg prosecutors, Benjamin B. Ferencz, described this second category as "less than slaves."[15] Slaves would normally be considered property by their masters, and therefore valuable enough to be kept alive. This was rarely true in the case of Jews forced to toil for German enterprises. That a few Jews, working in factories like those owned by the Krupp family, ultimately outlived the war was not merely unexpected; there is no reason to believe it was anything other than an unintended error.[16]

A senior Krupp doctor, who had visited many of the fenced-in compounds run by his employer, described in a report the treatment of the slave laborers he had seen: "Conditions . . . were greatly overcrowded. . . . The diet was extremely inadequate. . . . Only bad meat, such as horse meat or meat that had been rejected by veterinarians as infected with tuberculosis germs, was passed out in these camps. Clothing, too, was altogether inadequate. Foreigners from the east worked and slept in the same clothing in which they arrived. Normally all of them had to use their blankets as coats in cold and wet weather. Many had to walk to work barefoot, even in winter." He concluded that "tuberculosis was particularly prevalent" and estimated its rate to be "four times the normal."[17]

Though there is no way to determine during which of their various confinements any of the slave laborers contracted this disease, my mother was one of the many infected.

Almost exactly half a century later, doctors at Cedars-Sinai Hospital in Los Angeles would mistakenly diagnose her as having lung cancer when a doctor misinterpreted the ancient tuberculosis scars left on her lungs.

Thanks in part to cost-cutting strategies, the Krupp family amassed staggering wartime wealth.[18] Even in the contemptible company of other manufacturers who also made us of forced workers, the Krupps' role stood out for its size and often even its cruelty.

Living conditions for Jews in most Krupp factories were typically primitive at best. While in some locales these inmates did live in sturdy buildings, in others they had to survive in heatless huts, old ruins, or under tents, and some were even forced to sleep unprotected on open ground. In these latter cases, it is difficult not to recognize the goal of "extermination through work."[19]

On the other hand, I cannot remember ever hearing my mother complain about the housing at the Neukölln factory in Berlin, which was considerably better than those normally provided to Jews working at slave labor.

The Jewish prisoners at that particular plant lived in rooms that held between four and fourteen women who slept in double-decker bunks. There were working toilets, and even showers with the surprising luxury of hot water.[20] The women were each given a toothbrush and overalls affixed with a yellow Star of David, along with wooden shoes and socks to be worn during their ten-to-twelve-hour day or night work shift.[21] Though they received only one factory-cooked meal a day, it was apparently the same food served to the paid German employees as well as the non-Jewish conscripted workers who were made up of Italian, French, Polish, and some Russian war prisoners.[22] While each of the three barracks in which the factory's Jews lived was surrounded by barbed wire fences in order to prevent escape; this soon proved to be an unnecessary precaution since the terrifying intensity of Allied bombings against Berlin suppressed any thoughts of attempted flight.[23]

The better than normally allotted living conditions provided to the Jews of this Berlin factory may in part be explained by the plant having requested only non-Jewish laborers. Given the normal hierarchy of German forced labor, had Jews been expected, the factory might have been allocated lesser resources for each such worker. Yet, though the accommodations may have been better, the work required of some of the Jews in this Berlin plant could still be arduous, painful, and dangerous. One of the women would years later recount:

> It was impossible to do all that was demanded of us. . . . I worked in a galvanizing section, dipping hot irons into cold water. The sparks flew into my eyes and burned my hands. It was terrible. . . . I can hardly believe that I'm still alive today. The German civilian foreman of the Krupp Company kept rushing us and we were all so terrified that if we stopped or slowed down we would be put in [a] crematorium, that we worked to the last ounce of our strength. I endured this for nine months. . . . When I think of the time I had to work for Krupp it seems like another world.[24]

It is a testament to how nightmarish was the standard treatment of Jews that even these horrible conditions were better than those experienced in other SS-run work camps. For example, it was typical for Krupp factories to ask the camps to supply them with foreign women in lots of approximately five hundred; and on the same day my mother's group was being transported to Neukölln in Berlin, another group of five hundred young Jewish women had been sent from Auschwitz to the Krupp plant at Essen in the Ruhr.[25] Author William Manchester recounts:

> These Jewesses . . . first marched past Humboldtstrasse's new watchtowers on August 25, 1944. . . . By all accounts [the Lagerführer (the SS officer in charge of the women) Oskar] Rieck seems to have stepped straight from a wartime B-movie. Short, scar-faced, and jackbooted, he always carried a rubber hose in one hand and a long leather whip in the other [which he would use on the Jewish prisoners]. If this description were based solely on the recollections of his victims, one might wonder, but it is supported in every

detail by the Commandant staff [who confirmed the prisoners' characterization].[26]

The horror stories of the mistreatment of Jews taking place at Krupp's plant in the Ruhr Valley at the same time demonstrates how "comparatively benign" a camp was the Neukölln, where Jews were neither murdered nor severely beaten.[27] Though once fall and winter came they possessed neither enough clothing nor food to properly cope with the elements or the work, none of the Jewish women perished from cold or starvation as was the case in many other factories.[28] In fact, the women lucky enough to have been assigned to assembling mechanisms or creating molds, rather than the dangerous and exhausting work of galvanizing, understood how much worse their lives might have been.

That is not to say that things began well for these five hundred Jews. With their arrival at the Berlin Krupp factory came a warning from the guards who delivered them that their prisoners had better be watched carefully because they were criminals. As they marched onto the factory grounds, some German employees could be heard shouting, "Murderers!"

At first one of the female SS, who was the cruelest of the guards, was so brutal toward the women that they began secretly referring to her as "the Blonde Poison."[29] Given the women's fear and hatred of this guard, my mother relished describing the night when she and the "Blonde Poison" were in the same underground shelter during one of the many Allied nighttime raids. To the surprise of the prisoners, this normally frightening guard was the only one cowering in a corner and whimpering as the threatening explosions shook the wooden timbers. Seeing this, Malka turned to a fellow prisoner and, while motioning discreetly with her head toward their tormentor, whispered "Now Nazi, now who's afraid?"

I heard the story only once and I can still remember a rare rueful smile on her face as she told it.

Soon after their arrival, however, the manner in which these Jews were treated started to soften a bit, when the supervisors and other personnel began to doubt that there was anything dangerous about their new workers. The young women, almost all of whom were under twenty-five,[30] looked and acted like traumatized victims, not evil perpetrators. In addition, unlike most other ss-run factories, which continued to treat Jewish workers as easily expendable, the Neukölln management seems to have understood and accepted that, with labor in increasingly short supply, and replacements difficult to come by, no less properly train, they actually needed these Jews whom they quickly recognized as possessing unexpectedly highly adaptive job skills.[31] Four decades later, one of the Jewish women would actually say that she and her fellow Jewish workers had "rescued" the factory.[32]

One incident demonstrated the plant management's atypical concern for maintaining a functioning Jewish workforce. One day the "Blonde Poison's" behavior had grown so menacing to her prisoners that a head supervisor intervened and startlingly informed her, in the presence of a number of her charges, that he would consider unnecessary mistreatment of his workers tantamount to sabotage.[33]

A few survivors opined that, along with recognizing the difficulty of replacing them, a possible reason for the general absence of excessive cruelty was that some of those employed as overseers at the factory were neither German nor Austrian but rather Czechoslovakian, and that they may not have shared the same degree of anti-Semitic fervor as most of those ss who governed other camps. Additionally, the factory was located in an area that had been, and perhaps today still is, home to what was considered a politically left-leaning workforce. Some of the Jewish women speculated to interviewers that the local worker's politics might have accounted for their non-Nazi-like predisposition to pity rather than hate their oppressed coworkers.[34]

Whatever the reason—be it politics, practicality, or simple humanity—unlike at other forced labor facilities, most of the ss and the employed German workers in Neukölln did not gratuitously mistreat their Jewish captives. While some of those assigned to the most difficult work may have still been living in a kind of hell, even for those treated worst, it was better than the barbaric treatment meted out almost everywhere else the ss controlled a Jew's fate.

It is also possible that the single most important factor distinguishing this slave labor factory from others under SS control may have been the man and woman in charge of the Jewish prisoners.[35] Though Bruno Kreitich (the head of the factory) and Margarete Trampnan (an older woman in charge of supervising the female captives) were both members of the SS who were running a factory manufacturing bombs for the Reich, neither showed much interest in frightening or making these young women suffer.

As the supervisors of a small factory, physically separated from any camp, they may have felt little external pressure from SS norms in their treatment of Jews.[36] Many of the survivors when interviewed decades later recalled small acts of kindness performed by one or both of these head supervisors, who actually encouraged their prisoners to simply call them "Vati" (papa) and "Mutti" (mama).[37] It was a small gesture, but allowing Jews to call SS officers by such or any nicknames wasn't happening anywhere else. After the war, Kreitich, though not his subordinate, Trampnan, was arrested by Allied troops.[38] Before he could be tried for war crimes, he was released thanks to a series of positive testimonials provided by these Jewish workers.[39] There is a case to be made that, like Otto Schindler, Kreitich (and perhaps Trampnan) deserve credit for the eventual survival of at least some of the Jews in their employ. On the other hand, there is also a chance that the prisoners' positive image of their jailers may have been colored by a type of Stockholm syndrome whereby captives, feeling the need to identify with their captors, overly magnify the significance of the smallest and only sporadically offered gestures of kindness.

Under standard SS practice, for example, any Jew who was injured or who became ill while working at a labor camp was to be immediately shipped to the nearest concentration camp, with execution rather than treatment as the likely consequence.[40] One woman with a heart condition was sent from the factory to the camp at Sachsenhausen and never seen again. It seems improbable that Kreitich would not have understood that he was sending the young woman to her death. Though this appears to have been the only time he followed this merciless procedure, it may have been the reason why some of the women constantly feared transport to death camps.

Apart from this one incident, however, almost all of the other Jews who were injured or ill, including those suffering from severe health problems, appear to have been kept on the premises for treatment. Kreitich even violated ss protocol by taking one girl out of the plant to be treated for a bad toothache, and again by transporting to a nearby hospital in Berlin a young woman who had lost a finger while working.[41]

How does one explain such paradoxical behavior, in which the head of an ss factory consigns one ill woman to likely death, while risking the disapproval of his superiors by going out of his way to help others? Perhaps, though indifferent to their lives at first, he grew sympathetic as he began to know them. There is, however, a more cynical explanation in which such seemingly contradictory behavior can be rendered consistent. The young woman with a heart ailment was simply too sick to be of any further use and was thus a drain on limited resources, while someone with a toothache or a missing finger, once administered proper medical treatment, was still capable of contributing. Those who could serve the factory lived, while those who could not would be cast off.

Similarly, while it is unclear whether Kreitich and Trampnan could have done more to feed and clothe their slaves, what is known is that the women were never given enough to wear to keep them warm in the winter, nor were they fed enough to keep them much above starvation levels. Some of those who survived seemed never to have outgrown the fear of cold and hunger. When interviewed, Jewish survivors of the camps and slave labor speak of their persistent dreams in the war of bread and being able to eat as much of it as they could.[42]

There was never room in my mother's freezer for anything other than the loaves of frozen bread she always stored but never used. When they began to show signs of their long frost, they were discarded and continually replaced with new bread to be similarly frozen and eventually

thrown away. Finally, as a teenager, after years of frustration, I asked
her, "Why? Why do we have to have so much bread in the freezer all the
time when we never eat any of it?" She paused for a moment and then,
avoiding eye contact as she always did whenever a subject was difficult
for her, said, "Ven I vaz starving during da var, I promised myself that
if I lived I vood never be mitout bread." Her phobia exposed, she soon
emptied the freezer and never froze bread again. Perhaps I had done
her a favor, and yet, half a century later, I still cannot escape the guilt
of having asked.

CHAPTER 5

The Children of Luck

Protection from Allied bombing raids was rarely provided to Krupp's Jews. Though in a few locations they were permitted to take refuge "in the remnant of pulverized cellars behind the barbwire," normally their only safeguard from aerial bombardment was the primitive asylum afforded by hand-dug trenches.[1] Similarly, the Jews at Neukölln, although sometimes allowed to take cover in the factory's air raid bunkers from deadly nighttime bombardments, were rarely permitted into these shelters during the day, when a large number of non-Jewish workers were at the plant. As a consequence, the women dug deep ditches in which to hide from the daylight barrages.

Yet despite the peril from the constant air assaults against the German capital in which they worked and lived, especially in February, March, and into April 1945 when upward of fifty thousand were killed in the city, none of the Neukölln Jews died or was seriously wounded during the attacks.[2]

The company's German employees regarded the Jews' streak of improbable good fortune as something of a miracle, and started calling them *Gluckskinder* (lucky children).[3] Some began to speak about them as if they were the factory's mascots who might bring all of them good luck. Normally forbidden from even talking to Jewish prisoners, some workers, along with one surprisingly sympathetic ss guard, began to occasionally share parts of their sandwiches with the undernourished women.[4]

Even as I had entered early middle age, oblivious to the strength and resiliency that remained beneath the façade, I was utterly convinced that my mother was, and always had been, so weak and fragile that she had owed her life exclusively to fate. I was wrong.

Contrary to a popular assumption, for a Jew in the custody of the Germans to have survived required more than simply good fortune. There would often also have to be present a preternatural will to live, a mind agile enough to take advantage when opportunities presented themselves, and truly uncommon physical powers. For example, though based only upon my own experiences, every survivor I have ever personally known, unless they were suffering from some severe malady, possessed surprising and improbable physical strength.

Additionally, the willingness to partner and help one another, rather than go it alone, may be one of the insufficiently explored reasons why women had better success living through the Holocaust than did men. Access to resources and opportunities were increased when burdens were shared, and anecdotal evidence would suggest that women were somewhat more likely than their male counterparts to team up in the struggle to survive.

Malka had developed a close bond and friendship with a younger woman who, perhaps not so coincidentally, shared the same first name of her now lost daughter, Genya. They had both lived in Brzeziny before and during the two-and-a-half-year German occupation, and had been among the four thousand able-bodied Jews shipped to Łódź.

Himmler had ordered that, in his death camps, any sick or infirm Jew was to be killed.[5] In Auschwitz, where a limp could be a sentence to death, my mother was suffering from a badly pinched sciatic nerve but succeeded in covering up the problem by holding onto Genya as she walked. They had sat next to each other in the line to the gas chamber in Auschwitz; and by the time they had reached the Krupp plant, they had lost everything but each other and the desire to survive the German war against them. They were both left with demons that would never be overcome.

Genya was a bit larger than the petite Malka, who stood a fraction less than five feet tall and who, even when dwelling in well-nourished America in her forties and fifties, never tipped the scales at more than about ninety pounds. At about twenty-five, Genya was several years younger than Malka who, at thirty-four, was one of the older Jewish women. When one was able to scavenge food, both would eat. Even though in her later years she claimed that she never went looking for food, Genya proved to be the better at providing. Astonishingly, she had somehow managed to keep a small watch hidden through Auschwitz and into the slave labor camp, and traded it to a German guard at Neukölln, who, in exchange, good to his word, gave the two women occasional extra bits of food.

Genya also had the good fortune of having been assigned to the part of the factory that assembled timing mechanisms for Krupp bombs. Though detailed and stressful, it was not as physically taxing or as dangerous as were other jobs assigned to most of the Jewish women.

In 2016, I sat with Genya and her husband of nearly seventy years in their Tel Aviv suburb apartment. She told me of the elderly German factory supervisor who seemed concerned about his young workers. He would often bring Genya small portions of bread and sausage, which she would save and, once back in the barracks, share with my mother. Told by the old German not to speak of his rule-violating generosity, she was not certain if other women were also receiving extra food but came to believe that at one point or another he had likely helped all of the Jews working for him. Whether the older German's largess arose from compassion or out of a practical concern that starving workers would be less able to perform their assignments can never be known. Regardless, Genya and Malka would always be grateful to the old man.

One day in early 1945, there was a torrential downpour in Neukölln. By nighttime the grounds were flooded just as American planes began to rain bombs on Berlin. Malka followed Genya as they ran in the darkness across the open grounds toward the shelter when the younger woman stepped into what had looked like a puddle but proved to be one of the deep trenches dug by some of the Jewish women for protection from bombardment. The rain had poured in until it overflowed. Struggling in black water high enough to cover her face, Genya could neither feel the surface, nor grip the sides, nor breathe. Drowning in the middle of a Berlin factory, she suddenly felt an agonizing pain in her head and cold air on her face. Malka was dragging her from the ditch by her hair.

My mother described the experience to me in 1993. "I couldn't swim. I vas screaming and she didn't answer me, so I thought I'd try dis way, you know, they cut off our hair anyway so I figgered if I pulled it out it didn't matter."

Genya later, and independently, recounted a part of the story my mother hadn't. Malka, demonstrating her gift of unusual physical strength, had with one hand pulled her from the trench. Exhausted and unable to catch her breath, Genya begged Malka to leave her and save herself. My mother, refusing her companion's pleas to let her die, lifted and dragged her friend to the entrance of the air raid shelter just as a bomb exploded where the two had been lying moments before.

Genya would later tell her eldest daughter, Dvora, and me that in that moment she had given up and wanted to die, but Malka had forced her to live. The Germans had taken my mother's husband and ripped her children from her. She would never again let go of a loved one.

The bond forged by Genya and Malka would color their relationship for the rest of their lives. When I was visiting Israel in 1999, Dvora asked me if I knew why her mother always displayed a deference toward my mother that she never showed anyone else. Genya, who had never yet spoken to her children about the details of her experiences in the Holocaust, had always seemed to be the toughest, most independent woman Dvora had ever known. She prided herself on never catering to anyone. The joking suggestion was that if the president of Israel himself had ever come to visit, Genya would have surely told him that if he wanted anything to eat or drink he was free to "look in the kitchen."

However, when my mother had stayed with them, Genya was like a different person. While Malka (by then Molly) would sit quietly in the living room watching television, Genya would frequently come tiptoeing over and very hesitantly ask her old friend whether she would "like a piece of cake?" My mother would simply reply, "No thank you." A few moments later her prior partner-in-survival would return and ask if maybe she could bring her a cup of tea, which my mother would again politely decline.

To Dvora's bewilderment, this scene of her mother attending to my mother's every possible need would then be repeated throughout the day. Dvora asked me if I could provide any explanation as to why, of all the people in the world, her mother seemed cowed by the presence of my tiny parent.

I suppose the simple answer to Genya's daughter's question was that Malka, as the older of the two, had apparently acted as a kind of big sister or young aunt. Age had not withered her mother's memory of a time when Genya had survived simply because my mother would not allow either of them to die. Maybe this determination to survive and to force those she loved to carry on with her was in part a product of the guilt she felt at having been unable to save her children; or perhaps it was also a kind of retribution born of anger. Her revenge against the Germans was to live. Long after the war was over, this attitude and determination remained.

In the late 1990s, as my mother's health worsened and she grew weaker and I could no longer hide the concern on my face, she would proclaim matter-of-factly: "Don't vorry Stanley, Hitler couldn't kill me, dis von't." The source of her survival was in significant part simply a refusal to even consider the possibility of dying, or even speak of death. It wasn't that she thought she was immortal; it's just having lived through so many close calls, she wouldn't allow the thought of her own death to enter her mind; and having lost so many, she could not abide the very mention of anyone else dying.

I was about five or six years old and had a best friend named Edwin. The son of Polish Holocaust survivors, he was slightly younger than me and the closest thing I felt I had to a little brother. Edwin was a happy child, and I was always excited to see him. One day, my mother was acting strangely as we boarded the trolley bound for East Los Angeles where Edwin lived. She seemed angry or at least very upset about something.

When we arrived I could see Edwin's mother sitting at the dining room table with some other women. They were crying. Edwin's father sat in the living room surrounded by several men, none of whom seemed to be saying much of anything. I looked around, and not finding my friend I asked, quite loudly, "Where's Edwin?" There was a silence, interrupted after a few moments by his mother's wail. I didn't know what I had done wrong, but I was afraid to say anything else the rest of the day. I would learn some years later that my best friend had suffered an unusual spike in his temperature, and, before the ambulance could get him to the hospital, the wonderful little boy had passed away. At the time, however, I was simply disappointed not to have been able to play with him, so the following day, as my mother took me down the block to the local grocery store, I asked her why Edwin hadn't been at home. My mother, without looking at me, quickly answered,

"He's gone away."

"When is he coming back?" I eagerly inquired.

"He's not coming back," she responded.

Frightened by the thought of not being able to play with my friend, I questioned,

"What da you mean?"

Still not looking in my direction, she rapidly declared, "He's gone away and he's never coming back."

Confused, and after a long pause, I asked, "Even when he's old?"

"No." She answered.

Unable to comprehend, I bewilderingly followed up, with what proved to be the last query she would allow me to ask, "Even to see his parents?"

"No," she retorted, "he's dead and he's never coming back."

This answer was impenetrable to me, yet she was not capable of explaining or continuing. I had never heard about death before; after Edwin was gone, I started thinking about it a lot. Perhaps it would lead to my long puzzlement as to whether life is worth dying for.

Of course, my mother's refusal to consider even the very subject of death was not the attitude of every survivor, especially once they approached their end-of-life. Nearly sixty years after my childhood friend Edwin's passing, his parents, aided by their two surviving children and five grandchildren, took up residency at a Jewish Home for the Aged in the San Fernando Valley. Edwin's, by then, eighty-four-year-old mother, Sally, was suffering from dementia that allowed her to retain thoughts for only a minute or so before beginning everything again, while his ninety-six-year-old father, Sam, though still possessing the power of recall, was suddenly either unwilling or unable to speak English. Instead, all his attempts at conversation were only in the Yiddish of his youth. This made his daily existence even more solitary. Since seemingly not a single employee at this Jewish Home understood this Jewish language, the still philosophical old man appeared to the staff to have simply lost the ability to coherently communicate. When I was visiting one Sunday afternoon, Sam (who had survived more than five years in the Nazi camps and as their slave labor and whose first wife and child had been murdered by the Germans) ruminated to me in Yiddish his thoughts on life and his approaching end. "You know," he said, "we come to this place; we wander around for a little while [as he pantomimed a walking figure with the index and middle fingers of his right hand], and soon it's time to leave." Then he added, his head nodding, "I think it's time for me to leave." He actually stayed two more years.

In 2017, while I was visiting the ninety-nine-year-old Genya at her apartment in the outskirts of Tel Aviv, she said that she was now ready to die but was only afraid because she could not bear the guilt of seeing again her own younger sister, whom she had been unable to save more than three-quarters of a century before. Two weeks later, on the day before I was to return home from my eighteen-day summer visit to Israel, my mother's last living friend passed away. I had seen her three days earlier when she had held my hand as we briefly said our good-byes. It would prove to be the last afternoon she would be able to speak to anyone. While attending her funeral the morning following her passing, and just before I was to leave for the airport, her children and grandchildren commented to me how strange it was that their matriarch had died not only while I was in the country but also that she was being buried just

a few hours before I would be flying back to Los Angeles. I responded
sentimentally that maybe she had wanted a little of Malka there.
    Perhaps if my mother had lived into her mid-nineties she might have
felt differently about death, but I doubt it.

THE NEW AUSCHWITZ

In the first or second week of April 1945, having ordered most of the corporation's files destroyed in anticipation of a likely Allied arrival, Alfried Krupp seems to have concluded that it was time to also eliminate the human evidence of his crimes. The Jewish women of Neukölln were ordered transferred to the camp at Ravensbrück.[6] Located more than ninety kilometers north of Berlin, it was outside the zone of the most intense Allied bombardment of the capital, but it had not been selected as the women's destination in order to keep them safe. Rather, in April 1945 Ravensbrück was a functioning "extermination" camp with operating gas chambers and crematorium. My mother was being sent there to be murdered.

On the way, they first stopped briefly in the camp at Oranienburg, where they were to have their heads shaved as had been done in Auschwitz.[7] Bruno Kreitich, who was traveling with the women along with Margarete Trampnan, refused the order and allowed them to keep their hair.[8] Here was an act of human decency that could no longer be explained by a desire to satisfy production quotas. Perhaps these ss officers were truly looking after the young women. However, to the more skeptical observer, though he could not yet have known for certain that he would eventually be arrested, as the war was reaching its end any member of the ss in charge of a facility staffed by a large number of Jewish slaves might very well have suspected there could soon be consequences. Kreitich's motivation could have been to generate sufficient goodwill to secure exactly the kind of testimonials that did, in fact, save him from a war crimes tribunal.

After a day and night in Oranienburg, the women were moved the short distance to Ravensbrück.[9] In both camps, in which Jews were still being killed, they were shocked to have returned to a place reminiscent of the seeming lifetime they had spent in one week at Auschwitz.[10] The treatment they had received as slave laborers was benevolent compared to what they were now again to experience.[11]

Ravensbrück had become a smaller version of Auschwitz. Sabine Kittel in her essay "Liberation—Survival—Freedom: The Jewish Prisoners of Ravensbrück Concentration Camp Recall Their Liberation," summarized one survivor's 1945 experience and its lingering effects on her: "Because she had already been in other camps, she knew what could happen. The memory of her terrifying arrival and her constant fear of dying is carved into her emotions and seems to be present even when she relates her story much later."[12]

Since Ravensbrück had originally been intended as the Nazis' only exclusively female concentration camp; most of the guards were women. As one survivor put it, "The women guards," with their "big leather boots, flannel skirts, and big leather coats," "were worse than the men."[13] While postwar Allied prosecutors upheld a high threshold of proof of cruelty before bringing charges against low-ranking concentration camp guards, the extreme brutality of twenty-one of Ravensbrück's guards would later render them defendants before war crimes tribunals.[14]

At first the women from the Neukölln factory were kept outdoors, but they were eventually locked inside what was considered a punishment stockade amid filth and without food or water.[15] They were, as they had been in Auschwitz, so tightly packed that there was no space to lie down.[16]

An inmate who had been there since October 1943 described the final weeks of the camp as having been "a period of methodical extermination and horror that defied imagination."[17] One prisoner declared that, by April 1945, the ss guards had become terrifyingly "hysterical."[18] By the beginning of the fourth week of April, the camp was in utter chaos. The Germans were killing prisoners and selecting others for what were to be death marches.

Then something happened as implausible as was the clerical error that had saved my mother from the gas chamber in Auschwitz. Her life was about to be spared by a man who, in history's most homicidal regime, was its most terrifying murderer.

PART 2

The Jew Who Met Himmler

CHAPTER 6

The Last Party of the Third Reich

April 20, 1945: Adolf Hitler's birthday / Berlin

Trees broken and craters gouged by the force of explosions could be seen from the entrance to the New Reich Chancellery building. At about noon, air raid sirens shrieked, as they had for months. In fact in response to the significance of the day, more than the usual number of Allied bombs whistled downward against that morning's cool, clear spring air. Since the beginning of February eighty-three raids on the German capital, and now over 6,300 acres had been reduced to rubble.[1] Yet there were still sufficient loyal supporters, however, to raise Nazi flags and placards announcing their Führer's birthday on the ruins of Berlin.[2] An incongruous combination of chaos and order reigned in the capital. As foreign workers, some forcibly brought to the city, along with Russian POWs and Polish Jews cleared away debris from the most recent attacks, tuxedoed waiters still elegantly served their guests off of silver platters in the city's most prestigious hotel.[3]

Like many other buildings in the German capital, the Chancellery showed the effects of the continuous Allied bombing runs. Emptied of its extravagant furnishings, its carpets had been rolled-up, tapestries and paintings removed from stained walls and, along with valuable furniture, stowed in the air raid shelter.[4] The former grandeur of this seat of Nazi power now appeared a tawdry, haunted symbol of an imminent fall. Yet the few rooms that had been spared destruction were spacious compared to Hitler's narrow, poorly lit bunker, which lay beneath this structure and could only be reached by climbing down a perilously long iron spiral staircase.[5] Though the thunder of Russian infantry and tank fire could be heard, organizers felt the building would provide a more festive atmosphere in which to celebrate their Führer's fifty-sixth birthday.[6]

To anyone who knew the unspeakable horrors this Nazi leadership had inflicted, it would have appeared a macabre and chilling gathering.[7] At three o'clock in the afternoon, shriveled "up like an old man" twenty years his senior, his face swollen and complexion sallow, Germany's supreme leader slowly shook the hands of rows of exhausted soldiers and Hitler Youth.[8] The latter were arrayed in black caps and matching uniforms with bright metal buttons, as their Führer cupped their cheeks and ears in his trembling hand.[9] Though the Reich's elite praised and tried to congratulate the host, Albert Speer would later write that "no one knew quite what to say."[10] Like visitors at the bedside of an ailing elderly relative, they were tensely eager to leave.[11] This particular anxiety, however, grew not so much out of boredom but rather from a frightened awareness that the last remaining avenue of escape from Berlin was soon to be blocked by advancing Soviet troops. They could recognize that some sort of cataclysmic event would soon occur. During the course of that day, more than two thousand of the rare travel permits required to exit the besieged city had been issued, with a number of them going to this event's guests and their families.[12]

While the Nazi head of state ranted about his latest unrealistic plan to snatch victory from defeat, his propagandist, Joseph Goebbels, who worshiped his leader, and whose anti-Semitic rhetoric rivaled and sometimes even surpassed that of Hitler, lobbied that even if it meant dying there, his Führer could only make a lasting statement on the world stage by remaining in his capital. In stark contrast, Hermann Göring, a famous World War I fighter pilot who headed Germany's air force, insisted upon "a realistic estimate of how much longer" it would be safe for him to stay in the city before the anticipated, though unmentioned, arrival of the rapidly approaching enemy.[13]

Göring was right to worry. Supreme Allied Commander Dwight David Eisenhower had agreed to allow Berlin to be taken by Soviet forces.[14] The morning of April 21 would see the end of the Allied bombing raids against Berlin, as rapidly approaching Soviet artillery fire, which had begun on the twentieth, would supplant the need for aerial assault.[15] The sight and sound of approaching planes had provided some warning of attack, but cannon fire did not. By mid-afternoon on the day after Hitler's birthday, the blood and body parts of those who had not had time to reach shelter would litter the streets. Only four days later, when nine Soviet armies would complete their encircling of the capital, escape would become all but impossible.[16] In the next dozen days after Hitler's party, 1.8 million shells struck the soon to be captured city.[17]

To the shock of most of those present at their Führer's last party, Hitler suddenly announced that he agreed with Goebbels. He was not going anywhere. The Battle for Berlin had to be won at all costs; but if it was to be lost, he would rather order the city destroyed than let it fall to the Soviets.[18] Only if the enemy actually took his capital would he consider retreating to the still heavily garrisoned Bavaria in southern Germany, where General Schörner's army remained more or less intact.[19] The last days of the Third Reich were now upon it.

Hearing the surprise that his seemingly delusional Führer was not yet prepared to flee the capital, a nervously self-concerned Göring quickly announced that he was urgently needed in the country's South. As Hitler absently gazed at him, the man whom he had once designated as his successor declared that "he would leave Berlin [that] very night." [20]

With the precipitous departure of his nation's titular second-in-command, along with other frightened guests, Hitler found himself with fewer advisors whose loyalty he could rely on. Goebbels and Heinrich Himmler, who had been the ones to flank their Führer as he entered the Chancellery that evening, were now the German leader's two most trusted and important confidants.[21] Though Goebbels, a compelling speaker, had always been the more visible of the two, it was the easily underestimated, private, dull, and pedantic Himmler who had acquired the real power.[22]

HIMMLER THE NAZI

Beginning in about 1919, Himmler had accepted the right-wing tenet that Germany's defeat in World War I was caused by the Jews, the Socialists, and the Bolsheviks. He joined the Nazi Party in August 1923 and, even before he first came into direct personal contact with Adolf Hitler in 1926, as his biographer Richard Breitman concludes, Himmler had long believed in "German racial superiority, [as well as] the menace of the Jews, and had become a tireless worker on behalf of the Party's anti-Semitic platform.[23] To the Nazis, it was not the Jews' religion nor their ideologies but rather their race that had inevitably led them to perpetrate evil, and therefore it was the immutability of heredity that necessitated their elimination from Germany and then the world.[24]

Himmler was so obsessed with what he believed to be the secretive conspiracy of the "Semites" that he saw these "hidden enemies wherever he looked," wondering if those with slightly Jewish-sounding names were secretly of "Semitic" descent.[25]

Insisting his organization be populated by only those of pure Nordic bone structure who could trace their Aryan ancestry to 1800, and requiring that his officers establish their racial lineage back to 1750, he strove to ensure that the ss was racially as well as ideologically elite.[26] It also proved to be a marketing strategy that appealed to many Germans. When, as a young man in 1929, the leadership of the ss was assigned to Himmler, the organization's membership totaled fewer than three hundred.[27] In the first four years of his control, its numbers grew to fifty thousand.[28]

HIMMLER AND THE HOLOCAUST

Most of the specific plans implemented by the Nazi leadership had been attempts to bring to fruition their interpretations of the general desires of their Führer.[29] It was Himmler, revering his leader as a prophet, who proved most successful in this system of what Hitler biographer Ian Kershaw referred to as "working towards the Führer."[30] For example, while there is no record of Hitler having visited a concentration camp, the Nazi "Final Solution" was "the direct expression of Hitler's ideology and frequently expressed wish to destroy the Jewish race," and he assigned the implementation of this genocidal goal to the dedicated and efficient Heinrich Himmler.[31]

By the end of 1940 Himmler "had established the major elements of a general policy to resolve the Jewish question in Europe." He personally selected the isolated and easily camouflaged location at Auschwitz as the largest center for the total destruction of the Jewish people, and documents in his own handwriting provide some of the very "earliest evidence of the plan for a kind of death factory, with poison gas as the killing agent and crematoria to dispose of the bodies."[32] In August 1941, he approved the specifics of a plan, guided by him and drawn up by his subordinates, for the continent-wide complete elimination of the Jews.[33] He traveled across Eastern Europe encouraging, and sometimes witnessing, his SS's murder of the Jewish populous.[34] By the end of the war, he had "ordered more executions and massacres than any other man in history."[35]

Even those scholars who disagree as to whether the liquidation of the Jews had been planned by the Nazis long before the war or had been an improvised reaction to wartime events, all concur that had Himmler not existed, it is unlikely that the horrors inflicted by the Nazis on the Jews would have occurred as they did.[36] Simply put, there was no one more responsible for the implementation of the Holocaust than was Heinrich Himmler.

Nor were his chilling works limited to the destruction of European Jewry. He was also chief of the terrorizing Gestapo and therefore able to decide the fate of most everyone in Germany and much of occupied Europe.[37] His August 10, 1943, appointment as interior minister made him, second only to Hitler, the most important of all Nazi politicians, and just after the July 20, 1944, failed assassination attempt on Hitler's life, Himmler gained the power to command even the generals.[38] Given the scope of his portfolio, there had been periods in late 1944 and into 1945 when on a day-to-day basis it was he and not Hitler or Göring who had been the true ruler of Nazi Germany.[39]

Luckily for the non-Germanic world, Himmler lacked an understanding of military strategy commensurate with his new authority. A German colonel would record in his memoirs that when listening to Himmler discuss tactics, "It was difficult to avoid the reaction that this was a blind man discoursing on color."[40] Seemingly too frightened to approach actual fighting, he never ventured beyond the protected rear of any battle.[41]

Simultaneously also suffering from an all-but-paralyzing fear of admitting to his Führer how precarious their war effort had become, his reports to Berlin could be optimistically misleading. By mid-March 1945, Hitler had begun to understand and resent the scope of Himmler's combat failures and relieved him of much of his strategy-related military leadership.[42]

Nonetheless, Germany's supreme leader continued to see his interior minister as an astute political advisor, a merciless enforcer, and a fanatical driver of men personifying the highest principles of the "Aryan Germanic Men's Order of the ss."[43] At the time of Hitler's last birthday, Himmler still controlled the Reserve Army in the territory not yet occupied by the Allies, the "Werwolf" terror organization that remained active behind their enemy's lines, and he still maintained his leadership over the entirety of both the ss and the Gestapo.[44] He thus commanded a significant portion of Germany's still-functioning land forces. Only forty-five years of age, he appeared the likely successor to his Führer if the Reich were to survive its founder's death.[45]

CHAPTER 7

Meeting Himmler

With the birthday revelation of Hitler's suicidal plan to remain in the capital, the struggle for succession and survival had begun. Given the impending loss of the war, along with his Führer's declining health and disengagement from reality, Himmler had weeks before recognized that his future now hung by a slender thread.[1] Recalling that many World War I German politicians "had continued their careers under the Weimar Republic,"[2] he fancifully and fantastically dreamt that his ability to still order a significant cease-fire on the western front might be of enough practical value to the British and the Americans that they would overlook his prominent role in Nazi aggression and the murder of millions of innocent civilians. As Himmler biographer Richard Breitman concludes, "In spite of all he had done, he still hoped to be given a position of substance in a new German regime."[3] As he bid farewell to his Führer for what proved to be the last time,[4] his plans for the rest of that night, arranged a month earlier, were part of his ongoing effort to present himself to the West as a reasonable Nazi leader with whom they could negotiate.

Thus after departing the Reich Chancellery, Himmler would make his way to perhaps the strangest and most enigmatic encounter of the war—a meeting that could prove life threatening to even the powerful head of the Gestapo if word of it were ever to reach Adolf Hitler.[5] Already waiting for him at the house of a friend was Norbert Masur, a German-born representative of the Swedish section of the World Jewish Congress, who, acting as a private citizen, had flown from the safety of neutral Sweden into the heart of war-torn Germany in the hope of persuading the SS leader to free some of the Jews still surviving under Himmler's control.[6]

Masur would recall that waiting with him for Himmler's appearance was the head of the SS intelligence service, Brigadeführer Walter Schellenberg, who sardonically commented to the Jewish representative: "Hitler should only have known that Himmler, after the birthday party, would be negotiating with a Jew!"[7] Known for being cultured, ambitious, and dangerous, the Brigadeführer also proved prophetic in predicting his Führer's reaction. Eight days later, when Hitler learned of his interior minister's negotiations with a Western representative, he would fire Himmler from all of his political and official positions.

This impending fall from his Führer's grace meant that, in addition to all the other obstacles confronting this Jewish emissary successfully negotiating the freeing of captive Jews, there was a deadline that neither Himmler nor Masur were, or could have been, aware. What value would there be in an agreement with Himmler to free Jews if he no longer had the power to authorize either their release or safe passage out of Germany? An unknown clock was ticking—any cooperation by the Reichsführer in freeing Jewish prisoners would have to be performed before Hitler's April 29, 1945, discharging of the SS chief.

A VERY CONFIDENT MAN

He wasn't even supposed to be there. Norbert Masur, the Jew who sat with Himmler negotiating my mother's fate, was a last-minute substitute. The face-to-face encounter with Germany's interior minister had been painstakingly arranged and was supposed to have been performed by a wealthy Latvian Jewish refugee named Gilel Storch.[8]

Storch had always been something of a risk taker. The day he turned twenty-four, in 1926, he took control of his recently deceased father's company. He expanded the family business across Europe and the Middle East. He cultivated oranges in Cyprus, manufactured toys in Palestine, and produced fertilizer in Sweden. Out of Russia he exported pouches of diamonds as well as tons of raw materials, including phosphorus and lime chloride, into the rest of Europe.[9] He made a fortune betting that even a young communist regime would want to preserve its credit by honoring its obligations. So gambling much of his family's wealth, he bought up Soviet government bonds at 50 percent (fifty cents on the dollar) of their face value, and soon doubled his investment when Moscow paid off the debt at full price.[10]

Ironically, it was the Red Army's 1940 takeover of his homeland that led him to attempt a move to nearby Sweden. At first, the Soviets believed that Storch was too valuable to their economic program to be allowed to leave. Finally, he was given permission to exit Latvia for what was supposed to be a brief business visit and only on condition that he left his family behind. Then, even though they suspected he might be "a Soviet spy,"[11] Swedish authorities approved his entry after he similarly assured that country's foreign ministry that his visit would be short and financially related.

Within a few months, however, he used his considerable financial connections in both countries to secure not only transport to Stockholm for his young wife and their two-year-old daughter but also permanent residency status for all of them.[12] The family reunion took place just a few weeks before Germany's invasion of their native land, to which they would never return. Out of an estimated 94,000 Jews in Latvia, the Storch family were among the approximately 2,000 who would find refuge in Sweden.[13]

Storch would suffer the murders of seventeen close family members at the hands of the Nazis. His daughter later said that even when her father received word that his relatives had been taken away or simply disappeared, no one ever saw him cry. He had a different response to tragedy. While he had previously shown interest in saving Jewish lives, once he learned the likely fate of his own family, he became obsessed with liberating Jews.[14] Financially independent, he began ignoring his business and concentrating on a multitude of speculative rescue efforts.[15] He would spend little time at home in those war years. According to his daughter, the phone would ring and he would be off and not return until four or five in the morning.[16]

He was able to establish working relationships with men like Norbert Masur in these efforts to save Jews, but the aggressive, undiplomatic, and often disorganized Storch easily irritated those around him. Even the way he spoke, with his entire body emphatically acting out every word, would put people off.

While those he associated with either admired or hated him, it was said that he made no close friends.[17] Yet those successes he did achieve were undoubtedly the result of his fiercely individualistic attitudes and refusal to toe the line when it came to following his new country's bureaucratic procedures. Gilel Storch made waves.[18]

It took more than a year of work before he and Masur were finally authorized by the World Jewish Congress to establish an officially recognized Swedish section; and even after the two men had helped arrange for the boats used in the successful October 1943 exodus of Danish Jews to Sweden, neither Sweden nor the Allies appeared eager to support any of Storch's other proposed rescues.[19]

Nonetheless, always believing that if something was worth doing, it was worth doing on a large scale, Storch concluded that he needed to find a way to communicate directly with Heinrich Himmler.[20] Though this grandiose idea garnered little support from the Swedish government, there is evidence that Storch was eventually encouraged to pursue a meeting by a representative of the U.S. government's interdepartmental War Refugee Board.[21]

Established by presidential executive order in January 1944 with the goal of forestalling the Nazi plan to "exterminate" Europe's Jews and other persecuted minorities, the Refugee Board had placed a representative of Norwegian descent, Iver C. Olson, in neutral Stockholm to provide assistance and, if needed, to help cut through red tape.[22] Olson may have concluded that while no Allied government would allow any of its representatives to even communicate with Germany's interior minister, a private citizen such as Storch might be able to negotiate a prisoner release.[23]

Storch's efforts to communicate with the head of the SS may have first succeeded in the early morning hours of April 8, 1945. A last-minute phone call to Himmler, placed according to some reports on Storch's behalf, may have been the single act averting the implementation of a German plan to blow up the Bergen-Belsen camp and kill its remaining inmates. Though some have suggested that the threat was a false alarm, firsthand prisoner accounts describe seeing dynamite being laid beneath the camp's barracks.[24] That fateful call to the ss leader's private phone number was made by Himmler's confidant Felix Kersten.[25]

THE DEVIL'S THERAPIST

Kersten was an Estonian-born German from a well-to-do family who had become a prominent physical therapist in Berlin.[26] Although Heinrich Himmler may have been the second-most powerful man in Germany, he was terrified of the first: His fear of Adolf Hitler was so great that after each meeting with his nation's leader, the ruthless head of the dreaded Gestapo was seized by agonizing stomach pains.[27] Kersten proved to be the only one whose methods alleviated the minister's affliction.[28] Along with his eventual confederate Walter Schellenberg, the physical therapist would become a trusted advisor to the interior minister, for whom he also acted as a kind of "father confessor."[29]

In 1944, as Allied victory grew more likely, Himmler allowed Kersten to take up residency in Stockholm on condition that he return to Germany when summoned to treat his most important patient. The move gave Himmler a confidential aide in Sweden whose job it was to develop relationships with Western representatives in hopes of establishing a discreet line of communication between them and the ss chief.[30] Himmler, failing to grasp "the hatred and contempt felt towards him by the West," hoped covert offers of compromise and a willingness to clandestinely negotiate peace might save him from what he already understood could be postwar execution.[31]

Kersten, who was being handsomely compensated by Himmler out of foreign-exchange accounts as well as from the Reichsbank, was not only pleased to spend most of his time living well in a neutral nation, he also proved "eager to establish his own relationships with prominent Western officials."[32] He was growing fearful that, as a confidant to the mass-murdering head of the ss, he might also be exposed to eventual Allied justice.[33] At a Sunday afternoon tea party in Stockholm in late February 1945, as the already disproportionately overweight physiotherapist sat consuming an entire bowl of orange marmalade directly from its communal serving dish, he was introduced to Gilel Storch.[34]

Storch's larger-than-life personality, as well as the Jewish businessman's aggressive sales pitch, soon convinced Kersten that this wealthy and enthusiastic Latvian industrialist was the most influential member of the World Jewish Congress and the Zionist movement. This was an image Storch would exploit in his efforts to arrange a meeting with the physiotherapist's patron.

Storch and Masur had apparently bribed a South American consulate official into selling them a few passports, which they then disseminated to Jews in occupied Scandinavian countries just before those Jews were deported to Bergen-Belsen.[35] Some of the documents they gave out were real, while others had been clever duplicates forged in Sweden to resemble the few originals they had bought. This ostensible evidence of citizenship, seemingly issued by a neutral Latin American nation, may have given those prisoners possessing them at least a modicum of temporary protection from the harshest treatment in the camp, and, perhaps thanks to the documents, some of the captives survived their imprisonment.[36]

Storch bragged to Kersten that he had provided passports to Latin America for a number of Jewish refugees. It was a boast with a strategic purpose.[37] Given the specter of possible war crimes prosecution, Kersten realized that he might soon have a use for such papers if he should attempt to escape from Europe. He even seems to have fantasized that this rich Jew might even be able to provide him with entry into the United States, where the physical therapist dreamt of opening a practice.[38]

Overestimating the political influence of Jews in general and this Jew in particular, Kersten quickly concluded that Storch was exactly the kind of connection he had been hoping to make. On March 17, 1945, the physiotherapist proposed to the SS leader that the latter meet Storch. At first skeptical, Himmler agreed to sit down with this unofficial representative of the World Jewish Congress, but only in Germany and on condition that the encounter be kept secret. On March 23, a self-satisfied Kersten simply announced to Storch, "Himmler invites you for coffee."[39]

There remains the unanswerable question as to whether Storch would have been the right emissary for the job. The emphatic industrialist was not fluent in German, nor did he possess the (at least superficial) protection of neutral Swedish citizenship, his last-minute request for a Swedish passport having been turned down by Foreign Minister Christian Gunther, who even at that late date was afraid of deceiving Himmler.[40] There was also an additional complication that, according to Storch's colleague Fritz Hollander, seems to have most influenced the Latvian businessman's eventual course of action.[41] Fearing that the father of her three small children would suffer the same terrible fate as the relatives they had left behind, Storch's frantic wife Anja demanded that he not go.

Slow to learn the language of this foreign world, Anja Storch had never felt truly secure in Sweden. Born to a wealthy family and famous in her former Latvian social circles for her exquisite taste and beauty, she had been an accomplished musician who had hoped to become a concert pianist. Anja was accustomed to a comfortable life even before, as a twenty-four-year-old bride, she had married the wealthy thirty-five-year-old Gilel. Their wedding, as one might have expected, had been an extravagant affair.[42]

As news arrived from Latvia of the deaths or disappearances of her closest relatives, she reacted, unlike her husband, with long periods of crying and depression. The thought of now losing him was too much to bear. She first attempted to hide Gilel's Swedish refugee status papers and, when that proved not to matter, threatened to drown herself if he undertook what she believed to be a suicidal trip.[43] Thus, a mere two hours before his scheduled departure for Berlin, Storch asked his colleague, the German-born Swedish citizen Norbert Masur, if he would undertake the treacherous journey in his stead.[44]

The forty-four-year-old Masur was married and a father; but though his wife Ella also feared that her husband might never return, she appears not to have attempted to dissuade him from the audacious mission.[45] The concentration camps at Bergen-Belsen and Buchenwald had been liberated within only the preceding week or two, and their horrific conditions, likely replicated elsewhere, were suddenly well documented.[46] Perhaps Ella understood that the personal risk and even potential sacrifice were justified.

Something of a prodigy, Masur was just nineteen when he had traveled from Hamburg, Germany, to Scandinavia in order to establish a branch of his family's Baltic Fur Company, of which he would then become director. Unlike the often hot-tempered and aggressive Storch, Masur was reclusive, humble, self-controlled, and always polite. Most importantly, he was known to be a keen judge of people.[47] The slightly built, fervent chess player had already shown himself to be an astute, and even natural, diplomat in prior endeavors to save some of Europe's Jews.[48] All of these qualities would prove essential when negotiating with Heinrich Himmler.

Kersten would write that when he first learned of the substitution of Masur for Storch he feared that there was little hope for any successful outcome from a negotiation between such "an unassuming Jewish gentleman . . . with frightened eyes" and the Machiavellian head of the Gestapo.[49] With the benefit of twenty-twenty hindsight, however, the physical therapist would later revise this estimation and describe his traveling companion as having been "a young man, tall, slender, and well-dressed [with] a handsome, dark, thin face, which showed strong intelligence, energetic determination, and complete self-control."[50] (From the safety of the postwar world, Kersten would also pronounce his defeated former employer to have been a "Mephistopheles," with a capacity for cruelty" and yet "weak" of character.)[51]

Storch, who had proven to be a successful negotiator in various business and political settings, would always regret the decision not to go himself, and, in later years, having grown estranged from Masur, he felt his accomplishments were underappreciated.[52] Yet, it is arguable that his last-minute replacement may have been the better choice.

THE WORST PLACE ON EARTH

At 2:00 p.m., April 19, 1945, flying from Stockholm to Copenhagen aboard a Swedish plane, then transferring to a small German aircraft bearing a large swastika, Norbert Masur and Felix Kersten left Sweden with ravaged Berlin as their destination.[53] They were the only passengers aboard. This was Masur's first assignment outside the safe confines of Stockholm, and he not only had to perform it in a nation where being a Jew was a capital offense, he was going there to meet with the head executioner.[54]

The previous July, Masur sat with Raoul Wallenberg a few days before the latter left on a mission of mercy to Budapest, the idea for which had originated with Masur, in hope of saving some of Hungary's Jews.[55] Also present at that meeting with Wallenberg was Sweden's seventy-five-year-old chief rabbi, Marcus Ehrenpreis, who quoted a few words from the Talmud to the departing Swedish Lutheran: "Those who travel in the service of mankind do so under the special protection of the Lord."[56] Perhaps Masur had the same text in his mind as he made his dangerous journey.

Wallenberg would heroically survive the Germans whose genocidal campaign against the Jews he was traveling to circumvent, but, suspected of being an American spy, he would soon after be arrested and eventually executed by the Soviets.[57] While Masur could not, of course, know Wallenberg's fate, he did understand how treacherous was his own mission.

While Masur knew who Himmler was, and the risk he was taking by going to Germany to meet with him, he may have optimistically underestimated the virulent nature of the interior minister's antisemitism when he wrote that while "Hitler had a definite idiosyncrasy with respect to the Jews, Himmler never acted in accordance with his feelings. He would order cold-blooded killings as long as it fit in with his purposes, and he would change his ways as long as that was in agreement with his new purposes."[58] Masur surmised that, throughout the war, it had served Himmler's purposes to systematically murder millions. The Jewish envoy's life and the lives of an indeterminate number of captives now depended on whether this mass murderer's goals had changed from the slaughtering of all Jews to a willingness to sit across a table and negotiate with one.

In reality, Masur would have to surmount Himmler's deeply held antisemitism, which was so intense that he had long disapproved of the moderation he saw even in some members of his party and the army's aristocratic officers. Though anti-Semitic, even they could be surprised by how extreme were Himmler's policies toward the Jews.[59]

As Masur and Kersten approached Tempelhof airfield in Berlin just before 6:00 p.m., they could hear a few sporadic explosions and could see a city now dominated by ruins rather than buildings.[60] The German capital looked, in Masur's words, "as if it was dead."[61] His visit was a guarded secret from the Nazi leadership, who were preparing to gather to celebrate their Führer's April 20 birthday. Masur carried neither a visa nor any other legal papers justifying his presence in Germany. Himmler's Gestapo had simply ordered Passport Control to admit the man traveling with Dr. Kersten.[62] Soon after landing, the Jewish furrier was greeted by half a dozen well-groomed uniformed Germans who crisply saluted: "Heil Hitler." Out of either discretion or recognition of the surreal irony of the moment, Norbert Masur removed his hat and politely responded: "Good evening."

Their car was late. As they sat in the waiting room, the rabidly anti-Semitic orator Goebbels could be heard broadcasting over the airport's loudspeakers.[63] In celebration of the dictator's birthday, Goebbels was extolling the virtues and accomplishments of his Führer, whom he described as "defiant and combative."[64] Though somewhat subdued compared to his former style and no longer exuding confidence, he still spoke in the boisterously hectoring tone and with frequent use of slogans as was common for the Nazi leadership's propaganda speeches.[65] Regardless of the circumstances, the goal was not merely to persuade but also to preemptively drown out the voices or thoughts of any opposition.

Kersten would later say that at that moment he was "astonished by Masur's calm."[66] Seemingly unfazed, the only Jew in the Berlin airport prepared for his appointment. After a couple of hours' delay, a Gestapo car arrived and picked up the two men for the seventy-kilometer drive north to Kersten's German estate at Hartzwalde, which Himmler had given to him.[67]

Large regions of Germany remained unscarred by the conflict, but not the areas Masur was now traveling through. For an hour-and-a-half he passed ghostlike ruins of bombed-out buildings.[68] Taking detours to avoid streets filled with debris and closures caused by recent bombings, they reached the highway as the nightly Allied bombardment of Berlin was beginning. From the car, as they turned to look out at the capital, the flashes of bombs exploding appeared to lay unbroken before them. Both passengers feared that at any moment their moving vehicle would similarly be targeted for destruction.[69] Driving in darkness and with their lights off so as not to tempt Allied attack, they could hear the whirring of airplanes coming from every direction, but there was no sound of a German artillery response. The last of the antiaircraft batteries had been relocated closer to the front.

They drove by the town of Oranienburg, where the Germans had built a concentration camp and where an Allied bombing raid had recently all but destroyed the small city.[70] They next passed the camp at Ravensbrück, where my mother lingered in uncertainty. Located in a picturesque setting fifty-five miles north of Berlin and just thirty kilometers from Kersten's estate, Ravensbrück was still populated almost exclusively by female prisoners.

For most of its existence Ravensbrück had been a labor camp as well as a kind of way-station where Jewish women would be held briefly before being sent to death camps like Auschwitz.[71] Established on May 15, 1939, to house three thousand inmates, by 1944 there were thirty thousand prisoners in the camp.[72] A large number of seemingly permanent inmates, who sometimes resided there for years, were non-Jewish female members of resistance movements, or suspected criminals, from all over occupied Europe.[73] Jews seem always to have constituted approximately 20 percent of the population.

Kersten was well aware of the conditions in this camp. Since 1942, like other farm owners in the area, he had been allocated some of the paroled non-Jewish prisoners to help work on his crops. Many of these parolees were Jehovah's Witnesses who were still laboring for Kersten and from whom he had learned of the filth, illness, mistreatment, bare subsistence diet, and abusive guards dominating the lives of those confined in this prison so near his home.[74]

Storch and Masur had chosen to concentrate their extraordinary efforts on the rescue of the Jewish prisoners still surviving at Ravensbrück.[75] Not only was this camp located near to where the Jewish envoy was to meet with Himmler, it was also close enough to the Scandinavian countries to make ground transit, as well as access across the Baltic Sea, acceptable routes for a short journey to Sweden.[76] In addition to the proximity of Ravensbrück making a successful rescue more practicable than it might have been from other camps, there were also compelling and urgent reasons behind negotiating for its liberation.

On March 19, 1945, Storch had written a letter to Sweden's Department of Foreign Affairs, declaring that "in Ravensbrück, there are [thousands of] Jewish women literally starving to death," and demanding immediate action.[77] As if the lives of these captives had not been horrific before, German writer Sabine Kittel concludes in her study of Ravensbrück that "the westward shift [of] the front line had a terrible impact on those who [were] still clinging to life in the camp."[78] Masur would similarly warn that "the last days of the death struggle of the Third Reich could . . . be the death knell of the few remaining inmates, who [had managed to come] through all the tortures alive."[79] Each day women in this camp were slipping beyond hope, and disease and starvation were not the only maladies from which these Jews were dying.

As Soviet forces moved toward their January 27, 1945, liberation of Auschwitz, and the gas chambers in that most infamous of all murder factories had ceased operation, many of the Jews were marched out of the camp with Bergen-Belsen and Ravensbrück as their destinations.[80] Those who lived to arrive at Ravensbrück would discover that, beginning that January, this women's prison had been converted into a death camp where the Nazi gassing of Jews could continue.[81] At first these gassings took place in trucks and vans as had been widely used in Poland during the first years of the German occupation. Then a wooden gas chamber was built and began operation.[82] This installation, along with the deadly trucks, was used to supplement unceasing murders by lethal injection and poison, which were used to eliminate a significant though unrecorded number of captives.[83] One prisoner managed to smuggle a letter out of the camp describing how some of her fellow inmates were being killed in those last months of the war: "Thousands have been picked out and sent to the gas chamber. A number of them were ill, but some of them were quite well, though older. It was almost enough just to have gray hair. The saddest scenes have been enacted here. Many had dyed their hair with shoe black or soot. By a miracle, I have escaped."[84]

On April 2, 1945, a week or so before my mother's arrival, a different group of five hundred women had been executed.[85] The bodies burned in the three ovens of the camp's crematorium.[86] In the last three to four months of the war, more than two thousand, and perhaps as many as six thousand, mostly Jews were murdered in this room. Though some accounts suggest that the permanent death chamber may have been dismantled in the early part of April, at a minimum, mobile gas chambers continued operating for most of that month.[87]

A mere four days before Masur's flight (and only a few days after my mother's arrival in the camp), Gemma La Guardia Gluck, the sister of New York mayor Fiorello La Guardia, had been sent from Ravensbrück to Berlin in an unsuccessful attempt to use her as some sort of bargaining chip.[88] Born to the same Jewish mother who had given birth to the mayor, Gemma had married a Hungarian Jew and moved to Budapest, where she had been arrested in June 1944 on direct orders of Himmler. The Reichsführer had long mistakenly assumed that Jewish prisoners with influential relatives in the United States might prove useful as part of some sort of barter.[89]

Her supposed trade value had made her the camp's most prominent prisoner, and instructions had been given that she was not to be dealt with harshly. There were thousands of other captives who had no such currency and whose lives were rapidly deteriorating. La Guardia Gluck would recount how the other Jewish women were not treated like human beings but like animals.[90] Yet while prisoners like my mother may have had no individual exchange value, Himmler had begun to believe that, in large enough numbers, they might be bartered in order to pry open an avenue of communication with the West.[91] To exploit this possible option, he would need to maintain control over a sufficient quantity of Jewish captives whose freedom could be offered to the Allies in exchange for something that might improve the ss leader's postwar fate.[92]

Masur was right that it no longer served Himmler's purposes to have all of Jews in the camps be killed outright; unfortunately this did not require that they all be kept alive.[93] Toward that end, Himmler concluded that a substantial number of prisoners would have to be moved out of any camps in immediate jeopardy of falling into Allied hands, lest too many captives be liberated from his ss control. Though it would cost the lives of thousands of Jews, some of whom died in the final days of the war, forced evacuations from his camps would allow Himmler to maintain his imagined negotiating leverage.[94] As his biographer Peter Longerich cautioned, any "supposed humanitarian pose that Himmler adopted in conducting negotiations towards the end of the war for the release of Jews must be viewed against the background of this brutal and cynical evacuation process."[95]

In hindsight, and unknown to Masur, there was one other factor adding to the urgency of his mission: A "final death march from Ravensbrück was being prepared by the ss administration" to begin on April 27, with the intent "to empty the camp before its imminent Soviet takeover."[96]

CHAPTER 8

Appointment with the Executioner

As Norbert Masur and Felix Kersten arrived at the latter's home just before midnight, they were greeted by Himmler's astrologer (yes, astrologer), Wilhelm Wulff, who would later recall that both Kersten and Masur (the latter whom he described as "a small, slender man with a narrow head and intelligent eyes") appeared terrorized by their trip from the airport.[1] That morning's Allied bombing raids of Berlin and Oranienburg had been so heavy that they had severely damaged the area's power stations, plunging Kersten's home into darkness, without radio, and with only a direct phone line to Himmler's headquarters still working.[2] The interior minister was not there yet, and would not be arriving any time soon.

From the balcony, black clouds of smoke could be seen in the distance, rising above Berlin.[3] The morning of April 20, the waiting Masur was jolted by the reverberation of Allied bombs exploding on railroad tracks no more than two kilometers from the house.[4] An hour and a half from Berlin, muffled artillery fire could be heard from the approaching Russian front, and with the passage of every hour the sounds were coming closer. There was also an ammunitions dump just outside of the town where Germans were intentionally setting off a few smaller unexploded bombs as the easiest method of disarming them. Yet Masur would later recount that his inability to sleep was not caused by the sound of attacking planes or cannons or the fear of the nearby explosions, but rather by the fate of the Jews whose lives might depend on him.[5]

Present in the house, along with Masur, Kersten, and Wulff, was the head of Himmler's intelligence service, SS Brigadeführer Walter Schellenberg. Though now long dead and buried, the young and infamous Brigadeführer has for decades remained a fixture especially in spy novels and movies set in World War II. Appearing under various names, in different guises, and likely sometimes even penned by authors too young or uninformed to be aware of whom the character was originally based upon, Schellenberg has become the archetypical model of the suave, educated, rationally cold-blooded, evil, and opportunistic intelligence officer. He is the smart one in the room. Cynically recognizing his masters' all too apparent flaws and challenged acumen, he did their bidding as long as it served his own objectives.[6]

If you were a Jew in wartime Europe, however, there was nothing entertaining about Walter Schellenberg. Early in the war he had earned his ss credentials and Himmler's confidence. Antisemitism was customary among the army's aristocratic officers, but Himmler's ss went far beyond what they expected. Based upon information provided by Schellenberg, Himmler ordered the German High Command to cease what he interpreted as leniencies in their treatment of the Jews in Belgium and the Netherlands. Then, on May 20, 1941, Schellenberg instructed the police officials of occupied Belgium and France to prevent any Jewish emigration because Himmler insisted that all the Jews of Western Europe, without exception, were to be rounded up and sent to camps. It was also this charming and persuasive young intelligence officer who secured an agreement with German generals leading to their eventual cooperation so that Einsatzgruppen mass-murdering units would not be interfered with as they proceeded to murder hundreds of thousands of Jews in Eastern Europe.[7]

After the war, Schellenberg's survival instincts led him to cooperate with Nuremberg prosecutors by giving evidence against various former Nazi colleagues in exchange for a mere six-year prison sentence. Released early for health reasons, and (as if scripted for the karmic ending of a Hollywood film) looking old before his time, he died at age forty-two, soon after the 1952 completion of his memoirs.[8]

Schellenberg had been a clever, ambitious, and extremely dangerous Nazi, but on April 20, 1945, Masur gained unexpected confidence from his brief conversation with this SS officer. The Brigadeführer's change out of his uniform into civilian clothes had given the cultured thirty-five-year-old an unexpectedly gentle and approachable appearance. He confessed to Masur his concern for the future of Germany now that the conflict was lost. While in hindsight the imminent end of the war might seem to have been obvious to all, it was not so clear at the time to those outside the German High Command. Hearing Schellenberg's words was the first time Masur understood how close to total collapse was his enemy.

We can only speculate as to why the young Brigadeführer would have shared this valuable bit of insight with an enemy who was about to enter negotiations with his immediate superior. Perhaps as a result of not having slept in several days, exhausted and depressed, he may have simply been indiscreet in his admission; or perhaps the Machiavellian espionage expert was hoping that the Jew would use the information to secure concessions. By demonstrating his having cooperated in an enterprise culminating in the freeing of Jews, he might have hoped to improve his own, surely precarious postwar position.

Irrespective of Schellenberg's motives, Masur now understood he could bargain from a position of strength.[9] No longer fearful for his own safety or his ability to hold his own in the upcoming negotiations, Masur was simply nervous about whether Reichsführer Himmler would actually show up, and if he did appear, whether Masur would be able to control himself in a face-to-face meeting with the man responsible for the murder of millions of his people.[10]

As night became day, and day again turned into night, all of those present began to worry that the SS chief might never appear. Could he have changed his mind about the risky meeting? Had Hitler given him a new assignment? They were in an active war zone and Masur's own drive from the airport had been fraught with peril. He now feared that Himmler, on his way to discuss the freeing of Jewish captives, might have fallen victim to what would prove to be the last night of the Allied bombing raids against Berlin.[11] As he waited, he was in the unimaginable position of being the only Jew in the world hoping that Heinrich Himmler was safe and near.

At two thirty in the morning the anxious visitor from Sweden heard something moving over the gravel road and then the sound of car doors slamming. Herr Himmler had arrived for coffee.

IT BEGINS

Impeccably dressed in his best uniform and regaled with military medals, the narrow-lipped Nazi Reichsführer surprised his Jewish guest by greeting him with "Guten Tag" (good day) instead of "Heil Hitler" as Masur had expected after his SS greeting at the airport.[12] The SS chief had, in fact, been concerned about the hazardous drive from Berlin. Not until just past 1:00 a.m. on April 21, when the night's sky was no longer brightened into daylight by Allied flares, was he sufficiently confident in the cessation of the air bombardment to begin his journey.[13]

They now bowed slightly to each other, as their extended right hands momentarily touched but they did not shake.[14] Near-sighted, Himmler's gray, closely set eyes appeared sad behind steel-framed glasses that sat perched in the midst of a plump, shiny face of unexpectedly soft-looking skin and a strikingly receding chin.[15] Short to medium height, pudgy, balding, and not at all athletic, he was physically far from "the Nordic ideal to which he was so devoted."[16] Yet, in spite of the hour and reports of ill health, he gave the opposite impression by exuding a kind of freshness as well as appearing "outwardly quiet, and in control."[17]

Those who watched the 1961 Israeli trial of Himmler's subordinate Adolf Eichmann would make the same observation of Eichmann as Masur now did of Himmler: "Had I not known his past, I would have never believed that this man was singularly responsible for the most extensive mass murders in history."[18] That these men may have appeared and even behaved like bureaucrats did not disqualify them from being among history's most brutal mass executioners.[19] Their true malevolence, belied by commonplace features and bearing, lay within.

Himmler had been accompanied on the drive from the capital by his chief of staff, Standartenführer Rudolf Brandt. Trained as a lawyer, he provided a service to Himmler somewhat similar to the one afforded Hitler by his assistant Martin Bormann. He was the Reichsführer's eyes and ears. How Brandt chose to present a message or an issue crucially affected how his superior would react. Three years later, on his thirty-ninth birthday, Brandt would be hanged after being convicted by a U.S. Military Tribunal at Nuremberg for his participation in Germany's "Final Solution," and in particular his role in selecting eighty-six victims to be killed so that their skulls could be shown on exhibition (known as the Jewish Skeleton Collection) as examples of subhuman non-Aryan species.[20]

There were thus four close advisers to the second-most powerful man in German politics present in the home that night—Schellenberg (the prototypical foreign espionage expert), Wulff (an astrologer), Kersten (a masseur), and Brandt (a mass murderer who collected the skulls of his victims). Norbert Masur had stepped through the looking glass.

Immediately after the pro forma greetings, Masur and the interior minister's confidants started toward the dining room table, where refreshments had been set. Himmler, however, remained unexpectedly frozen as he stood staring into the fireplace. Then, distractedly, as if no one else were present, the Reichsführer spoke. He talked of how, for more than a generation, Germany had not experienced peace. No sooner had World War I ended, he said, then civil strife had broken out, with the Jews playing a predominant role. He turned and, for a moment, in a room lit only by the flames of the fire and the flickering of candles, looked directly at his Jewish visitor.[21] Then, seemingly for the first time noticing the food, he walked over and took a seat. There was silence as the Gestapo leader leaned over the table, selected a piece of cake, and began to eat.[22]

WEAK OF WILL

Masur and Himmler sat across from each other. Lying between them were "dishes of butter, jam, honey, and plates with cakes and brown bread," some of "which Kersten had brought from Sweden."[23] Himmler drank his coffee, while Masur sipped tea. My mother and the other Jewish women of Ravensbrück were a mere thirty kilometers away, dehydrated and starving and not knowing how much time they had before they too would be killed.

The usually irritable interior minister was initially well mannered at Kersten's table that night. At first he chatted as he had so often—

emphatically but dispassionately, and in a voice neither high-pitched nor particularly deep. The son of a school principal, Himmler was the most educated and pedagogically oriented of the Nazi Party leaders. When he spoke, he often reminded people of "a schoolmaster reviewing a long and somewhat complicated lesson for his pupils."[24] As he consumed his second slice of cake, however, his tone changed, and he began lecturing his Jewish guest at length in a speech salted with anti-Semitic comments.[25]

There is no record of how much he had had to drink just before driving to the meeting, and so it is impossible to conclude whether or not he could have been feeling the effects of alcohol as he droned on, lecturing Masur. It is documented, however, that during this period Himmler had been drinking more heavily than was his norm. On the eve of his Führer's birthday at the stroke of midnight between April 19 and 20, and "contrary to his usual custom," he had ordered a second bottle of champagne for a midnight toast.[26]

Whatever the reason, the Reichsführer went on for nearly three-quarters of an hour attempting to justify German behavior toward the Jewish people.[27] "The Jews were a foreign element in our midst, which always evoked irritation," he declared in his long tirade. "They were driven out of Germany several times, however, they always returned. After coming into power, we wanted to settle this issue once and for all, and I was in favor of a humane solution through emigration. I conferred with American organizations . . . but even countries who claim to be friendly towards the Jews did not want to admit Jews."[28] It was the kind of speech his aides, hoping for some accommodation with this Jewish representative, had feared.

The diatribe sent a shudder through Masur, but as he looked for the right moment to interrupt, he tried to control himself so that no one else in the room would notice his hatred of the Nazi leader and what Himmler was saying.[29] In spite of this effort to hide his reaction, it was nonetheless obvious to Kersten, who would write that he "could only admire Masur's self-control as he listened with scornful patience."[30] Eventually, the chess player from Sweden, seeing an opening, made his first move, and to Himmler's apparent surprise, the Gestapo leader found his monologue suddenly interrupted.

"It has never been contemplated under international laws and inherent human rights," Masur began, "to suddenly drive out people from a country where their fathers and forefathers had lived."[31] The intrusion seemed to puzzle Himmler and momentarily threw him off-balance. It had likely been a long time since anyone had even considered a face-to-face challenge of his doctrinaire view of the Jews and the Nazis' treatment of them. When had been the last time anyone, other than Hitler or a few of the highest Nazi officials, had dared interrupt the Gestapo chief while he spoke on any subject?

After a moment's confusion, the German official continued his defense of Nazi policies, only to be interrupted again. In spite of his complete awareness that, as the head of the SS and the Gestapo, the Reichsführer could have had him killed or sent him to a camp with a single word, the German Jewish businessman nonetheless demanded that they begin discussing practical matters. Himmler, however, obsessively needing to complete his long-winded explication, was not to be stopped.

The leader of the SS now lost the aura of control he had exhibited upon his arrival only an hour earlier. In an almost hysterical tone, he defended the concentration camps, which he claimed the world had misunderstood. The head of his nation's secret police insisted that Germany's crime rate had dramatically decreased as a result of such "educational" camps.[32]

Masur appreciated the utter uniqueness of his position. At that moment he was, as he would later write, "a free Jew face to face with the feared and unmerciful chief of the Gestapo, [with at least] 5 million Jews on his conscience."[33] "Mr. Himmler, I lost a large part of my family, my friends' families, and my childhood friends in these educational camps," interposed Masur, no longer able to control his rage.[34] When he then challenged the National Socialist program of mass murder, Himmler defensively retorted that the Jews had been working with partisans.

"Only by being harsh could [our] troops prevail," [Himmler responded]. "They were forced to destroy whole villages, if there was resistance and shooting from such a village. . . . If, because of these difficulties in the East, the Jewish people suffered great casualties, one needs to remember, that the German people also suffered severely."[35]

This was not the first time Himmler had similarly attempted to justify the indefensible. Unknown to Masur, the Reichsführer had delivered a 24,000-word speech on October 10, 1943, to high-ranking members of the SS at Posen, in which he had praised the wisdom of "exterminating" the Jewish people. Though realizing he was being recorded, he had mistakenly believed his remarks would be kept secret,[36] and thus it was one of the rare occasions when, in public, he had spoken candidly about Germany's "Final Solution" for the Jews: "This is an unwritten—never to be written—and yet glorious page in our history," Himmler had lectured his fellow SS. "For we know how difficult we would've made it for ourselves if, on top of the bombing raids, the burdens and the deprivations of the war, we still had Jews today in every town as secret saboteurs, as agitators and troublemakers.[37] . . . We had the moral right; we had the duty with regard to our people, to kill this race that wanted to kill us."[38]

Himmler was now, however, making similar claims to a rather different and unappreciative audience. Masur found it particularly difficult to restrain himself, especially when the Nazi minister described what Masur regarded as "the heroic fight of the Jews in the Warsaw ghetto" as just another example of Jews firing without cause upon "German troops."[39] He would continue to force himself to listen to the Reichsführer's ranting until he felt the time was right to respond, and then carefully choose his words.[40]

Finally, however, as Masur recalls in his report to the World Jewish Congress, when Himmler talked about the "just treatment" in the concentration camps: "I was not able to, nor did I want to, contain my agitation. . . . It was to my satisfaction, in the name of the suffering Jewish people, to tell him a thing or two about the atrocities in the concentration camps. At that moment, I felt that I had the upper hand. . . . And I believe that Himmler felt the weakness of his position."[41]

For most of the two-and-a-half hours Masur and Himmler spoke, two or three German advisors were always present, but for one half-hour the two principals were left alone. It was during this brief period that Masur began to understand something Himmler's closest confidants had long known: The interior minister, chief of the ss, and head of the Gestapo was more malleable and easier to persuade than his titles and offices would suggest.[42] The Third Reich's most murderous enforcer was simply weak of will. Perhaps it was this susceptibility to the strongly held views of others that led Himmler to his early conversion to the religion of National Socialism.[43]

Himmler's entire diatribe had actually been surprisingly self-justifying. Doubtlessly realizing, writes Masur, "that the days of his life, or at least the days of his freedom were numbered," Himmler spoke as if he needed "to express his defense to a Jew."[44] Masur would later describe how the ss leader's assertions and tone governed the Jewish emissary's negotiating strategies.[45] His predawn insights into Himmler's vulnerabilities, and the use he would make of them, would eventually establish this little-known Jew from Sweden as more than merely a quixotic figure: in fact, he was about to save my mother.

CHAPTER 9

Trading for Jewish Lives

This was not the first time high-ranking Nazis considered using Jews as bargaining chips for their particular political agendas. Beginning about the time of Kristallnacht in 1938, the Germans started suggesting the possibility of exporting large numbers of Jews out of the Reich and into Western nations. The earliest of these offers in the late 1930s may have been primarily a propaganda stunt. If the world refused to take Germany's Jewish refugees, then the Germans would use this fact to demonstrate that not even the liberal Western democracies wanted such people in their midst. However, if the West agreed to accept them, willingly mixing these despicable creatures into their overall populations, it would prove that America and Britain were mere puppets of their capitalist Jewish masters. And if in fact these nations actually did take in large numbers of Jews, then, under National Socialism's racial theories, the integration of subhumans within the populations of their potential enemies would lead directly to the societal decline of these adversaries, thus making their defeat at the hands of a pure Aryan nation even more of a certainty.[1]

In that prewar period of 1938–39, Himmler disapproved of releasing Jews, in part because any form of orderly release or even an organized transfer "would be too easy on the Jews themselves."[2] Contrary to his later assertions to Masur, he had issued unpublished orders limiting Jewish emigration to any country.[3] Even as he gave occasional lip service to the far-fetched, yet surprisingly long-considered proposal to ship hundreds of thousands of Jews to the island of Madagascar, he would never have accepted allowing those transported to escape Nazi control. Even if these potential hostages were relocated to this remote locale, a place where he imagined African conditions even less hospitable than those he could create in eastern Poland, there would have been no Jewish self-rule permitted.[4]

Himmler, as well as his Führer, had actually been more interested in keeping a large Jewish population as hostages to guarantee "the good behavior of international Jewry" and their allies.[5] Hitler warned the West that they would regret any military intervention against Germany, not only because the Allies would lose such a war against his powerful fatherland but also because it would mean "the destruction of the Jewish race in Europe."[6]

In January 1941, the American-British Lend-Lease program that authorized sending American destroyers and other military equipment to Britain without the immediate need for payment appears to have been interpreted by the German dictator as the first step toward American entry into the war. It could also have convinced Hitler of the urgent need to attack Russia and destroy the Jewish Bolsheviks in the East before having to confront another powerful Jewish-controlled capitalist opponent on its Western front.[7] Unfortunately, the conviction that war against America was now inevitable may have made the perceived enemy population of Jews in their midst less valuable as hostages. The Nazi "Final Solution" would now no longer involve elimination through eviction, but rather by "extermination."[8]

BARTERING FOR THE JEWS OF HUNGARY

In mid-1944, however, as the Nazi war effort began to deteriorate and their need for resources grew, the willingness to bargain for the lives of Jews in exchange for supplies or equipment had finally become acceptable, and, likely with Hitler's acquiescence, the SS were in charge of any negotiations. This was particularly true with respect to dangling the possible release of Hungary's Jews. Though Hungary was an Axis ally, in March 1944 the German army entered and occupied the country, where 750,000 Jews constituted Continental Europe's largest, and arguably last, remaining completely intact Jewish community. By the end of April 1944, however, massive transports to Auschwitz would begin.

Whether or not they were truly serious, the ss now made several proposals to exchange Hungary's Jews for money and/or materials. For this purpose, Himmler used two significant subordinates he had assigned to Budapest. One of these men was the infamous permanent head of the ss's Jewish Section, Lieutenant Colonel Adolf Eichmann. The other, and only slightly more junior, was Lieutenant Colonel Kurt Becher, whom Himmler had put in charge of economically exploiting the country. Both Eichmann and Becher appear to have seen themselves in competition with each other when it came to bartering the potential release of Jews, and both would eventually negotiate with the Romanian/Hungarian Zionist leader Rezso Kasztner.

One could plausibly argue that nowhere in German-occupied Europe was there anyone like Kasztner. Even after hundreds of thousands of Hungarian Jews had been shipped to the camps and killed, the Jewish Kasztner not only managed to remain free in Axis-allied (and then German-occupied) Hungary, he was able to broker the exchange of Jews for payments to willing Nazi officials. When he lacked the resources to bribe or barter, he attempted to stall by bluffing the ss into believing that he would soon gain access to massive funds from Western backers.[9] Both Kasztner as well as the representatives of the War Refugee Board believed that, so long as the Germans thought a major deal was in the offing, they were less likely to simply execute all of Hungary's Jews.

In the spring of 1944, Adolf Eichmann informed Kasztner that for $1,000 per person he would allow a "sample group" of a few hundred Jews to leave Budapest in a "rescue" train on which they would be delivered to neutral territory such as Lisbon, Portugal. The Nazis were testing the waters as to whether there might be future, and larger, exchanges of Jews for equipment such as trucks, in what would become known as the negotiations over "blood-for-goods."[10]

There have been varying reports as to how many Jews Eichmann, with Himmler's approval, had originally expressed a willingness to release. The highest number ever suggested was the extraordinary possibility of freeing nearly a million European Jews, in exchange for ten thousand trucks, which the Germans would guarantee to use only on the Eastern front.[11] Sadly, the West never expressed a willingness to barter with the Nazis for the release of civilian captives. The deal for trucks, for example, would have had to involve the cooperation of the British, whose reaction to even the suggestion of such a bargain seems to have been one of utter "astonishment"; though there are also reports suggesting that Britain's contemptuous rejection may have only occurred once word of the proposal reached the ears of Soviet officials.[12] Whatever the reason, no such exchange would ever take place.

In fact, for the entirety of the war, Western leaders adamantly maintained that they were not interested in negotiating anything less than total German surrender, a concession Hitler would never consider and Herr Himmler could not deliver. Even though the U.S. government belatedly created in early 1944 the interdepartmental War Refugee Board, signaling its blessing of efforts to obtain the release of Jewish captives, it would not sanction giving the Germans anything tangible, such as trucks, medical supplies, money, or even soap.

Kasztner learned of the Allies' refusal to give anything of substance to their enemy, even if it were the price for saving hundreds of thousands of Jewish lives. Nonetheless, although the War Refugee Board did not officially distribute dollars to aid or rescue European Jews, it was still possible for private citizens, using nonofficial sources, to pay small bribes to Nazis with the knowledge of, if not formal cooperation from, the board's representatives. These moneys were taken not from governmental funds but rather provided by an American Jewish charity known as the American Jewish Joint Distribution Committee (the "Joint"). The Joint had and would continue to discreetly supply funds when governments would not.[13]

One of the practical concerns always present during any such privately arranged exchange for the release of Jews was whether the Nazis would actually fulfill their part of any bargain. For example, while Eichmann spoke emphatically of trading lives for significant quantities of goods, Kasztner feared that the leader of the ss Jewish Section would find an excuse to renege on or sabotage such an agreement.[14] It was this anxiety that lead Kasztner to arrange his first private meeting with Lieutenant

Colonel Becher in May 1944.[15] It soon became clear that Becher was a German officer motivated more by personal greed and self-preservation than by the fanatical ideology that drove Eichmann. Here was a Nazi who might be turned into an inadvertent ally, or at least an induced accomplice.[16]

Eventually, in spite of Eichmann's threats to cancel the rescue train, Becher acquired enough authority from Himmler, or perhaps even from Hitler himself, to allow 1,684 Hungarian Jews safe rail passage from Budapest.[17] Becher had first demanded $2,000 for each passenger, but eventually settled for $1,000 as Himmler had instructed.[18] Just after midnight on the morning of July 1, 1944, the train pulled out of Budapest.[19]

By that first week in July, only about ten weeks after the first deportations had begun, between 434,000 and 475,000 Hungarian Jews had already been shipped to Auschwitz-Birkenau, with most being murdered within an hour of their arrival.[20] The passengers aboard Kasztner's train, as it would be called, had paid in the hope of being spared.

Unfortunately, after an eight-day journey, instead of safe transport to Portugal or Spain as promised, the train was delivered to the Bergen-Belsen concentration camp. There the frightened travelers would be prisoners, though separated from the rest of the camp into one of the "privileged areas" designated for "exchange Jews," who were not to be killed because they were seen as having value. On August 21, 1944, and then again on December 3, partially in exchange for additional payments to the SS, several hundred of those who had boarded the rescue train in Budapest were provided safe German transit to Switzerland. Most of those left behind in the camp would outlive the war, but some would not.

One of the prisoners, a young teenage girl suffering from scarlet fever who barely survived, later recounted how she had been sent outside her restricted zone into the camp's neighboring Dutch-Jewish enclosure. Lying near her in a hospital bed was a pale, dark-haired, dark-eyed fifteen-year-old girl about her own age who had been brought to the camp from Amsterdam, and who was also terribly ill with fever. The young "exchange Jew" from Budapest would recover, but Anne Frank was dying.[21] The "Dutch girl," whose story lives on as the personification of all Jewish children trapped in the Shoah, would not survive to be saved by the strange partnership between the Jew Kasztner and the Nazi Becher.

SAVING BERGEN-BELSEN

On April 10 or 11, 1945, (only two or three days after the camp had likely been spared being blown up),[22] Becher, at the urging of and accompanied by Kasztner, appears to have induced Bergen-Belsen's SS commander, Captain Josef Kramer, to peacefully surrender the prisoners to the advancing British, who would arrive on April 15.[23] Captured German records reveal that, in its last month of operation, an average of five hundred captives died each day in Bergen-Belsen, and it is possible that many more would have perished without the intervention of Becher and Kasztner.[24] It should be understood, however, that when later interrogated, Becher could not explain (after observing the condition of its prisoners) why he had never ordered the distribution of stockpiled Red Cross food and clothing to the desperate inmates of the camp.[25] Self-preservation, rather than preserving the lives, or well-being, of Jews does seem to have been the principal factor motivating the young German colonel's late-war actions.

Becher's belated interest in at least appearing to save Jewish lives may well have originated as the result of a clandestine Sunday, November 5, 1944, meeting with a representative of the War Refugee Board in a conference room in Zurich's Savoy Hotel. The meeting had been arranged by Kasztner and the Joint representative in Switzerland, Saly Mayer. Both Jewish men attended, though neither took part in the actual discussions.[26]

The War Refugee Board's envoy, the "composed" and "erudite" American Quaker Roswell McClelland,[27] informed Becher that cooperation in efforts to rescue Jews might work to the benefit of even high-ranking members of the SS. With German defeat on the horizon, McClelland advised the Nazi representative that if he would begin working to save lives it "would count in his favor in the war criminals trials at the end of hostilities."[28] This may well have been the first time an official of a Western government had informed a Himmler surrogate that even high-ranking SS officials might yet receive leniency if they cooperated in the late-war rescue of Jews. Becher immediately cabled Himmler,[29] who two months later promoted the German lieutenant colonel to the rank of full colonel.

In gratitude for his end-of-war cooperation, Kasztner intervened in Becher's case just as Allied officers were interrogating the Nazi colonel on July 7, 1947.[30] Leniency was granted to Becher, even though, in summer and fall of 1941, he had helped carry out Himmler's order to round up and execute masses of Jews in Russia's Pripet Marshes.[31]

There were numerous later attempts to formally charge the man who had always made certain to sign any correspondence to his SS chief "the Reichsführer's most obedient Becher."[32] Yet, in spite of the fact that the ex-henchman's belated humanitarian efforts had been accompanied by extorting substantial and largely unrecovered sums from Jewish individuals and organizations, the wealthy Becher was never brought to justice and died in his own bed fifty years after the end of World War II.[33]

Rezso Kasztner, on the other hand, was assassinated in Israel in 1957 by fellow Jews who believed that their target had been a Nazi collaborator.[34] One of the lawyers working on the prosecution of the killers had also previously been part of an Israeli government investigation of whether Kasztner had cooperated with the Nazis. The former prosecutor, who would later present the Israeli case against Adolf Eichmann, reiterated to me in a meeting in Jerusalem in May 2015 that there had never been any basis for the allegation that the Hungarian Jew was a traitor to his people. Only decades after his death did the official Israeli body in charge of Holocaust remembrance, Yad Vashem, even acknowledge Kasztner's wartime efforts, and it was still hesitant to bestow upon him the well-deserved official title of having been a "hero" of the Shoah.

CHAPTER 10

A True Believer

Kurt Becher, apparently following the advice delivered to him in his Zurich meeting by the representative of the War Refugee Board, would succeed in saving himself from conviction at Nuremberg by demonstrating his cooperation in both the ransoming and sparing of Hungarian Jews,[1] but could there be any rational basis for Allied prosecutors to show leniency to the man who not only headed the SS and the Gestapo but who, as his Führer's most trusted and dependable advisor, was one of those leading Germany in its wars of aggression?

Yet, by spring 1945, no longer interested in obtaining cash or trucks from the Allies in exchange for the release of Jews, Himmler's most immediate priority was now the desperate attempt to cultivate Allied contacts so that he could convince them that he was a reasonable German leader who could prove valuable in both speedily ending hostilities as well as acting as a stabilizing force in the postwar world.[2]

Though in the eyes of the Allies, he would be the primary Nazi war criminal, second only to Hitler himself, Himmler still imagined that a series of token acts of mercy might gain him both goodwill and avenues of communication through which he might barter for his future.[3] Perhaps the irrational belief that such a gesture could placate his inevitable prosecutors was as much a part of Himmler's pathological delusions as was the racist philosophy that had resolved itself into the "Final Solution."

Whatever his thoughts might have been, Himmler's newly found eagerness to cultivate favor with the Western powers clearly did not lessen and may even have intensified the demands he placed upon his troops to fight to the death in order to give him time to negotiate his own fate.[4] As late as April 15, 1945, less than a week before his encounter with the Jew from Sweden, he had ordered those troops still under his control that "every village and town will be defended and held by every means possible. Any German man who fails to uphold his fundamental national duty will forfeit his honor and his life."[5] He had always fervently maintained that members of the Jewish race were prepared to sacrifice others in order to protect them, yet it would be Himmler who now attempted to save himself at the cost of his own soldiers and by offering to betray his revered Führer.

THE BEWILDERING CREED OF THE NAZI

If we accept that Himmler hoped to save himself by finding an avenue of communication with Western leaders, it still remains something of an enigma why one of Nazi Germany's most powerful men was interested in negotiating with and cultivating the goodwill of a Jewish representative like Norbert Masur or an organization like the World Jewish Congress.[6] The simplest explanation is that Himmler may have believed that since the Jews had been the group most targeted by the Nazis, and particularly by his SS, that he might later benefit from any Jewish testimonial.

There is, however, another equally straightforward, if perhaps now difficult to appreciate, explanation of the Gestapo chief's motivation. By April 1945, Himmler may still have been a true believer in National Socialism or simply a worried pragmatist. But whether fanatic or opportunist, he had spent over two decades as a principal exponent of the propaganda central to Nazism: that the world was run by a clandestine Jewish order.[7]

Like the followers of a religious cult, Himmler and his fellow National Socialists filtered everything through the prism of what they had been indoctrinated to believe: that behind any group that the Nazis saw as the enemies of their fatherland, and therefore of all civilization, lurked the Jews. They were "masterfully organized throughout the world," always extending their powerful networks.[8]

Though objective observers might immediately recognize the irrationality of such beliefs, to Nazis like Himmler as well as even many non-Nazi Germans, the Jews posed a dual, contradictory, but equally menacing danger in their controlling both the Communists in Moscow and the Western capitalist governments in London, Paris, and Washington.[9] The German Führer had once "told the grand mufti of Jerusalem, Haj Anin el-Huseini, that . . . Britain and Russia were both . . . power bases of Jewry, and he would carry on the fight until the last trace . . . was eliminated."[10]

This grandiose credit and blame, as well as the depth of the hatred shared by many Germans against Jews, seems particularly bewildering, given the paucity of Germany's Jewish population.[11] Jews made up less than 1 percent of the population of the Weimar Republic, and, with 70 percent of that Jewish 1 percent residing in large urban centers, only a relatively small proportion of Germans had ever knowingly met a Jew.[12]

Yet, even among that segment of the German population who were not rabidly anti-Semitic, there was nonetheless a staggering overestimation of Jewish influence. A demonstration of how ingrained was the German perception of the mythical might of the Jew is unintentionally revealed in the reminiscences of Felix Kersten. Here was a man who was not prosecuted for any war crimes, and had never even joined the Nazi Party, yet he rendered the negotiations between his Nazi employer and the Jewish Norbert Masur as having involved the "peacefully seated representatives of two races who had been at daggers drawn, each regarding the other as its mortal enemy; [an] attitude [that] had demanded the sacrifice of millions."[13] How readily he adopts a tenet central to the anti-Semitic biases he claims to have disdained as he casually appears to conflate the Jewish and German "races" as equivalently responsible for the "sacrifice" of the millions who had perished in the war.

In reality, in the 1930s, Jewish influence was of no consequence in the Stalinist Soviet Union, of little or no significance to the politics of Churchill's Great Britain, and of only minimal importance even in Roosevelt's America. While any sort of world Jewish hegemony was chimerical before the war, once the conflict had actually begun and true power was measured by military prowess, Jewish influence was even more tragically impotent.[14]

Yet, though the battle between Jews and Germans was always a one-sided war waged by Europe's most powerful military nation against a politically powerless and unarmed civilian minority, Hitler was not alone in referring to the Allies' armies as "troops of Jewry."[15] The renowned and pro-Nazi German philosopher Martin Heidegger, as learned from his posthumously published private papers, also avowed that his nation's principal enemy was the Jews, who he asserted needed no armies to impose their will since they used others to fight their battles for them.[16]

As Germany's position began to weaken, the desire to speak to the Jews in order to reach the leadership of the Allied powers, or at least the Western media, would have been a logical course for a self-concerned Nazi leader. If foreign ministers and generals would not speak with the head of the Gestapo, then it made perfect sense to communicate directly with their puppet masters. While it should have been clear to any educated, rational being that Gilel Storch and Norbert Masur were sadly insignificant players on the world stage, to Himmler they were representatives of the true power behind the thrones.

Once safely back in Sweden, Masur summarized his tactical use of at least one of these Nazi assumptions about the power of the Jews: "Without a doubt Himmler believed . . . that we Jews really had the power to control the world press, as stated by the Nazi line propaganda. And maybe he thought that I as a representative of the Jews could influence the press of the allied and neutral countries, even though he had been told that I had come as a private citizen."[17]

Having caught the Nazi leader in the midst of what proved to be increasingly frantic and far-fetched efforts to avert his inevitable downfall, it was Masur's ability to exploit Himmler's fanatical anti-Semitic belief in the scope of Jewish influence that would allow him to achieve at least part of his goal of saving the Jewish women of Ravensbrück.

A GESTURE OF GOOD FAITH

Knowing that Himmler's hope for postwar leniency was a delusion born of denial and desperation,[18] Masur purposefully assured the Reichführer that cooperation in rescue efforts would increase his chances for survival.

Though pure fantasy, the malleable Gestapo chief was sufficiently prepared to believe that he might yet avert postwar prosecution that he agreed to several of Masur's requests.

In exchange for no more than the delivery of the interior minister's good auspices to the West,[19] Masur obtained assurances from Himmler that he would make an effort to stop the death marches of Jewish captives and attempt to prevent the camps from being blown up, thus allowing them to remain intact for eventual surrender to advancing Allied forces. "With respect to stopping the forced evacuation and surrendering of the camps to the allies, I will endeavor to do my best,"[20] pledged the man Hitler had charged with responsibility for implementing the Holocaust itself. These were basically the same promises that Himmler had Kersten deliver to Storch on March 12, 1945, but they were only officially sent to Himmler's subordinates on April 21.[21]

Yet how much value was there in these promises? On April 18, only three days prior to this meeting with the Jewish emissary, Himmler had commanded his underlings "that no living prisoners were to fall into enemy hands" (Kein Haftling darf lebend in die Hande des Feindes fallen). Despite his April 21 promise to Masur agreeing to reverse these orders, Himmler appears to have taken no new action with respect to the camp at Flossenburg, which would be liberated by American troops two days later, on April 23. Nor is there proof that Himmler acted to save the lives of any Jews at Dachau.[22] The commandant of Dachau's decision to execute all of the camp's inmates appears to have been stymied only as a result of the liberation by Americans soldiers on April 29.[23]

While it is possible that the April 21 promises made to Norbert Masur did result in some camps not being blown up, and the timing of events makes it also plausible that this agreement had an effect on stopping some death marches, a direct causal connection to the meeting at Kersten's home remains difficult to establish with any certainty.[24]

Masur was not, however, so gullible as to simply accept Himmler's personal promises. He knew the kind of man he was dealing with, and that Himmler could not be trusted to fulfill all or even any of his sweeping assurances. The chief planner of the Holocaust was, after all, "a master of deceit."[25] For years Himmler had orchestrated the misleading of his victims as to their true fate. Even now he was trying to represent himself to the West as the reasonable German leader with whom they could negotiate a peace, while hiding the effort from his Führer and urging the troops under his control to continue fighting to the death. In bargaining for broad generalized concessions, such as stopping the death marches and surrendering the camps, Masur understood that, though hoping for success, he was running the risk that the promises might not be kept. However, if an order to do one specific act was given by the SS leader to those underlings in attendance at the meeting, Masur believed they would follow through, not only because their leader had commanded it but also because they too seemed to believe that such cooperation could mitigate the war crimes charges that would likely be brought against them in the soon-to-be postwar world.[26]

While Himmler was not yet willing to reduce his bargaining position by immediately freeing tens of thousands of Jews, the perspicacious businessman from Sweden insisted that if a significant number of the internees at Ravensbrück were to be freed within a few days, it could give the SS leader "the chance of establishing politically useful connections with the enemy."[27] He assured the organizer of the Holocaust that "without a doubt" freeing these women "would make an excellent impression with the governments of the allies. And before the judgment of history, the release of remaining Jews is of great importance."[28]

According to Walter Schellenberg's memoirs, there was, however, one problem with Masur's specific request. Hitler had given Himmler authority to release Polish Christians from Ravensbrück, but he never would have condoned his interior minister's freeing Polish Jews.[29] Demonstrating how far such a gesture deviated from Hitler's wishes, and just how concerned Himmler was that his Führer not learn of the concession, the minister of the interior added the following caveat: "The Jewish women in Ravensbrück [who I will order released], however, will be designated as Polish women, rather than Jewish. It is very necessary that not only your visit here must remain secret, but also the arrival of the Jews in Sweden must remain that way."[30] Given the one stipulation that the official designation was to be that of Poles and not Jews, the head of the ss promised Masur that he would free "1,000 Jewish women from the Ravensbrück concentration camp," and that he would see to it that the Red Cross was guaranteed safe passage in order to transport them into Sweden.[31] According to the Reichsführer's astrologer, Wilhelm Wulff, in his 1973 memoir, *Zodiac and Swastika*, Himmler then added what, if he actually did say it, would be as remarkable a statement as has ever been uttered: "You know, if we had met ten years ago, Herr Masur, this war would never have taken place."[32]

Six million Jews had been murdered as part of the Nazis' "Final Solution."[33] Perhaps as many as five million non-Jewish civilians (including Roma [Gypsies], homosexuals, Jehovah's Witnesses, resistance fighters, political opponents, Polish intellectuals, and those the German government labeled as "anti-social") were annihilated.[34] In those last days of April 1945, hundreds of thousands of Jewish prisoners still remained under Himmler's control.[35] Assuming Storch and Masur can be directly credited with no more than negotiating the freeing of these one thousand women, an event of which history seemed to have long taken little note, were their efforts a significant achievement? Though I cannot speak for anyone else, but in April 1945 this was an act crucial to my mother's survival. Fritz Hollander, a World Jewish Congress confederate of Masur, reflected that "if 10 million would have [each] saved one, then no one would have perished."[36] The only proper yardstick I can personally recommend for measuring the accomplishment of the two Jews from Sweden is the value we choose to place on a single human life.

CHAPTER 11

The Count of the Red Cross

Almost immediately following the conclusion of the meeting between
Masur and Himmler, Count Folke Bernadotte was contacted.[1] As vice
president and acting head of the Swedish Red Cross, Bernadotte could
arrange transit to Sweden for the one thousand Jewish women soon to
be freed.[2] In addition, as the nephew of King Gustav of Sweden, and
a charmingly natural diplomat, he had developed relationships with a
number of governmental and military leaders.[3] The Swedish count was
thus not only crucial to providing transportation for prisoners freed from
Ravensbrück, but, unlike Masur or Storch, he was in a position to have
a message delivered from Himmler to the Western powers.[4]

The count had already negotiated with the ss leader in February and
March of 1945 for the release of nearly 7,800 non-Jewish Scandinavian
prisoners from concentration camps. During those meetings, Bernadotte
had also dealt with Brigadeführer Schellenberg.[5] Schellenberg arranged
for Himmler to meet Bernadotte on the morning of April 21 and then
again on the night of April 23 into the morning of April 24 at the Swedish Consulate in the German town of Lübeck, where the Swedish Red
Cross had already established a headquarters.[6]

The two meetings appear to have gone as follows: On April 21 Bernadotte began by asking Himmler if the ss chief would agree to release
the French women prisoners (who were gentiles) from Ravensbrück.
Himmler, fresh from his negotiations with Masur and most likely because
of the commitment he had already made to that emissary of the Jews, was
now prepared to promise even more. He first informed the Swedish Count

of his middle-of-the-night agreement with the Jewish envoy to release a thousand women and allow the Red Cross to transport them to Sweden. The head of the Gestapo then (either at their meeting on April 21 or the subsequent meeting of the twenty-third and twenty-fourth) promised the Swedish count that he would also free the other women in the camp. This would mean the release of French, Dutch, Polish gentile prisoners, and perhaps even the Jewish captives not selected as part of the thousand he had already agreed to free.[7] Though Bernadotte had been hesitant in the past to risk the safety of his Red Cross workers, he agreed to provide the buses and drivers for these potentially dangerous rescue missions.[8]

At that April 23–24 meeting with Bernadotte, Himmler was more specific than he had been three days earlier with the Jewish emissary about the particularities of what he expected in exchange for these prisoner releases. Himmler "asked the Count to convey to the Swedish government," and then to General Eisenhower, his willingness to surrender his "German forces on the Western front."[9] He may not have been offering total unconditional surrender, but, if Himmler could actually accomplish what he was proffering, it was not an insignificant proposal, and Bernadotte agreed to have the message delivered.[10]

Without the count and his Red Cross, the rescue of the women of Ravensbrück could not have taken place. Not only did he arrange transport for my mother and the nearly one thousand women freed with her,[11] he appears to have participated in the negotiation that would a few days later also emancipate most of the rest of the women from the camp. He accomplished much, and much gratitude is owed him.

Yet, though a minor criticism compared to what he actually accomplished, there is at least some plausible evidence to suggest that the count may have had a penchant for not always sharing credit with others who also participated in the rescuing of prisoners.[12]

Bernadotte authored three separate books about his own humanitarian contributions as a leader of the Swedish Red Cross. The first of these, *Last Days of the Third Reich: The Diary of Count Folke Bernadotte*, was published a mere six weeks after the end of the war and is therefore perhaps the most reliable account of Bernadotte's exploits. Though he discusses his involvement in many rescues, there is "total absence of any mention of the Jews."[13] This is particularly interesting when compared to Masur's report to the World Jewish Congress, apparently written April 22, 1945, detailing his own negotiations and agreement with Heinrich Himmler to free Jewish women from Ravensbrück.[14]

Even a strong advocate of the credit justifiably owed the count for his efforts to free prisoners also concedes that this particular diary published by the count unfortunately reveals the author to have been quite "self-absorbed."[15] If in fact Bernadotte was the one who negotiated the release of the group of a thousand Jewish women that included my mother, it is unlikely that modesty would have prevented him from including so significant an accomplishment.

There would seem to be only two reasonable explanations for why the count would not even mention such a success. The first possibility is that perhaps Bernadotte feared a negative reaction from his countrymen if they learned he had spent any of his diplomatic capital rescuing Jews. On the other hand, the second possible reason for his failure to even mention his negotiations to save the Jewish women of Ravensbrück could be that his part was actually so small as to not warrant inclusion, even by a "self-absorbed" writer.

As the postwar months passed, and the true enormity of the Holocaust revealed, the failure of organizations like the Red Cross to save Jews became a liability to the reputation of not only the Red Cross but also its leaders, like Bernadotte. In Bernadotte's next book, *The Curtain Falls*, published later in 1945, he not only recalls having played a part in the freeing of non-Scandinavian Jews from the camps but also claims "exclusive credit for negotiating the release of" all the Jews freed from Ravensbrück.[16] Nowhere in any of Bernadotte's writings can be found any mention of the significant contribution of Masur, or the part played by Kersten, in persuading Himmler to emancipate Jewish women from that camp.[17] As a result, for decades, history often credited Bernadotte with having instigated and negotiated the freeing of all Ravensbrück's inmates, when it is more likely that it was Masur who first led Himmler into a promise to free those first thousand women.[18]

So completely accepted was his version of the events that whenever my mother was asked how she came to have spent eighteen months in Sweden after the war, the answer was that she had been "ransomed by the Swedes, a vonderful people." She seemed unaware, as was I, that Jewish negotiators had been involved.[19] In May 2014, while at Jerusalem's Yad Vashem museum, I struck up a conversation with a Holocaust scholar. When I told her that I was there doing research on the circumstances surrounding my mother's late-war release from Ravensbrück, she responded: "Ah, the Bernadotte rescue."

SWEDEN AND THE JEWS

While the Swedish government and Red Cross were eventually instrumental in bringing thousands of Jewish women to Sweden from Ravensbrück and Bergen-Belsen, this appears not to have been a policy they pursued aggressively until very near the end of the war.[20] Until then the International Committee of the Red Cross, believing that it possessed no mandate or authority to interfere in the internal affairs of any nation, nor in the behavior of nations working in concert, failed to take a firm stand on the concentration camps.[21]

On behalf of the Swedish Red Cross, Bernadotte, a "nationalist and a . . . promoter of Nordic unity," had concentrated the bulk of his rescue efforts on the completely legitimate goal of saving Scandinavians from German captivity.[22] Initially he did not even participate in negotiations for the release of Jewish, French, or Polish prisoners under the apparent assumption that he had his government's authority to rescue only Scandinavians.[23] Not until the very end of March 1945 and perhaps later did Bernadotte ever write a single report suggesting that he had ever spoken to the Germans about freeing any Jews, other than perhaps a few from Nordic countries.[24] It was on April 11, 1945, that a frenzied Gilel Storch pressed Bernadotte as to whether, during the latter's negotiations with Himmler about freeing Scandinavian prisoners, he had ever brought up the subject of the Jews.[25] There is no definitive evidence that he had.

Felix Kersten (who seems to have been prone to occasional exaggeration as to his own role in saving Jewish lives) would later write that

Bernadotte had asked him, in a threatening tone, not to include any Jews among the prisoners released as part of any agreement with which the count was personally involved.[26] The count may have felt that he was in something of a zero-sum proposition in which negotiating the release of imprisoned Jews would interfere with, or at least limit, the number of those from Nordic countries the Germans would be willing to free.[27] Kersten, however, would also assert that the nephew of the king feared that using his prestige and position to negotiate on behalf of Jews, instead of Scandinavians, might result in "difficulties for himself and his family in Sweden."[28] *If* Himmler's physical therapist is to be believed, the count may have even tried to have Kersten's memoirs removed from bookstores because it did not portray Bernadotte in a sufficiently favorable light.[29]

It is certainly plausible that Himmler's former therapist had a personal animus against the Swedish aristocrat, whom he claimed blocked his attempts to obtain postwar Swedish citizenship. Or, perhaps Kersten was denigrating the involvement of the count in order to make his own role in the freeing of captive Jews appear more crucial. There is, however, some historical basis for at least considering the physiotherapist's claims about Bernadotte's alleged concerns.

Just as a racist and nationalistic current had been sweeping Germany in the 1920s and 1930s, it was also rising in other Western countries, including Sweden. Swedish newspapers were filled with stories written by those convinced that the evil Jews were running the world,[30] and negative attitudes directed at the Jews seem to have been common even in those Swedish communities where it would have been difficult to find a single Jewish resident. While we should not extrapolate the attitudes of an entire country based on random newspaper stories and editorials, there are more concrete illustrations of widespread anti-Jewish policies in Sweden during the period between the wars.

In the late 1920s, before the Nazis came to power, Sweden introduced immigration laws intended to limit possible future Jewish influx. A government bill presented as early as 1927 extolled the virtues of the nation's unmixed race. When Hitler took control and hoped to force Jews out of his fatherland, the Swedish government clearly did not want to take them in. While Aryan Germans and Austrians seem to have been welcome, Sweden appears to have been eager, as were other nations like Switzerland, for Germany to stamp a large red "J" in the passports of German Jews so that they could more efficiently be denied entry.[31]

In addition, though Sweden may have claimed official neutrality, this did not stop the country from becoming, until late in the war, Germany's principal wartime iron ore and ball bearings supplier. Its railways were used by the Germans well into 1943. Swedish trains had carried German troops into Norway as that country was being conquered and occupied by the Third Reich, and there is evidence that they also transported Jews from occupied nations across Sweden to death camps.[32]

On the other hand, it would certainly not be correct to suggest that Sweden did nothing during the war to help Jews survive German oppression. Ninety percent of Denmark's Jews (7,200) found refuge in Sweden.[33] There were also significant Swedish efforts in the last year of the war to save the Jews of Hungary, including a June 1944 appeal by the king to Hungary's ruler, Admiral Horthy, to stop the deportation of Hungarian Jews to "extermination" camps.[34] It should be noted, however, that by the spring and summer of 1944 there were other world leaders who also expressed such displeasure, including that of President Roosevelt, whose request was followed a few days later by a heavy American air bombardment of Budapest. Even Horthy himself seems to have been uncomfortable by what he appears to have understood to be the mass murders of his citizens.[35] Though his having made the effort is extremely significant, it is unclear whether the Swedish king's message played any actual role in what would prove to be the brief reprieve given Hungarian Jews from shipment to the death camps.

RAOUL WALLENBERG'S ATTEMPTS TO
SAVE THE JEWS OF HUNGARY

Clearly the most famous and arguably consequential Swedish action to save the Jews of Europe was the appointment of Raoul Wallenberg as third secretary to their embassy in Budapest.[36] Arriving in Hungary in July

1944 (as the deportations were coming to a temporary halt), he started creating passports, which he issued to as many Jews as he could reach.[37] He even designated buildings to be covered by diplomatic immunity in which some of these new Jewish/Swedish subjects were able to find safe refuge, and to which Wallenberg would eventually direct the delivery of life-sustaining food rations.[38] By mid-October, Wallenberg instructed his staff to issue Swedish papers to any Jew who applied. By the end of October (when Germans troops would wrest control of Hungary from its native ruler), more than 4,500 Hungarian Jews carried Swedish papers along with another 3,000 possessing fake Swedish certificates handed out by a Jewish organization known as the Aid and Rescue Committee, one of whose leaders was Reszo Kasztner.[39]

In October, when the deportations had resumed, Wallenberg would drive to the sites from which the Jews were to be shipped and bluff the armed guards into believing that some of the deportees were actually Swedish subjects. He stood on the rail tracks or climbed the train wagons, handing out protective passes even as warning shots buzzed by him, and succeeded in having a significant number of prisoners returned to Budapest.[40] His legendarily heroic work likely saved the lives of 20,000 to 30,000 of Hungary's Jews, with some estimates suggesting that as many as 100,000, in one form or another, may have owed their survival to him.[41]

There is a question, however, as to whether it is the Swedish government that deserves the bulk of the credit for having the wisdom and compassion to send Wallenberg on his mission. In reality, the Swedish Foreign Ministry seems to have shown little interest when Wallenberg was selected and assigned to Budapest. His ministry's leadership gave him no instructions, and, contrary to normal procedures, they neglected (perhaps out of either indifference or some unexplained desire to avoid a paper trail) to create even a dossier on their thirty-one-year-old attaché. An American representative in Stockholm reported back to the U.S. government that it was not likely Sweden would ever provide the newly appointed diplomat with anything resembling a concrete program, because in making the assignment, the Swedish Foreign Office simply believed it was cooperating in the furtherance of "an American program."[42]

It was American authorities who would have to fulfill any promises of lenient postwar treatment offered by Wallenberg to Hungarian or German officials in exchange for their cooperation in saving Jews. Sweden may have paid Wallenberg's salary and provided him diplomatic status, but it was the American War Refugee Board's instructions that Wallenberg would be following. It was Washington, not Stockholm, that gave the young Swedish diplomatic aide permission to build a camp in Budapest in which Jews could reside under some protection.[43] And, as was the case with most of the other funds distributed by the War Refugee Board, the majority of the money used for Hungarian rescue efforts was not drawn from either American or Swedish governmental sources, but was provided by the privately funded American Jewish Joint Distribution Committee.[44] As his biographer Ingrid Carlberg concisely concluded, "Wallenberg was a Swedish diplomat, working on an American assignment."[45]

The Swedish Foreign Office would in fact grow uneasy over Wallenberg's activities in Budapest, with many in the office raising a disconcerted eyebrow as his mission began to gather momentum. They feared that his issuance of credentials to Hungarian Jews would result in a kind of passport inflation, which might reduce the value of all Swedish passports and thus undermine the security of their own citizens traveling abroad.[46]

Why and how, with no diplomatic experience and little support or enthusiasm from the corridors of the Swedish Foreign Office, this young businessman came to be selected for his legendary mission actually began with Norbert Masur.

MASUR'S ROLE IN THE SENDING OF WALLENBERG

On April 18, 1944, a year and a day before his own treacherous journey to meet Himmler, Masur sent a letter to Stockholm's chief rabbi, Marcus Ehrenpreis, suggesting that it was time to find a non-Jew who is "clever, with a good reputation, [and] willing to travel to Romania/Hungary to lead a rescue mission."[47] He went on to propose that the man would need to be provided with a Swedish diplomatic passport and be assigned by the Foreign Ministry to the legation in Budapest. Masur added that even large sums of money could be provided, as they would come from American Jewish sources, as needed. He believed, given such a position, the right man could save hundreds of lives.[48] Other than his underestimation of how many lives the actual emissary would in fact save, his sage-like suggestion proved prescient.

Rabbi Ehrenpreis immediately recognized the wisdom in Masur's plan and asked the advice of the well-connected Koloman Lauer, a Calvinist Hungarian businessman of Jewish parentage who had escaped to Stockholm but whose relatives were still living precariously in Budapest. Lauer suggested that the youthful and energetic Wallenberg fit the description.[49] A Lutheran, Raoul Wallenberg was the great-great-grandson of Jews who had settled in Sweden. Though only one-sixteenth Jewish, he was known to refer to himself as being a half Jew.[50] At the time of the war, "his family controlled the Eskilda Bank, a financial institution that continued to deal with both the Allies and the Axis."[51]

In April 1944, Iver C. Olson was designated as the American War Refugee Board's attaché in Sweden with responsibility for refugee issues. As the Jewish situation rapidly deteriorated in Hungary, the Americans had also been hoping that the Swedish Foreign Ministry might strengthen its diplomatic representation in Budapest. As luck would have it, soon after hearing from Rabbi Ehrenpreis, Koloman Lauer encountered Olson and recommended that the United States urge the Swedish Foreign Ministry to dispatch the energetic and willing Wallenberg on the diplomatic assignment Masur had suggested.[52]

CREDIT DUE

There is no doubt that without the Swedish government's cooperation in sending Wallenberg, thousands of additional Jews would have been murdered. Yet there seems to be little public awareness that there were other players in addition to who government officials in Stockholm deserve some of the credit.

Similarly, it cannot be denied that without Bernadotte arranging for Red Cross transportation, Masur's April 1945 negotiations with Heinrich Himmler might likely have yielded little practical result. The Swedish count clearly deserves credit for having participated in the saving of thousands of lives, eventually including many Jews. Yet, had Masur not first laid the groundwork during his daring meeting with the head of the ss, would the Swedish count or his government have negotiated for the release of Jewish captives? Without Masur, would Himmler have made Bernadotte the offer to also release most of Ravensbrück's other prisoners in exchange for delivering his offer of a cease-fire to Western leaders as and when he did?[53]

These questions cannot be answered with absolute surety. Yet, perhaps in some small part due to the count's own version of the events as well as the general admiration in which he was held, the efforts of the unofficial representatives of the World Jewish Congress were for decades too often ignored or literally relegated to a footnote in history, only to be more fully recognized much later.[54] Masur's 1971 obituary in the *Jerusalem Post* included the following telling sentence: "There must be quite a number of people alive today who do not even know that they owe their lives to Norbert Masur."[55]

With unfortunate and dreadful irony, the extent of the credit Bernadotte received for freeing Jews from Ravensbrück might have played a small role in the Swedish count's tragic and violent death. His reputation for having successfully negotiated for the lives of Jews may have been part of the reason why he seemed a logical person to be tasked as a neutral representative of the Red Cross to assist in brokering a peace in the wartorn Palestine of 1948. In September of that year, in the middle of the Arab-Israeli war fought over Israel's nationhood, Bernadotte would die in Jerusalem from a bullet fired by a member of a Jewish fringe group of the era, pejoratively known as the "Stern Gang."[56] The count's fervent advocacy for establishing Jerusalem as an international city, as well as his support for the "right of return" of some 300,000 Arab refugees, was perceived as a danger to his killer's vision for the future of Israel.[57]

CHAPTER 12

The Buses Were White

By the beginning of the fourth week in April 1945, Fritz Suhren had been commandant of Ravensbrück for three years.[1] By all accounts he had created "a special hell for women." He ordered Jewish inmates murdered by "torture, lethal injection, medical experiments, starvation or gassing." He worked some to death, and had others shot in an alley specifically designated for the purpose.[2]

As the war was ending he was arrested by the British, but on the very eve of what was to be his 1946 trial he escaped his captors and remained on the run for the next three years until he was apprehended by the Americans. After conviction by a French military court, he was executed in June 1950.[3]

On what was most likely April 22, 1945 (the day after Himmler's April 21 meeting with Masur and the first of his two meetings with Bernadotte), Schellenberg's aide Franz Göring delivered to Commandant Suhren Himmler's order to free one thousand (Polish Jewish) women. Göring was surprised by the ss commandant's refusal to comply. Suhren had just received instructions from his Führer's office not to release any inmate, and to liquidate all of the prisoners before the arrival of Allied troops.[4]

Franz Göring would later claim that Suhren reluctantly agreed to release the thousand Jews only after Himmler's assistant Rudolf Brandt personally reaffirmed the interior minister's directive and informed the commandant that Himmler himself countermanded all other prior instructions, including the one previously issued by Hitler's office.[5] Masur's assessment had been correct; if the ss leader gave a specific order to his underlings, they would do everything they could to see it carried out. Although the camp's prisoners would continue to be murdered through at least April 27, it appears that the gassing of inmates ceased on approximately April 22.[6]

In anticipation of the Himmler-approved buses spiriting away some of his prisoners, the Ravensbrück commandant reluctantly followed the dictates of his ss superiors and instructed the camp population that all Polish Jewish women were to step forward for potential selection. At first many were unwilling to identify themselves as Jews. Most had seen how other selection processes, particularly those in Auschwitz, had often ended. One Ravensbrück prisoner chosen for transport said that some of her fellow selectees had to be dragged, while other inmates who were to remain in the camp appeared from "behind . . . the barbwire looking at us, [knowing] that 'transport' usually means death."[7]

Decades later, one survivor described the women's condition, confusion, and finally her decision to cooperate.

> Suddenly they took some of us. . . . We didn't know how, what, why. . . . We didn't know a thing. . . . And there were rumors. They didn't give us food or water, nothing. We were just lying there, one day, two nights or two days. I only know that suddenly they opened the door and the white buses arrived. . . . Someone suddenly says: "Who wants to go to Sweden? The Red Cross buses are waiting outside."
>
> [A woman] said: "They'll trick you.". . . And I said: "Anything will be better than this. Let's go!". . . We just went . . . in the bus, . . . we were crying, they gave us food.[8]

Amazingly, almost every one of the original five hundred prisoners from the Krupp factory near Berlin was selected to be among the first group evacuated.[9] Having barely escaped the gas chamber at Auschwitz exactly nine months earlier, they now became part of the private bargain struck between a Jew from Sweden and Heinrich Himmler. The arrangement was so secret that apparently most of those freed would never learn the true circumstances leading to their release.[10]

Though a few who investigated the incident believed that the selection of those to be transported was done haphazardly, since Kreitich and

Trampnan were present in the camp when the decisions were made, some of the Neukölln survivors speculated that their two former supervisors had arranged to have their group chosen.[11] Had Kreitich and Trampnan been ordered to stay, or had they chosen to remain in order to look after the young women? If they were not at least in part responsible for their former workers going first, how can we explain that seemingly all of them were included? If these SS officers did influence the selection, was it out of their attachment to the women or to provide themselves with mitigating evidence if they were ever brought before a postwar tribunal? The answers become even more complicated when we learn that many of the women did not believe that their former supervisors played any part in who was chosen to board the buses. Rather, they were convinced the choice had been made because of how they looked.

Many of Ravensbrück's Jewish prisoners had been brought there from labor camps like Rechlin-Retzow. Malka's group from Neukölln called them "Shadow Women" because many of them were so thin, weak, and malnourished that they were unable to even stand.[12] The survivors of Krupp's Berlin munitions plant, though severely undernourished, had not been starved to death or near-death as had these "shadows."

It is true that as the least-emaciated Jewish women at the camp, the women from Neukölln were, of course, more capable of making the journey to Sweden, but my mother and her friend Genya more cynically believed that the Germans had selected them for release not because they would be more likely to survive the trip but rather because the SS were simply afraid to let anyone else see these "shadow women."[13] They hoped to mislead the world into believing that the undernourished yet comparatively healthier women from the Neukölln plant were typical examples of how the Third Reich had treated its Jews.

Like the memory of a dream, the details of exactly when the women left remain elusive. The best evidence is that on what was likely April 25, or possibly April 26, a thousand Jewish women, including approximately 490 of those from the Krupp-Neukölln factory, were evacuated from the camp, where they appear to have spent approximately the previous twelve days.[14]

Since Himmler had insisted that their identity as Jews be kept confidential, the women were ordered to remove any markings or identifications that might label them as Jewish.[15] At the camp's gates, in the midst of terrifying uncertainty and confusion, and with some female SS guards still taunting women by telling them they were on their way to be gassed one thousand women boarded white buses whose polite Swedish drivers offered them cigarettes.[16] In spite of this small gesture of kindness, fearing the buses might themselves be disguised gas chambers, the women were still concerned, and some remained suspicious even after they were being driven from their last concentration camp toward a promise of liberty.[17] In reality, they had yet to awaken from the nightmare, and a few never would.

A DANGEROUS JOURNEY TO FREEDOM

One survivor would tell an interviewer that when finally on the bus, she had "hoped it was over. . . . but [then] we saw in the sky the planes. One of our buses was attacked. . . . The next bus . . . was bombed."[18] Himmler's astrologer, Wilhelm Wulff, who traveled the same route three days later, described the experience as "just like being at the front," the road strewn with "burned-out vehicles strafed by low-level attacks."[19]

Exhausted and terrified, the women poured out of their transports, running into the surrounding woods as they fled bullets and bombs. Some found shelter in a barn, where they hid for the night.[20] Remarkably, the next day all managed to walk safely to nearby Lubeck. Their luck was holding, but the delay had created added risks and unforeseen complications to their exodus.

The Lübeck of April 26 and 27 in 1945 was a very dangerous place to be stranded if you were a Jew. On April 27, three barges of prisoners from Eastern European camps landed near the city. As the inmates struggled ashore, they were gunned down by SS men as well as members of the crew.[21]

In addition, the longer the women remained on German soil, the closer they were to the day when Adolf Hitler would fire Heinrich Himmler from all of his government and party offices.[22] With this dismissal, Himmler would lose all official authority to approve the releasing of anyone, especially Jews, out of the "fatherland." Time had now become even more of the essence as my mother and those with her anxiously waited in Lubeck for the arrival of replacement vehicles.

To Bernadotte's credit, the Red Cross quickly arranged for trucks to carry the Jewish women into German-occupied Denmark and then on to his home nation. On the rescue vehicles was affixed the flag of neutral Sweden. In the latter days of the war, however, the Germans had been known to use emblems such as the Red Cross and the symbols of other countries as camouflage for their military. These new displays of Swedish neutrality proved no better shield from the chaos at war's end than the red crosses that had been painted on the buses originally carrying them from Ravensbrück.[23]

Once on the open road, and within hours of actual freedom from the horror, the young Jews who had survived months of Allied bombing raids without a single casualty were again strafed and shelled by British planes.[24] Three of the women from the Neukölln factory were killed. Three others were badly hurt but would eventually recover in a Danish hospital,[25] while a number of less seriously injured would wait to be treated in Sweden. When shrapnel tore through her right leg, Malka joined the wounded. Though she bore no tattooed serial numbers, for the rest of her life she carried a three-inch-long purple gash on the back of her calf as her external memento of a war that had been waged against her.

When their convoy finally reached Denmark, the survivors were surprised by the warmth of the greeting.[26] The same was true the next day when they arrived by ferry at Malmo in southern Sweden, where they made first contact with relief workers from the American Jewish Joint Distribution Committee and the free Jews of the city.[27] The date was April 28, 1945, a day that would prove to be the beginning of a new hope for my mother and the end of hope for Heinrich Himmler and Adolf Hitler.[28]

1. Malka's father, Samuel Repstein, in Poland in the
very early 1900s. Author's collection.

2. Malka's first husband, Hamel Wolf, in Poland in the mid-1930s.
Author's collection.

BL № 021875

Attiecības pret kaṛaklausību:

Zemessargs.

Pamats:

Daugavpils kara apr.

pr-ka 1926 g. rīd.

apliecība № 97/2099

— 4 —

BL № 021875

Pases
īpašnieka
paraksti:

Pases īpašnieka labās rokas
rādītāja pirksta nospiedums:

— 5 —

3. Gilel Storch.

4. Norbert Masur.

5. Genya and Malka in Sweden in 1946. Author's collection.

6. Malka (center) flanked by Genya to her right and Genya's future
husband to her left, in a group that includes other survivors and
Swedish supporters near the end of 1946. Author's collection.

7. Morris and Molly Goldman's wedding photograph
in Los Angeles 1947. Author's collection.

8. Stanley in Boyle Heights in the mid-1950s. Author's collection.

9. Genya and Molly in Los Angeles in 1990. Author's collection.

10. Mother and son in Los Angeles in 1994. Author's collection.

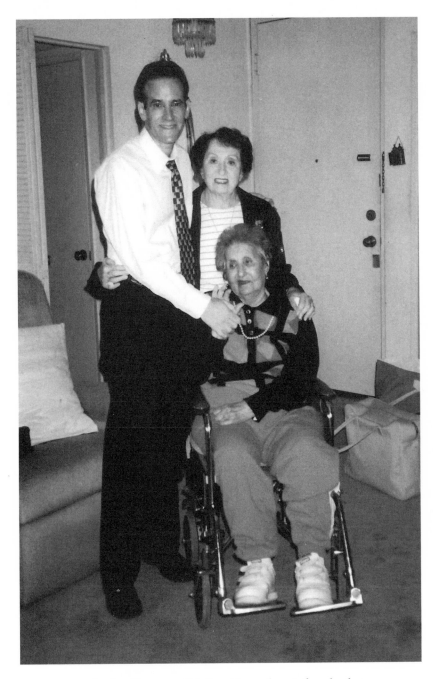

11. Stanley, Genya, and Molly as Genya departs from her last
visit to Los Angeles in 1998. Author's collection.

12. Genya returns to Auschwitz in 2001. Author's collection.

CHAPTER 13

Time Brings on All Revenges

LÜNEBURG HEATH

All his desperate efforts to secure a deal for himself with the Allies proved futile; when all was said and done, Himmler "stood empty-handed" and on the run.[1] If it were not for the monstrous crimes from which he was attempting to flee, his efforts would be laughable. Like someone unable to conjure the image of his own demise and so forever postpones putting his affairs in order, Himmler never actually prepared either an escape or a believable new identity.[2] He acquired forged papers identifying him as a German sergeant named Heinrich Hitzinger. His disguise was simply to shave his mustache, don a patch over one eye, and (oblivious to the reality that any member of the Gestapo was likely to be stopped and arrested) substitute his SS Reichsführer uniform for that of a Gestapo sergeant-major.[3]

It proved to be a ruse so patently transparent that it left him still readily recognizable as the same Heinrich Himmler whose likeness had for years appeared in newspapers, magazines, and newsreels. On May 11, with five compatriots and wearing his ineffectual disguise, the now former head of the SS took to the road in hopes of avoiding Allied capture.[4] Within a few days the group divided in two.

On May 21, exactly a month after his April 21 meeting with Norbert Masur, Himmler and a couple of remaining companions were taken captive by a pair of freed Soviet POWs deployed to reinforce a British patrol at a checkpoint near Bremervorde.[5] Two days later he identified himself as Heinrich Himmler to a British officer who seemed to already know exactly to whom he was speaking. A captain later described his prisoner as having "behaved perfectly correctly and gave me the impression that he realized things had caught up with him." The captain added (similar to how Masur had felt when first meeting the SS leader a month earlier) that he "found it impossible to believe that this man was the notorious Heinrich Himmler."[6]

The army medical staff began a physical examination. As a doctor was about to search his prisoner's mouth, Himmler understood that his captors were seconds away from uncovering his only remaining avenue of avoiding enemy retribution. His last moment had come.[7]

Every now and then there appears the slightest remnant of controversy surrounding the exact circumstances of Himmler's death. For a brief period of time in the early 2000s, for example, it was reported that various British memos and telegrams allegedly authored in May 1945 indicated that a secret execution ordered by His Majesty's government had terminated the life of the Gestapo leader.[8] These letters caused a stir until even the Himmler biographer whose claimed discovery of the alleged conspiratorial papers had seemed suspicious to a number of experts, eventually conceded that the documents were likely "inauthentic."[9]

The idea that the British secretly executed Himmler for fear that the Reichsführer would reveal the existence of clandestine wartime negotiations, which Churchill's government adamantly denied, makes for an intriguing storyline. However, what history has long recorded remains the unimpeachable truth: While in an internment camp undergoing medical examination, Himmler chose to end his life with a bite to the cyanide capsule that had long been embedded in his tooth. His body buried in an unmarked grave near Lüneburg Heath, his Berlin Villa torn to the ground, and his land used to build housing for occupying American soldiers.[10]

THE FALL OF THE UNREPENTANT ALFRIED KRUPP

On April 11, 1945, as the advancing Allied forces captured the German town of Essen, "a squad of steel-helmeted American infantrymen" found Alfried Krupp, in whose Berlin factory my mother had labored for nearly nine months, still in the office of his enormous mansion, carrying on business as usual for the benefit of his Führer and the Reich.[11] His captors inquired why, though he must have received reports of the approaching Allied soldiers, he had not chosen to flee the Ruhr Valley? He responded simply, "I wanted to stay with my factory, where I belong." When placed under house arrest, he blithely assumed it would be for no more than a few days.[12]

At his Nuremberg trial, Krupp's attorneys argued (as did the lawyers for other manufacturers) that if their client had not accepted slave laborers or had he failed to meet the required quotas of munitions, he would have been punished. To rebut such claims, the prosecution offered testimony from Karl Otto Saur, the former chief of Albert Speer's ministry's technical office.[13] A prisoner of the Allies from 1945 to 1948, Saur had been granted immunity in exchange for his cooperation at Nuremberg. William Manchester wrote that Saur's "appearance out of the past . . . stunned the thirty-three German lawyers [who sat] before Alfried like a protective black shield. They were helpless against Saur. He had been too close to the Führer, he knew too much and he swore under oath that Alfried's personal intervention with Hitler was directly responsible for Krupp's use of Auschwitz Jews."[14]

In 1948 the U.S. Military Tribunal at Nuremberg, in a sixty-thousand-word written opinion, found Krupp guilty of, among other crimes, the use of slave laborers like my mother.[15] Krupp continued to show as little emotion when sentenced to twelve years in prison as he had during the course of his lengthy trial. However, when the tribunal pronounced the unexpected order that his corporate assets, the significant bulk of his fortune, were to be forfeited (a punishment not even the prosecution had requested), "he went as white as a sheet [and] seemed to be on the point of collapse."[16]

Like so many of those convicted at Nuremberg, however, Krupp would not serve anything approaching his pronounced sentence. A book quickly authored by two of his attorneys along with the former National Socialist constitutional lawyer Ernest Rudolf Huber and entitled *Why Was Krupp Condemned?* convinced West German chancellor Konrad Adenauer, as well as a large segment of the already sympathetic German public, that Alfried had been wrongfully convicted.[17]

Though in 1951 only a handful of years had passed since the gas chambers had ceased and the killing camps closed, the Nazi regime was already being thought of as a remnant of an aberrant warp in time. Acting as if half a dozen years were an epoch, the unpleasant subject of the Holocaust was appearing less and less as a topic of public discussion in Germany, as well as in the United States.[18]

This optimism and historical amnesia was promoted by Western governments' opportunistic efforts to align public opinion with what they saw as the new world order. A strong West German democracy was deemed vital to confronting the Soviets' expansion into Europe. Obsessing about the Nazi atrocities of the last decade succeeded only in awkwardly stirring up anti-German feeling in the West at a time when that former enemy was becoming an important new partner.[19] Britain and the United States, in particular, wanted the industrial potency of the coal and factories of the Ruhr Valley to reinvigorate their new ally, and the heart of the Ruhr Valley's industrial strength had long been the Krupp works at Essen. With its surviving population of skilled workers, engineers, and supervisors, Krupp's company still possessed the potential of an enormous economic engine.[20]

On February 3, 1951, Alfried Krupp, along with all other imprisoned German industrialists, was officially released from prison. In addition, personally believing that "property forfeiture was somehow repugnant to American justice," U.S. High Commissioner for Occupied Germany John J. McCloy also ordered that the vast holdings that the tribunal at Nuremberg had forced Krupp to surrender be returned.[21] None of the prosecutors who had tried him, or the judges who had found him guilty, or the slaves who had toiled in his factories were consulted before his release and the restoration of his financial empire. No alleged trial errors, which were claimed as the justification for the amnesty, were ever identified.[22] The trial records seem never to have even been examined by those entrusted with making what proved to be a political decision to commute the sentences of Krupp and the scores of others granted early release.[23]

Having been reinstated as the head of his conglomerate by the American high commissioner, Alfried Krupp would become the German public's most popular industrialist. He appeared on the August 19, 1957, cover of *Time* magazine—not as part of an exposé on the exploitation of wartime slave labor, or because of the murders he had ordered, the thefts he had perpetrated, or his mass-produced weapons, which had played a significant role in Hitler's wartime successes. Rather, the publication hailed Krupp, "the wealthiest man in Europe—and perhaps the world," as a symbol of the economic miracle that was postwar West Germany.[24] As the 1950s approached its end, he was about to become Europe's only billionaire.

A QUEST FOR REPARATIONS

In the late 1950s, four decades before the better-known and more all-encompassing German slave labor reparations cases of the late 1990s, a legal brief entitled "The Forced Labor of Jewish Concentration Camp Inmates within the Krupp Combine," authored by the Conference on Jewish War Material Claims (hereafter, the Claims Conference) arrived at the Krupp corporation. It was a request, or demand, that the company provide a financial settlement to those who had been made to toil in Krupp's wartime factories.[25] The document included the following allegations: "The firm of Krupp [had] exploited the prisoners' labor without ever paying them for it, nor did it ever attempt to compensate its forced laborers for the injuries to life, health, freedom, and honor which were sustained."[26]

In response, the corporation's representatives were adamant that any discussions of settlement that they might agree to participate in could not involve possible payments to the heirs of those already deceased, nor would they consider making any charitable contributions on their behalf.[27] In other words, in order for talks to begin, the plaintiffs would have to agree that there would be neither debt, nor justice, owed the dead.

Furthermore, perhaps fearing that it could involve tens of millions of dollars in additional payouts, the company took the position that a Conference on Jewish war claims was not empowered to negotiate on behalf of potential gentile, as opposed to Jewish, plaintiffs. This refusal to allow the Claims Conference to negotiate payments to anyone other than Jews was contrary to the position previously agreed to by the Farben corporation. Farben was a major German company that had also used slave labor, as well as having operated a plant near Auschwitz-Birkenau, and had recently reached a settlement agreement with the Claims Conference.[28]

The plaintiffs' pro bono counsel in the negotiations, Benjamin B. Ferencz, who had been the youngest of the Nuremberg lead prosecutors, was appalled by the prenegotiation restrictions demanded by the Krupp company.[29] During the war, Ferencz, a Hungarian-born Jewish American, was a sergeant who survived the landing at Normandy and the Battle of the Bulge and arrived in the camps in time to witness Jewish bodies still burning in the crematoriums. Three years later, he was twenty-eight years old and a general leading the 1948 Nuremberg prosecution of the Nazi murderers of a million Jews, and was subsequently one of the trial court prosecutors of Krupp himself.

Ferencz was particularly eager that formerly subjugated Jews and gentiles should remain unified whenever possible and detested the suggestion that the discussions be limited to only certain former slaves. However, he sadly concluded that Krupp (still apparently believing Jews to be a people separate from the rest of the world) would never make payments to non-Jewish victims based on a claim asserted by a Jewish organization. In the end, Ferencz agreed to the company's demands. In exchange for limiting plaintiffs' claims by not including deceased Jews or any gentiles among their ranks, the corporation agreed to begin negotiations.

NEGOTIATING A SETTLEMENT

Krupp had been quite generous when providing retroactive compensation to his former German employees. In 1953, once he had felt secure at the head of his family business again, he sold off some of his land in order to make good on back payments owed to the company's pensioners.[30] Since Farben had recently agreed to pay each of its surviving slave laborers $1,250, Ferencz believed a quick settlement could be reached by requesting the same relatively modest sum from Krupp's representatives.

Unfortunately, the very thought of compensation to non-German forced laborers, even in such a minimal amount, was abhorrent to Krupp, and negotiations between his designated agents and the plaintiffs' Jewish lawyers proved fierce and unpleasant. "Each session was marred by recriminations, accusations of bad faith," and even with what Ferencz later described as "anti-Semitic remarks" from the corporation's representatives.[31]

Alfried had spent much of the 1950s denying that he had done anything wrong, while simultaneously eliminating the visible evidence and reminders of his crimes. "One by one, Krupp bulldozers leveled most of Alfried's wartime concentration camps,"[32] with the company typically building new housing developments in their place. It was a time when no one in Germany seemed to talk "about the Jews anymore, partly because there were so few to attract attention,"[33] and Krupp's demolition of the facility and barracks at Neukölln where my mother's group had labored for him seems to have occurred without comment.

Krupp could deny anything he wanted, but the claim that he had never been responsible for the treatment of his former slave-laborers was, of course, both legally and factually false. Legally, the verdicts of guilt rendered against him, which had never been overturned, established his legal responsibility under German law; and his 1951 release from confinement had not absolved him from convictions for his use and treatment of slave labor.[34] Factually, it had been proven in court that he had signed detailed contracts giving the SS the authority to supervise and inflict punishment on the forced laborers at his enterprises. He had admitted in affidavits to having, on several occasions, personally inspected the clearly abused and exploited slaves at a number of his factories. It had been on his personal orders that his foreman entered Auschwitz to select laborers fit to work while those rejected were consigned to die in the gas chambers; and it was at his insistence, and over the protests of even other Nazis, that a munitions plant was constructed in Auschwitz itself. In addition, "so shocking" had been the proof of the company's treatment of slave labor that, in the first few years immediately following the war, "all the allies, East and West, were [initially] determined to purge Europe of the Krupp name."[35]

In the end, Krupp did grudgingly, as a consequence of external pressure and advice, agree that he would make some payment to each of his surviving Jewish former workers. There was, however, a disagreement as to the number of plaintiffs likely to qualify for compensation. The intentional destruction of the company's business records as the war approached its end had made an accurate count of exactly how many Jews had gone into his labor camps difficult to determine. Calculating the number that had actually survived to the time of the settlement appears to have involved a fair amount of educated guess work. The Claims Conference estimated that their class of surviving Jewish former Krupp slaves totaled approximately two thousand, while the corporation maintained that far fewer potential recipients were still alive.[36]

On December 23, 1959, a compromise was reached when the corporation agreed that 1,200 (the company's estimate of the number of claimants) multiplied by just under $1,200 per claimant (for a total close to $1.5 million) would be immediately provided in compensation.[37] The corporation's representatives also stated that an extra nearly $1 million would be set aside by the company in the unlikely event that their predicted number of survivors proved to be an underestimation.[38] The understanding included an acceptance by the prospective plaintiffs that the maximum Krupp could be held responsible for would not exceed 10 million Deutschmarks ($2,380,000) and that by agreeing to such payment the potential civil defendant was not admitting liability or responsibility for any alleged past misconduct.[39]

A MEAGER BARGAIN UNFULFILLED

Alfried seems to have been little affected by the negative foreign comments, such as those of the *London Sunday Dispatch*, which suggested the meagerness of this settlement should be compared to the enormous wartime profits Krupp had made on "the blood and misery and starvation of . . . Jewish slaves who worked for him during the war."[40] He also appears to have been confident that he would never have to provide the additional $1 million he had agreed to if more than 1,200 claimants qualified for payment.

In the last months of the war, Krupp's own squads had dispatched box-car after boxcar of his Jewish workers to various death camps. It would have seemed unlikely to him that as many as 1,200 Jews, no less 2,000, had outlived both their captivity in his factories and the likely death sentence inherent in those spring 1945 transports to extermination camps as well as having had the added good fortune not to have perished in the ensuing fifteen years.

It is possible that Krupp may have lacked an adequate understanding that during the waning weeks of the war "extermination" facilities had no longer been functioning efficiently. The commander at Buchenwald, for example, had refused to accept delivery of any additional Jews, since by the spring of 1945 his underlings no longer had time to murder all of those already in confinement. Thus, more Jews than Alfried had likely assumed had outlived his death camp deliveries.[41] In the end, more than seven thousand applied for the funds.[42] The vast majority would be disappointed.

Though, due to an insufficiency of records, only a small percentage of those claiming to have worked in Krupp factories such as the one at Reichenbach were ever able to establish their eligibility; nearly 75 percent of the Jewish women who had survived slave labor at plants in Neukölln, Essen, and a factory at Geisenheim were qualified for compensation.[43] Thus, it quickly became clear that, while many of the 7,000 petitioners could not sufficiently establish their right to collect, considerably more than the corporation's estimated 1,200 Jewish survivors would be able to corroborate that they were entitled to the reparations.

Each of the first group of applicants deemed eligible (including my mother) was sent $750, with a few receiving as much as $825, and told that more money would hopefully follow. However, in spite of no fees being charged by the Claims Conference or its attorneys, as more Jewish survivors came forward and had their claims validated, each initial payment was temporarily reduced to $500 to insure that all would be provided some compensation. As the number of claimants approved approached the plaintiffs' original estimate of two thousand, the funds dwindled away, and payments had to be stopped until receipt of the antic-ipated additional $1 million promised.[44] "Claimants could not under-stand why some of their comrades had been paid while others were told to wait," writes Ferencz.[45]

As the reserves were running out, the plaintiffs' attorneys first learned that Krupp would not be contributing the additional money.[46] The cor-poration's top representative, who maintained that the original agree-ment had been merely a gratuitous promise and not a legally binding settlement, not only denied that the agreement required these funds, he also argued that the request itself was precluded by the understand-ing's financial limits.[47] Krupp believed that he had already been made to unjustly suffer enough. Having weathered the worst of the criticism as to the paltry nature of the restitution, as far as he was concerned giving away more money was unlikely to benefit his business. "We do not see ourselves in the position to make further sums available. I therefore do not consider even a discussion of this matter as appropriate,"[48] announced the corporation's spokesperson.

KRUPP RESURRECTS AN OLD ANSWER

When confronted with the question of why, if he were not guilty and bore no responsibility, Krupp had paid the $1.5 million in seeming rep-arations, his representatives continued to claim the payments had sim-ply been a voluntary "sacrifice" made in hopes of healing old wounds. The German populace proved receptive to their popular job creator's explanation. What could and should have been disastrous publicity was converted, at least in Germany, into a public relations success.[49]

Adding insult to the irreparable injury he had caused, when con-fronted in 1960 by requests for belated compensation from surviv-ing non-Jewish former slave laborers, Krupp responded that he was "unfortunately" unable to provide them with even a token amount.[50] His excuse, in spite of the entire settlement having cost him a mere one-fifth of 1 percent of his family's fortune, was that since "so much money has been used to the advantage of the Jews, we are not in a position to make voluntary contributions."[51]

Thus, in the National Socialist tradition, the explanation given by the richest man in Europe to the gentiles he had forced into the wretched conditions of his slave labor camps was that they were now to receive no compensation because the Jews had taken all the money for themselves.[52] The founders of the SS might have paid ready homage to their old friend's logic and tactic. The strategy achieved even more than what it may have set out to accomplish when there emerged palpable anti-Jewish resentment among the non-Jewish forced workers left out of the settlement.[53]

The agreement to pay reparations to Jewish survivors, perhaps as well as the fact that gentile survivors were not to be included, may also have sparked an even more widespread incarnation of the old hatred. It could have been coincidence, but within a month of the announced settlement, "there would be almost 700 reported cases of desecration of Jewish houses of worship and cemeteries [many of which had likely not been used in years] in every state of the Federal Republic of Germany." During this period, there were accounts of anti-Semitic incidents in "Vienna, Oslo, Antwerp, Brussels, East Berlin, Paris, Johannesburg, Cape Town, Melbourne, London, [and] New York."[54]

When, in the course of a personal correspondence with Benjamin Ferencz in January 2015, I mentioned to him that my mother had been a beneficiary of his late 1959 negotiations, the still angry ninety-five-year-old responded, "I am honored and pleased that your mother was one of the recipients of the meager sums we managed to squeeze out of the Krupp criminals."

THE FINAL FALL

There was eventually a small measure of ironic justice meted to Alfried Krupp. What constant Allied bombings and conviction at Nuremberg could not achieve, the hubris of his overconfidence would. A series of massive early to mid-1960s business deals in Communist nations proved to be a mistake destined to bring down his empire.[55]

In order to fund its colossal speculations, the Krupp company had been borrowing heavily against its assets and its future. In 1966, 270 very nervous lending institutions learned that their most significant debtor would be unable to meet scheduled interest payments on these massive loans. The banks, as well as the German government, were willing to provide assistance on the condition that the Krupp corporation, including its ownership, was significantly restructured.[56]

By the close of 1967, the house of Krupp ceased to exist as a private company. Its assets and debts were transformed to a so-called philanthropic foundation.[57] Without Alfried Krupp, the company would manufacture elevator systems, automotive parts, bobsleds, protective glass panels for ice hockey rinks, fireworks, and weaponry, including eventually supplying military submarines and warships to the government of Israel.[58] The last of these business arrangements gave rise to allegations of bribery of officials so highly placed that the Israeli press dubbed the scandal "The Submarine Affair."[59]

Time brings on all revenges.[60] The pressure had grown great. When it was already clear that his company could no longer survive as he had always known it, the embittered, twice-divorced, increasingly isolated, and unrepentant fifty-nine-year-old was dead. Reportedly succumbing to a cancerous tumor, though there is a certain mystery surrounding the cause of death, the man who had come close to making Adolf Hitler ruler of the world died in the company of only a nurse, with a copy of *Mein Kampf* on his bedside table.[61]

PART 3

Living with Survival

CHAPTER 14

There Was No Returning

Unable to rise without assistance, and at a time when I mistakenly believed she was in her last illness, my octogenarian mother was still pestering me about things seemingly as trivial as changing my eating habits. "Stanashe," she said from her bed, "you're a good Jew, an a good Jew doesn't eat pork."

"Ahh, Mom!" Her forty-eight-year-old son protested.

"You got ta promise me, you von't eat no more pork."

"Mom?" My resolve weakening.

"Promise me."

"Okay, I won't eat any more pork."

Obediently, I have not consumed the unsanctioned meat since. Luckily, she never mentioned shellfish.

It was not religious conviction that led her to insist that I follow this particular ancient dietary prohibition, but rather it was just (as it had been in the Poland of her youth) that we were Jews—a people with our own tradition—and that was the way it was. As for actual religion, if one sentence were needed to summarize how my parents raised me, it would have to be this: It was not that after the Holocaust we no longer believed in God, it was just that we were not prepared to talk to him until he apologized.

PROMISED LAND

Once in Sweden, my mother and her companions were hospitalized and, after a period of recuperation, housed and given employment in

Swedish factories.[1] All had suffered, and some of their number had been lost. Of the original 500 young women who together entered the Krupp munitions factory near Berlin, five had died and two others remained unaccounted for and presumed dead, leaving 493. In peacetime, the loss of 7 out of 500 young women workers in less than nine months would seem a scandalously improbable tragedy. Under the circumstances, it proved to be the highest survival rate of any of the numerous groups of Jews shipped from Auschwitz to an ss-controlled labor camp.[2]

In a report to the World Jewish Congress, Norbert Masur eloquently described his first meeting with Ravensbrück survivors, who seem not to have entirely understood that he was the one who had persuaded Heinrich Himmler to spare their lives:

> A visit to the rescued Jewish women in the receiving camps in southern Sweden affected and overwhelmed me deeply. It cannot be told what they had suffered during six years of incarceration. First, they were herded into a ghetto, then one concentration camp after the other, among them the horrible Auschwitz. During all these years, always hungry, always in mortal fear of total annihilation, [always] working very hard, and always tortured. It is a wonder that they were able to survive. Only a few of the hardiest could withstand the years of terrible agony. How could they resume something of a normal life? Most of them were alone in the world, their families scattered all over, most likely killed. Their homes and their milieu . . . completely destroyed. [F]or these Polish Jews . . . Palestine is probably their only chance to regain human dignity.[3]

In Sweden, the women were for the most part treated well. Though Swedish employers were rarely eager to take on the foreign workers, those with textile skills (as was the case for some of those from Łódź, including Malka and Genya) found it less difficult to obtain jobs. A few of the women, making new lives for themselves, chose to remain in Sweden.[4]

For most Holocaust survivors who returned to Poland, Masur's dour prediction unfortunately proved to be an understatement.[5] Hundreds of returning Jewish men and women were brutalized by Polish assailants infuriated that the Jews, whom they had assumed to be dead, had returned and dared attempt to reclaim their homes and property. In July 1946, the killings, which had been random and scattered, turned into a pogrom in which nearly fifty Jews were killed in the Polish town of Kielce.[6] In those years immediately following the war, more than one thousand Polish Jews were murdered, producing an exodus of many of the thousands who had attempted to return to the land where their families had lived for centuries.[7] My mother never forgave Poland.[8] As far as she was concerned, when it came to antisemitism, "da Poles, day vere as bad as da Germans, da Germans vere just bedder organized." A U.S. State Department restricted intelligence report dated May 15, 1946, and declassified in 1983, agrees with my mother's assessment. The report concludes that "there is evidence that Poles persecuted the Jews as vigorously as did the Germans during the occupation."[9]

In 1947, with returning to Poland no longer a realistic option, some of the Neukölln factory survivors, perhaps taking Masur's advice, chose to attempt illegal migration to Palestine.[10] Of the two boats they boarded, one successfully completed an uninterrupted journey to their Promised Land, while the other was stopped by the British Royal Navy. These latter passengers, including a number of the women who had survived the Łódź Ghetto, Auschwitz, the Krupp Berlin factory, and Ravensbrück, were then held for nearly a year at a detention camp in Cyprus.[11] At least they had not been sent to join the few thousand who, similarly captured, were shipped to an internment camp established by the British near Lübeck in Germany. In that period the United Kingdom believed it was justified in sending Holocaust survivors to Germany for incarceration. Those kept in each of these camps were eventually allowed to migrate to the newly formed state of Israel in 1948, where they would later be joined by others of my mother's fellow munitions factory workers, including her friend Genya, who arrived in 1949.

WELCOME TO LOS ANGELES

Though it was initially difficult to obtain entry to the United States, after a time, a majority of the remaining Neukölln workers were able to move to America, with most settling in New York and California.[12] After living for eighteen months in Sweden, my mother was one of the first to depart for the United States when she traveled alone to Los Angeles, where her eldest brother had moved years before. All of her European relatives had been swept away in the Shoah, leaving her parents' eldest offspring her only family. Finding her name in a list of the living, he had sent her a little money and tickets to sail to New York and then journey on to Los Angeles.

The testimonials of survivors are unfortunately filled with stories of American relations first welcoming the newcomers and then asking them to move out as soon as possible.[13] Eva Hoffman, a psychotherapist and herself a child of Holocaust survivors, observed that "the coldness of relatives who were supposed to provide a cushioning of hospitality and security" exacerbated the new immigrants' already palpable state of depression.[14]

Even among such unfortunate reports, the speed with which my uncle rejected his sister may have set something of a record. Perhaps he regretted his decision to accept the burden and expense of this seeming stranger he had neither met nor ever spoken with previously. Maybe he didn't like, or even dreaded, hearing stories of what she and the others he had left behind had suffered. On the drive from the Los Angeles airport to his apartment, they were involved in an automobile accident serious enough to put both of them in the hospital with broken bones, severe traumas, and contusions. Using a kind of logic that defies rational explanation, he considered the accident to have been her fault because he had been picking her up. Concluding that this foreign woman was obviously bad luck, her brother wanted nothing more to do with her, and though they lived in the same city for the next quarter of a century, he never again knowingly spoke to her.

I add the word "knowingly," because when I was a teenager, my mother confessed to me that she would occasionally call my uncle's phone number, let it ring until he answered, and then hang up. She just wanted to hear the voice of her only other relative. They would actually speak to each other several more times, but only after her ninety-year-old brother had slipped into dementia. He had no idea of the identity of the woman he described as "that lady," who would come regularly to sit with him in that last year of his life.

In 1939, Malka had a total of thirty-four close relatives in Europe. These brothers, sisters, nieces, nephews, first cousins, and of course her own husband and children, had lived between Poland and Belgium. By 1945, she alone was left alive, and in the Los Angeles of early 1947 Malka was without friends and ostracized by her only family. Yet, while she could not speak the language, she could sew. For several months, using the skills that kept her alive in the ghettos, she worked at a sewing machine in the city's downtown garment district until, at age thirty-seven, she met and married Morris Goldman.

In the years after his passing I never spoke with anyone who had known my father and failed to praise his goodness. Although he had suffered great deprivation and sacrifices growing up during World War I, having escaped Europe before the Shoah, he was my less damaged parent. An insightful man, he was capable of expressing parental affection in a way his wife could not. Although my mother was an attractive, extraordinarily intelligent woman and very aware that she surprisingly had continued to look years younger than her age, she would later tell me that my father had likely married her only out of pity. Watching them together when I was young, I had no doubt that he loved and was protective of his emotionally scarred spouse.

A Russian-Romanian-speaking Jew born in 1907 in that part of Romania that in the early 1990s was to become the nation of Moldova, he had studied in hope of becoming a doctor. Soon after his 1928 arrival in New York, however, he had been confronted by the Great Depression and the need to support his widowed mother and younger sister and brother who had joined him. Together they moved to Winnipeg, Canada, in the early 1930s, and then, as the war was nearing its end, he relocated on his own to Los Angeles. Looking for a way to make a living, he would become the barrel man of East L.A.

In his rickety old black truck, Morris would seek out businesses interested in disposing of their emptied barrels and drums. Gathering them up, he would sell them to companies in need of his used merchandise. Arguably overqualified for the work, the man who could speak and write seven languages made something of a practical science out of determining which discarded containers would be best for which purposes, even when his customers had not known. It never made him wealthy, but his savvy and strenuous physical labor would eventually allow us to move from a $30-a-month apartment in the lower-income, blue-collar, recent immigrant neighborhood of Boyle Heights to the modest American middle-class of West Los Angeles.

Exactly five years from the very day (and perhaps the very hour) when my mother had waited to enter the gas chamber in Auschwitz, I was born. It appears I somewhat resembled my brother before me, or at least at age seven my hair was that same shade of golden blond. There are sometimes small mercies to be found even in the rudest of streams.

CHAPTER 15

Memory

Dvora, Genya's eldest daughter, herself the mother of a boy and girl, once told me that she had asked her mother how it was possible for Malka to have gone on living after the Nazis had taken her children. Malka's wartime companion answered that even she did not know how anyone could go on after suffering such loss.

It would have been nice if my mother had escaped the harsher psychological effects of the Shoah, but how could she? She had been strong enough to survive the dangers of the ghettos, the camps, and slave labor as well as months of the most saturated of the Allied bombings of Berlin. Constant dehydration cost her the use of a kidney. Damage to her back would periodically send her into fits of spasmodic agony. She had contracted tuberculosis and been wounded by shrapnel. Yet it was the scar that was her memory that most troubled the otherwise undefeatable little woman. Like many others, though she had survived the Shoah, she never escaped it; and to a much lesser degree, neither could I.

Like many survivors, once sufficient time had passed, my mother could look fine, dress well, behave sociably, and even be quite charismatic and charming.[1] More than being just victims, survivors could carry on seemingly normal lives, yet they could also exhibit a sadness that was usually only discernible by those who knew them well.[2] A few of those meeting my mother for the first time could sense that there was something slightly enigmatic about this little Jewish woman, which they hadn't expected. (One devoutly Catholic colleague of mine left her initial encounter a bit shaken by what she could only cryptically describe as a kind of "aura" she sensed surrounding my parent.)

The actual consequences visited on those who lived through genocide were slow to be recognized. In the first few decades after the war, it was still axiomatic among many psychotherapists that only childhood traumas produced lasting effects. It was the rare psychiatrist who would have suggested that all of those who came out of the Shoah generally needed psychological treatment.[3] A relatively small percentage of the victorious and honored Americans returning home after years of fighting the righteous war against the Axis powers persistently complained of psychiatric problems. Nor did many who came through the Shoah think of themselves as emotionally damaged. They were the lucky ones who had outlived Hitler. Still young, they rarely spoke of it and tried not to dwell on the suffering and loss. Instead they concentrated on their new lives and new families. The world appeared perfectly prepared to put the Holocaust behind it, and the victims of the Shoah tried to fit in. Survivors like my mother hardly ever received the help they needed.

In the 1940s, 1950s, and even into the 1960s, serious examination of the depressing subject of the camps and their survivors seldom appeared in the mainstream popular media of motion pictures, magazines, or television and the Holocaust was thus less likely to be considered and discussed by the public at large. Though sales of Elie Wiesel's well-reviewed *Night* would reach ten million copies fifty-five years after its 1960 U.S. release, the book was not at first a commercial success. It took years before *Night* began to gain its significant readership.

Wiesel later speculated that in the 1960s the public was not prepared for a realistic account of the Holocaust.[4] The 1959 *Playhouse 90* television production as well as the 1961 theatrically released and still powerful motion picture of *Judgment at Nuremberg* (which included no Jewish characters), and, more directly on point, director Sidney Lumet's depiction of a survivor in his 1964 film, *The Pawnbroker*, represented rare high-profile exceptions to the rule that the Holocaust was simply too downbeat a subject for mass audiences.

It was only in the last decades of the twentieth century, as the victims as well as the generation of their victimizers started to precipitously disappear, that the true impact of the Shoah prominently emerged into popular consciousness and as the knowledge of what they had suffered and continued to suffer came to be understood, the remaining and elderly survivors began to be viewed with a kind of reverence.

SURVIVOR

On a Tuesday afternoon in April 1961, with my sixth-grade lunch break about to end, the few students who had permission to go home to eat were returning. One of them came up to me and said that he just walked by my apartment building and saw an ambulance in front of it. I asked him if he could see who was in it, and he answered, "There was an old lady." I breathed easier. I had been afraid the ambulance was there for my dad. He had suffered heart attacks before, and his condition was always on our minds. Then I was gripped by the unsettling thought that the "old lady" could have been my frantic mother getting in the ambulance to be with my father. I worried the rest of the afternoon, but I didn't say anything to anyone. When class let out at three o'clock I was afraid to go home. All the other children had gone, but I stayed by myself, bouncing a basketball around the schoolyard, until about four thirty.

Finally, I started on the short, two-and-a-half-block walk to our apartment. As I rounded the last corner, leaving only one long block left to travel, I could see cars I recognized as belonging to several of my parents' friends parked in front of our building. I knew only a death could explain them all being there on a weekday afternoon. I started running. As I sprinted up the flight of stairs to our second-story apartment, I was already screaming "No!" Our apartment was filled with adults all too familiar with loss. My mother was in her bed moaning uncontrollably. She spent almost the entire week sedated, barely able to communicate. Emotionally distancing myself from all of it, from everything, was best. It would be two weeks before, waking up in the middle of a dream about my father, I would cry.

Yiddish writer Isaac Bashevis Singer's alter ego, narrator, and protagonist of his short story "The Cafeteria" gave his own answer to how survivors go on living and functioning:

> They greet me, and we talk about Yiddish literature, the Holocaust, the state of Israel, and often about acquaintances . . . [who] are in their graves. . . . Whose turn is it next? . . . I'm often reminded of a scene in a film about Africa. A lion attacks a herd of zebras and kills one. The frightened zebras run for a while and then they stop and start to graze again. Do they have a choice?[5]

After my father's passing, my mother would visit his grave regularly, and she never remarried. She supported the two of us aided by the money they had saved. We were never rich but neither did we want for essentials. She managed an apartment building, and we were assisted financially by the monthly arrival of small Social Security widow and child benefits as well as an almost identically sized and similarly sized reparations check sent from the West German government.

It would be misrepresentation to imply that Molly Goldman never again had good days. Her expectations for life were still the relatively simple ones of the small cities in Poland she had come from. Though she never dated after my father's passing, she relished being around people. She could spend hours wandering through department stores like the iconic Bullocks Wilshire and the May Company. She would visit friends, lunch out, or just talk endlessly on the phone. She hated it when there was no one to keep the loneliness at bay.

She had three truly close friends in Los Angeles over the years, none of whom really got along with each other but all of whom enjoyed spending long periods of one-on-one time with Molly. Unfortunately, two of those friends would predecease her by about a decade, while the third reluctantly moved to Jerusalem to join her four children who had immigrated to Israel. Not surprisingly, both before and after the loss of her closest friends, most of my mother's small joys involved the son on whom she doted.

Survivors would often treat their children as the entire reason for living, and this was especially true for those who had already lost a child.

While an intense need to conform to parental demands is hardly unique to the offspring of survivors, many of us in the second generation found it particularly difficult to reject the sometimes suffocating attention.[6]

THE SECOND GENERATION

Everyone now understands that tremendously traumatic events such as the Shoah can, of course, influence the lives of survivors' offspring.[7] Each generation, through even its most subtle behavior and attitudes, passes a bit of its experiences on to its children.

In the early twenty-first century some experts first concluded that, in addition to the already understood psychological component that comes with being a member of a second generation, there may also be physiological consequences to being the child of a mother who lived through cataclysmic events such as the Holocaust, the atomic bombing of Hiroshima, the killing fields of Cambodia, or the butchery of Rwanda. Rachel Yehuda, a neuroscientist at the Mount Sinai School of Medicine in New York, asserted that mothers—in particular Holocaust survivors—suffering from PTSD gave birth to children three to four times more likely to be depressed and anxious than children born to mothers who had not suffered such fates.[8] Using a relatively small number of subjects, she compared Holocaust survivors' children to a control group of offspring whose Jewish families were not in Europe during the war and made a concerted effort to eliminate any possibility that these genetic markers were the result of traumas experienced during the childhood of the second generation. The study controversially concluded that children had the same epigenetic tags, which potentially impact the production of a stress hormone, as did their survivor parents.[9] In a somewhat similar vein, researchers at Emory University in Atlanta maintained that their tests had demonstrated the strong possibility that fear can also be genetically inherited.[10]

I have no idea if I or any of the other children of survivors I knew growing up had high cortisol levels, and I have no gauge to now measure whether we were abnormally prone to depression, anxiety, or fear. For that matter, it cannot be said with absolute certainty that my mother's postwar behavior, or that of any other survivor, wouldn't have been substantially the same had they never experienced the Shoah, just as there can be no surety that I and other members of my second generation would not have been exactly the same had our parents never gone through the horror. Yet the evidence, in a number of confirming case studies, certainly does at a minimum endorse a strongly correlative cause and effect. For myself, although I may not be able to identify precise, if any, chemical origins, I do not seem to have escaped a small part of me being forever caught in the currents of that rude stream that had very nearly drowned my mother. I had inherited only the shadows of a memory, but the reverberations of that echo would shape my life.

When I started writing my mother's history it never occurred to me, until I was deep into the preparation, that I would make myself a character in the story. There are hazards when the children of survivors not only document their parents' harrowing experiences but also include their own postwar lives. There is a danger of displaying not only self-pity but, even worse, self-aggrandizement by interposing into survivors' narratives and appearing to shroud ourselves with the awe in which our ancestors are remembered. As Eva Hoffman writes, "seeing yourself as a victim of victims, as damaged by calamities that had been visited on somebody else, is not a sympathetic position, [and you just might] end up not so much illuminating the past as turning the searchlight on your own narcissism."[11] I write, aware of the dangers lurking in the penumbra of any such a memoir, but in the conviction that the telling is worth the risk.[12]

PAST MIDNIGHT

The awe-inspiring nature of what Holocaust survivors lived through has often left their offspring, as documented by Helen Epstein in *The Children of the Holocaust: Conversations with Sons and Daughters of Survivors*, with a heightened sense that their own concerns are woefully inconsequential compared to those of parents who might "shatter" at any moment.[13] By the fortuitous timing of my postwar birth, I had evaded the horror my mother and her dead children had suffered.[14] It seemed completely appropriate and reasonable to hesitate before putting any part of my life ahead of her wishes because to do otherwise would cause more pain to this woman that I saw as intractably delicate.

The story of a nervous, overly protective and controlling widowed mother of an easily cowed young son is hardly unique. What separated my mother and I from the norm was not only the circumstances giving rise to her behavior but also, to a lesser extent, how codependently long I let it dominate my life.

Many children of survivors have had to overcome a considerable psychological barrier of guilt before being able to even move out of their parents' homes, and this has proved especially true for those of us who have borne a conscious need to fill the role of perished siblings.[15] My mother was never able to purge herself of the pain and guilt of her children's kidnappings and murders or the fear that (even if no longer at the hands of the Nazis) it could happen again. In fact, as far as she was concerned, there would always be only two sides to any argument—her side and the Nazi's. Accepting her claim that moving out of the apartment we shared would completely destroy her, I continued to live with my mother while in college and law school, through my years as a public defender, and into a tenured professorship.

A thirtyish bachelor living with his lonely mother, though a bit odd, is certainly not extraordinary. What gave our relationship its most unusual character was her uncontrollable need to always be certain that I was safe. Whether at a party, the movies, or someone's home, I was supposed to find a phone and let her know that I was all right and give her a specific time when I would be home. I wasn't so much a prisoner as I was like a parolee or an aged teenager with an unarticulated but understood curfew.

She accepted my occasional need to be out of town for a few days for professional reasons such as delivering bar review lectures, or even for a brief vacation. However, on most nights when I was in Los Angeles, at some slightly varying point after midnight, if I wasn't back in our apartment, she would start to panic. Though embarrassing, the need for a grown man to be constantly checking in with his mother paled in comparison to my frequent acquiescence to her screaming demands that I quickly return home.

In that era before mobile phones, if I wasn't at work, my friends or acquaintances would call me at our—my mother's—apartment. When I wasn't home, she would sometimes answer, take a message, and routinely ask for the caller's number. Even when they would repeatedly demur, as I had sometimes advised them to do, she would politely insist until they, as often as not, surrendered the information. It was an unusual tool of which she would make use. On some nights, when I had rebelliously either not called her or had called but refused to return home as summoned, she would start phoning, one after another, the numbers she had collected over the years. More than a couple of times I arrived at the faculty lunch room at noon to find one of the professors describing, with understandable irritation, having been awoken randomly at two thirty in the morning by my mother frantically searching for me.

Whether planned or not, fear of such humiliation proved a valuable weapon in my mother's constant battle to have me check in with her and/or simply come home. Those late-night phone calls to my friends or colleagues, the sheer guilt-inducing power of her obviously pained recriminations (often yelled loud enough to awake the neighbors), and even suicidal threats to leap from our third-story balcony or run out into the street and oncoming traffic were part of her arsenal.

Perplexed girlfriends were not only confused but hurt that I would not, unless we were traveling together in a different city, be able to spend an entire night with them. At some point, often in the dark early morning hours, I would gather myself together and head home for what was still likely to be an ugly, recrimination-filled reception. Once, while dropping a girlfriend off at her place, we discovered that a pipe had burst in her apartment building, temporarily flooding her unit. Her staying there that night was out of the question. After settling her into a nearby hotel at one thirty, she was shocked when I told her that I would be leaving to go back to my apartment. Even risking, as I had many times before and would again, the end of a relationship with an attractive, well-educated young woman seemed less painful than the unpleasant consequences of my not returning home that night.

As if that didn't make things difficult enough for the women I dated, they would also soon discover that there was something missing, or at least unreachable, about me. Like many, I was emotionally stunted, and I certainly wasn't alone in fearing that any close relationship might result in my being controlled. Yet, having my mother's tragic life as my template, I was also concerned about ever risking love for anyone, when inevitable loss, or at best obsessive fear, would be its end. Given the potential downside that can accompany closeness, I have lived my life pondering why I should feel anything.[16]

Of course, try as I might, stoic indifference would be a goal I could not always achieve. Yet, unable or unwilling to risk committing beyond superficiality, I have become the final descendent of that grandfather who had returned from the New World to a waiting Holocaust. I write, at least in part, the history of a soon-to-be vanished clan of which I will be the last member.

CHAPTER 16

The Last Chapter

When I was thirty-four, still living at home and still unsuccessfully urging my mother to seek deeply needed psychiatric help, for the first time I sought out a psychotherapist that I hoped could advise me on how to deal with my impossible situation. He was my age or a little younger, and for our first half hour I recounted the injustices I had suffered at the hands of a parent who refused to stop treating me like I was fifteen. When I had finished my practiced opening statement, the young therapist simply advised, "Well, then you should do something about it. Move out. You can't really expect her to do anything, it's clear she's not going to change."

It seems unfathomable now, but, at the time, this statement came as an unprovoked solid jab to my stomach. The guilt and fear were immediate and overwhelming. Was he really suggesting I simply abandon my unbelievably victimized mother?[1] I had long ago been convinced that she would fall apart or harm herself if I walked out. I had consulted this therapist to learn the magic words that would get her to change. I left his office after the one session and never returned.

It would be five years before I would again seek therapy in a group exclusively for children of Holocaust survivors, followed by one-on-one sessions, and it was only then that I would come to realize that I had spent my life mistaking my mother's strength for fragility. I lived with her until the month after I turned forty, when one day I simply left for a condominium I had bought and furnished without mentioning it to her for fear she might still talk me out of the move. My mother didn't hurt herself, and she didn't die. She survived as she had her entire life. It had taken me decades to realize she was one of the strongest people I would ever know.

Three and a half years later, however, she would suffer a stroke that paralyzed the left side of her body but left her mind intact. Although I never moved back, if I wasn't traveling out of the city I visited her every day in the apartment where she had lived for years. She now had a sympathetic long-term caregiver who became not only her constant companion but also her closest friend in America.

I still received late-night phone calls with accompanying recriminations, but she grew used to my not always being there and could be grateful when I visited or drove her places. The mother who I could not recall having hugged me, even when I was a child, would now sometimes put her right arm around my shoulder when I would arrive and kiss me awkwardly on my cheek.

She was indomitable. It was simply not in the makeup of the little Jewish woman to ever give up. As she lay in bed, with her numb left arm positioned across her chest, she would occasionally pat it with her right hand as she would smile and jokingly say, "It's like my little babala (baby)." She would always remain the consummate survivor. Like the definition of "man" in Fyodor Dostoyevsky's *House of the Dead*, if it was necessary in order to stay alive, my mother could seemingly "get used" to any physical deprivation or disability.[2]

One evening, when I had just arrived, she began a predictable rant about not having been able to reach me. After just a few moments of yelling, however, she broke into uncontrollable crying. She never cried when scolding me. There was an unfamiliar tone and texture to her voice when she said "Stanley, Stanley, I'm sorry, I'm so sorry. I know what I'm doing to you, but I can't stop myself."

It was the only apology of its kind I would ever hear from her. Perhaps the awareness had occurred in that very moment, or maybe it had come slowly over time, like those tears, drop by drop and against her will.[3] Our co-dependent relationship had been the fault of us both and yet perhaps of neither.

In the late 1990s, fifty-seven restitution-based lawsuits were filed in American courts against more than twenty different German and Austrian companies on behalf of all the World War II slaves who had labored for them.[4] Fearing that suing a sovereign country might be perceived as an unconstitutional interference with the executive branch's control over foreign relations, and thus result in a dismissal, no nation was named as a defendant.

During the Shoah, approximately four hundred German companies could be described as having been major users of forced workers gathered from concentration camps, with a number of enterprises even insisting that the SS construct labor camps adjacent to their own factories.[5] Over fifty businesses used prisoners from Auschwitz.[6] At least half of the early twenty-first century's top twenty German companies previously made use of some of the estimated 8 million to 10 million Nazi-era slave laborers.[7]

Yet, there was little legal precedent on the question of whether U.S. courts possessed the authority (jurisdiction) to even hear a lawsuit against European-based corporations over wrongs allegedly committed in Europe nearly half a century before. The plaintiff's attorneys were predominately the same American class-action lawyers who had recently brought the then still pending case in the Southern District of New York against Swiss banks for their failure to pay the heirs of Jewish account holders who had been Nazi victims. In both lawsuits, these lawyers tenuously argued that since the defendant companies did business in the United States, they could be sued in this nation's courts.

Understanding the possible fragility of their position, plantiff's counsel hoped to pressure the defendants by pursuing a widespread and potent public relations campaign in the media. Full-page ads appeared in the *New York Times*. One attorney organized a demonstration of Holocaust survivors in Frankfurt. Former slaves were interviewed on the CBS news magazine *60 Minutes* as part of a segment broadcast about the litigation. California governor Gray Davis joined a lawsuit claiming that the defendants' refusal to settle amounted to an "unfair trade practice."[8] Though there was a significant chance that U.S. courts might eventually dismiss the cases, the plaintiffs were clearly winning the battle for public opinion.

In spite of all the negative publicity, the defendant corporations continued to maintain that, even if jurisdiction existed in American courts and reparations were due, the burden of any financial settlement should be borne by the German government. The corporate defendants again, as Alfried Krupp's lawyers had done at his criminal trial fifty years before, fatuously argued that it had been the Nazis who had coerced their companies into accepting forced labor.[9] This assertion was an easily refuted lie. Documents submitted into evidence during the Nuremberg trials proved that German manufacturers clearly had a choice as to whether or not to exploit prisoners.[10] A few who chose not to use such workers continued to run their companies and even successfully compete for various government contracts, though perhaps not as profitably as they might have otherwise.[11]

Yet, in late 1998, the newly elected chancellor of Germany, Gerhard Schroeder, reversed the position taken by his predecessor, Helmut Kohl, and agreed that his government would contribute to any settlement reached with their nation's former slaves.[12] Thus, principally at government and not corporate expense, the Germans agreed to pay $7,500 to every victim, whether Jew or gentile. However, just as the Krupp corporation had insisted in the late 1950s, payments would be made only to those who were still living as of the date a settlement was agreed upon. February 15, 1999, for example, was designated by one federal judge and was used as a triggering date, making plaintiffs still alive on that day eligible for compensation, and rendering ineligible the estates of those who had passed away before.

The $7,500 payment was far less than the $30,000–$40,000 per survivor initially demanded. In fact, given the rate of inflation over the intervening years, it represented almost exactly the same purchasing power as had the roughly $1,200 Krupp was supposed to have paid his former Jewish slave laborers almost forty years earlier. The plaintiffs nevertheless accepted. Their willingness to settle was motivated not only by the realistic possibility that they might still lose their yet-to-be-ruled-upon motions to pursue these cases in American courts but also by the sad recognition that in 1999, as compared to 1959, a significant number of the senior-citizen plaintiffs were dying each day the negotiations continued unresolved.[13]

My mother anxiously awaited the payment for which, by dint of tenacity in both her initial survival and subsequent longevity, she had applied and qualified. It wasn't that she was in desperate need of the funds, as was unfortunately the case for many survivors, it was just that she had always felt making the Germans pay for anything was something of a small victory over the nation she had never forgiven.

The check was mailed to her, but by the time it arrived she was no longer there to receive it. By then she was with my father in a place she had reserved thirty-eight years earlier, after he succumbed to a heart that had been slowly failing since rheumatic fever nearly took his life as a child. On my mother's gravestone I had inscribed: "Beloved mother of Archie and Genya lost to the Holocaust." Maybe death was invented so that memory could finally rest.

FINAL ACT

Now you know who the little Jewish woman was and why Heinrich Himmler spared her, but how did any of this come to break Adolf Hitler? Here is how it happened. Pursuant to the agreement reached during the April 21, 1945, negotiations between Himmler and the German-Jewish businessman from Sweden, Norbert Masur, and then Himmler's discussions with Count Bernadotte, a letter documenting Himmler's offer of a cease-fire passed from the count to the Swedish foreign minister, who in turn conveyed it to the intended recipients—the British and the Americans. The Allies immediately rejected the proposal, and either they, or the Swedish government, quickly released the proposed peace initiative to the press.[14] On April 28 (the day my mother arrived in Sweden), Reuters issued a wire story revealing that Heinrich Himmler had been involved in an attempt to negotiate with the Allied powers by using a Swedish diplomat as an intermediary.[15] Late on the night of April 28, or early April 29, Goebbels forwarded the Reuters reports to his isolated

Führer, who rarely paid any attention to the "lies" being broadcast by the Western press.[16] This, however, was a story he believed.

Firsthand accounts reveal that, upon hearing the news, Hitler "raved like a madman."[17] One witness described how the German leader at first "turned a dark red, and his face became almost unrecognizable," and a short time later he grew "white as chalk" as if he were no longer alive.[18] He shouted that "even faithful Himmler," his most trusted minister, who "had constantly talked of loyalty," had betrayed him.[19] It proved to be the final blow to Germany's Führer. Himmler's "treachery," writes Joachim Fest in his history *Inside Hitler's Bunker*, "signified the collapse of a world."[20]

On April 29, Germany's supreme leader penned what he labeled his "Political Testament," sending four copies by separate messengers from his bunker to increase the document's chances of survival.[21] In it he fired Himmler from the Party and all offices of State. The SS chief's unauthorized attempts at negotiation, he wrote, had "done untold damage to the country . . . quite apart from . . . treachery towards me personally."[22] On April 30, 1945, reportedly while simultaneously biting down on a cyanide tablet, Adolf Hitler put a bullet in his own head.[23]

He had been living in the hush of death's impending presence. The capital's defenses had collapsed, and Russian troops were entering the city.[24] If he had never learned of Himmler's betrayal, something else would have soon brought about his end. Yet, had the news of Himmler not sapped his final will to resist, might he have tried to live a few more days or, though less likely, even changed his mind and attempted an escape to the south, where a diminished but still active German army might have protected him a bit longer? How much longer might the war have lasted? Alexandra Richie notes in *Faust's Metropolis*, "It was the information about Himmler's attempt to negotiate with the West along with the news that his phantom armies had not moved in to save him, which finally convinced the Führer that he had no course but to commit suicide."[25] Even if other pressures were at work pushing him, Himmler's freeing of a tailor's daughter played its part in the death of Adolf Hitler.

Everyone who has ever lost loved ones knows that their apparitions return in sleep. I dreamt about my mother for years after her passing. Although details would vary, it was in substance basically the same dream. We were in her last apartment, the one we were living in when I moved out, the one she had remained in for the next ten years, and the one in which she died. My bedroom was to the immediate left of the unit's only entrance, which opened into the living room. To its immediate right was a small hallway down which you would first pass the master bath and then the door of, what had been until her last few years, her bedroom. Given my prior room having its own conveniently situated bathroom, once my mother had her stroke and needed assistance getting around, she switched rooms. Her bed positioned in the same spot where mine had previously sat for years, she passed away in her sleep one morning, a few hours after leaving me a middle-of-the-night never-to-be-answered distraught voice message.

Although her appearance in the dream would vary, she most often looked the way she had when she was about sixty or so—less than five feet tall and ninety pounds; her hair darkly dyed and set in a bubble-like permanent that was fashionable in the late 1950s and early 1960s, and which women of a certain age continued to wear long after it ceased to be the style; her eyes often seemed oddly much darker than the color-changing hazel they had been in life.

It would be daytime, with light streaming through the sliding balcony door while we stood in the living room speaking to each other about some subject I could never later recall. Suddenly someone would knock on the front door. Looking quizzically, she would ask, "Should I hide in my bed-room?" I would first answer, "Yes, if it's someone who was at your funeral, they won't understand." Then, after a moment, I would change my mind and add that "maybe it would be better if other people saw you." Relieved at the thought of finally sharing the secret of her latest feat of survival, and imagining the surprise on the visitor's face, I would move toward the door—but before I could reach it I would always wake.

Genug—Enough

Postscript

In 2008, after I had raised the funds from sympathetic alumni of my law school, I became the founding director of what we named the Loyola Center for the Study of Law and Genocide. In February 2009, we were scheduled to hold the center's first sponsored conference. It would feature lawyers and scholars delivering papers on various legal issues arising out of genocides, including restitution, retrieval of stolen property, and even criminal liability. I was planning to speak on the significance of the UN Genocide Convention, the origin of the term "genocide," and a man named Raphael Lemkin.

Lemkin was a Jew who had managed to escape Poland soon after the German invasion and come to the United States. As was true for my mother, with the exception of one brother, the Shoah would cost him his entire extended family. A Polish-trained legal scholar, he found employment in the United States teaching criminal law, initially part time at Yale and then at Duke. In 1944, for a scholarly work on the Nazis' European occupation, he was looking for just the right word to describe what was happening to his people as well as what had happened earlier in the century to the Armenians. Unable to find the term he was looking for, he simply made one up: "genocide."

I remember being particularly touched by the brief descriptions of him I earlier found in Samantha Powers's *A Problem from Hell*. Though unemployed and without diplomatic portfolio, in his tattered suit and shirt frayed at the collar and cuffs, too poor to buy a cafeteria lunch, he worked alone shepherding passage of the UN Genocide Convention for the Prevention and Punishment of the Crime of Genocide, which he had authored.[1]

His Genocide Convention, adopted by the UN in December 1948 and brought into law in January 1951, obligated all countries who signed the agreement to intervene whenever and wherever genocide was being committed as well as creating the right, though not the technical procedures, for any signatory nation to criminally prosecute all perpetrators of genocidal acts.[2] Lemkin was not a naïve idealist who expected that, as a consequence of this pact, all international human rights violations would suddenly come to an end. As Powers writes, "He simply believed that if the law was in place, it would have some effect—sooner or later."[3]

As I was driving to school on the morning of that 2009 conference, it occurred to me that the circumstance that had most likely saved my mother's life was actually an illustration of Lemkin's quest for deterrence. At least in part, the prospect of postwar prosecution and punishment influenced Heinrich Himmler, and certainly motivated his underlings like Felix Kersten and Walter Schellenberg, to free those thousand Jewish women from Ravensbrück. If the fear of consequences could stay the hand of even Heinrich Himmler, who else might it deter? An event that may have allowed my mother to live provided a pristine example in support of Lemkin's instincts.

Some months later I wrote and eventually published a short essay expressing exactly this point. I entitled it "The Jew Who Met Himmler."[4] In January 2012, I decided to expand that article into a book, but this time I focused neither upon law nor international politics, but rather on the saving of Malka Repstein, the one survivor to whom I was forever inextricably bound.

I had been gathering information and writing in my spare time for about three years when Dvora, the eldest daughter of my mother's wartime companion Genya, urged me to include my mother's postwar experiences, and therefore, by necessity, my life with her. It was a subject I had consciously avoided, yet I hesitantly took her advice. The strange relationship between Molly Goldman and me was, and is still, not a subject I comfortably confront. It was going to be the hardest thing I had ever written, and it not only significantly slowed the completion of the book, I believe it also added the first, if long overdue, grey hairs to my head.

It was at this point that I first picked up a copy of psychotherapist Eva Hoffman's *After Such Knowledge*. While reading it, I unexpectedly found myself the protagonist, or at least a poster child for a long list of the most dysfunctional symptoms reported in her second-generation case studies. These included my mother's excessive overprotectiveness and my mistaken conviction of her physical fragility, her treatment of me as a replacement for the children she had lost, my insurmountable guilt at the thought of abandoning her to grief, and my decision to capitulate to an infantilized captivity rather than simply take the independence I could have physically, though not emotionally, achieved. As I suspect is true for the children of many other genocide survivors, the older I grew the more I realized that my overprotected upbringing was hardly conventional, and my guilt-ridden adulthood, including my inability to create meaningful commitments, had not been what most would describe as "normal." I was not unique among my generation, though I was something of an extreme representative.

After years of research and writing, I am still unable to settle on any particular explanation as to why exactly I started and persisted so obsessively to complete a project so personally painful to produce. Hoffman partially credits the surge of twenty-first-century memoirs written by the children of survivors to their having reached what she describes as "the age of retrospective reflection" and the need to come to terms with both the Shoah and our relationship to parents victimized by it.[5] On the other hand, perhaps my motivation was simply born of the advice I was given by a gentile lawyer when I was a child: "Who else could be in a better position to write it?" All I can say with confidence is that, though I can only speculate about what others will think, I believe the telling of this story will be the most, and perhaps only, worthwhile thing I leave behind.

Though it may not be a particularly appealing admission, I must also concede that part of the reason I wrote this book is anger—both my mother's and mine—at the atrocities that shattered her life and apparently never stopped influencing my own. I have long understood that most of the responsibility for how my life has been lived is mine, but it is also clear that the consequences of the war against the Jews did not end in 1945.

There should also be no misunderstanding: for Molly Goldman there was never forgiveness for the perpetrators, their allies, or those who failed to aid, in spite of the ability of some to do so with little risk or discomfort to themselves. The bitterness ran deep. So many incomprehensible crimes had been committed against her and those like her, and, as is so often the case after genocide, few of those responsible were ever punished. Although she never cursed the descendants of her tormentors, neither did she wish them well. When the Berlin Wall fell and Germany formally reunited, my mother mourned. Having for decades gained rueful comfort from news reports of shortages and long lines in the German east, she could not bear watching them rejoice.

Anger was part of what kept her alive. No matter how grave her condition, she would determinedly stare me in the eye and say, "I'm not going to let those damn Germans off da hook from sending me my checks." And, for years longer than the doctors had predicted, she held on. I don't think it was a coincidence that she passed away the morning after we had received and I had deposited what proved to be the last of her monthly reparations checks. To some, the small payment made to their victims by the German government may have seemed no better than meager conscience-easing blood money to be contemptuously spurned by any but the neediest. Yet, for my mother, the arrival of each recompense was a small victory, and her continued survival to collect them, her last revenge.

Sometimes I do wonder how she would have felt about my writing this book. I think there would have been some pride that her story was being told and that I cared enough to tell it. If nothing else, she would have approved of my effort to keep the subject alive. Yet, I can hear her voice now scolding me about how the whole business is just too much trouble and that "Stanley, you should stop before it makes you too tired or upshet."

ACKNOWLEDGMENTS

It would require an unusually long list to thank all the people who have helped me produce this book, and if I tried I would be likely to unjustly leave off an important name or two. For more than half a dozen years I have managed to persuade just about every friend and close acquaintance I have, and thereby risked losing the association in the process, into reading and commenting on various primitive drafts. H. G. Wells once mused that "[no] passion on earth, neither love nor hate, is equal to the passion to alter someone else's draft." Though this may actually be far from a universal truth, it is common enough that I owe many for their honest critiques, from which I benefitted. There were, however, a handful of people who had such a seminal impact on the work that I must specifically thank them. My friend and colleague Professor Michael Bazyler was the first to suggest that I convert a short essay into a volume. My dear friend Dvora Morag persuaded me, against my will and for better or worse, to write the postwar portions of this book. My independent editor, Bonny V. Fetterman, not only ceaselessly encouraged me but also guided the way to my agent, Ronald Goldfarb, and then, through him, to Potomac Books editor Tom Swanson: Each of them were willing to take a chance on a difficult subject told in a somewhat unusual way.

I feel I must also add that I am not a psychologist, nor, though my undergraduate degree may have been in history, I make no claim to be a professional historian. Other than the sections dealing with my personal and family history, only a portion of the historical information used in the book comes from my own original research. Though the conclusions I draw from the work of others are often my own, I am grateful to the authors cited in the text and endnotes. Were it not for their efforts, no personal story like the one told herein could be placed in anything resembling an accurate historical context. Though it is difficult to single out any particular author, I would like to thank Lena Einhorn, whose work *Handelresande Liu*, documenting the Herculean efforts of Gilel Storch (Hillel Storche) and Norbert Masur, proved particularly valuable to the writing of this book.

Portions of this manuscript were previously published in articles I wrote for a student-run journal at Loyola Law School at which I teach. Parts of chapters 4 and 12 previously appeared as "A Führer of Industry: Krupp before, after, and during Nuremberg," *Loyola of Los Angeles International and Comparative Law Review* 39 (Winter 2017): 187–208; parts of chapters 7, 8, and 10 originally appeared in "The Jew Who Met Himmler, and Other Stories" *Loyola of Los Angeles International and Comparative Law Review* 32, no. 1 (Winter 2010): 1–18; and part of the postscript appeared in "The Man Who Made Genocide a Crime: The Legacy of Raphael Lemkin," *Loyola of Los Angeles International and Comparative Law Review* 34, no. 3 (Spring 2012): 295–300. All are reprinted with permission from the *Loyola Law School International and Comparative Law Review*.

NOTES

I have selected "left . . . to the mercy of a rude stream" from William Shakespeare's *Henry VIII*, act III, scene ii, as the title of this book because I saw it filling a dual purpose: The plain reading of the words describe well my mother's wartime plight. While on the other hand, in its original context and as once referenced in part by legendary novelist Henry Roth, the phrase is appropriately applied to myself as an admission by the speaker of having foolishly ignored his true circumstances until, finally understanding, it proved too late to change his course.

PREFACE

1. Hoffman, *After Such Knowledge*, 15.

1. "LEFT TO THE MERCY OF A RUDE STREAM"

1. Porter, *Kasztner's Train*, 244. See also Ohler, *Blitzed*, 232.
2. Agassi, *Jewish Women Prisoners*, 158.
3. Agassi, *Jewish Women Prisoners*, 158.
4. Agassi, *Jewish Women Prisoners*, 159.
5. Morag, "Thou Shalt Tell Your Daughter."
6. Agassi, *Jewish Women Prisoners*, 158.
7. Shaibowicz, "Brzeziny in History," 3–20.
8. Hendler-Gocial, "The Brzeziner Jewish Community," 156.
9. "Jews were kicked, beaten and humiliated; they were taken from their homes or from the streets to perform hard tasks which were often useless and senseless." Lipson, *Book of Radom*, 39.
10. Warhaft, "I Saw the Destruction of Our Shtetl," 135–38.
11. Zagon-Winer, "I Saw the Destruction," 148, 156.
12. Breitman, *Architect of Genocide*, 202; Gutman, "Introduction: Distinctiveness," xlvii; Dobroszycki, *Łódź Ghetto*, xx–xxii.
13. Miron, *Yad Vashem Encyclopedia*, 85.
14. Rosenberg, *Brief Stop*, 278–79.

15. "We are so strangely made; the memories that make us happy pass away, it is the memories that break our hearts that abide." Twain, *Personal Recollections*, 413.

16. "Our souls are like those orphans whose unwedded mothers die in bearing them: the secret of our paternity lies in their grave, and we must there to learn it." Melville, *Moby Dick*, 361.

17. See Singer, "Cafeteria," 287.

18. For an example of these German practices, see Lipson, *Book of Radom*, 53.

19. My mother heard this information from the eyewitness.

20. Blanket-Sulkowicz, "Destruction of Brzezin," 140–43.

2. "SALVATION THROUGH LABOR"

1. Dobroszycki, *Łódź Ghetto*, xxx.

2. Dobroszycki, *Łódź Ghetto*, xxxi. See also Singer, *Family Moscat*.

3. Dobroszycki, *Łódź Ghetto*, xlvii.

4. Dobroszycki, *Łódź Ghetto*, xxiii; Gutman, "Introduction: Distinctiveness," xxix.

5. Dobroszycki, *Łódź Ghetto*, xxxvi.

6. Neumann, "National Socialist Weltanschauung," 365–66.

7. Norimitsu Onishi, "Germany Grapples with Its African Genocide," *New York Times*, December 29, 2016.

8. Gutman, "Introduction: Distinctiveness," xxx; Dobroszycki, *Łódź Ghetto*, xxxvi.

9. Breitman, *Architect of Genocide*, 75.

10. Dobroszycki, *Łódź Ghetto*, xxxvi.

11. Gutman, "Introduction: Distinctiveness," xxx, xxxi.

12. Dobroszycki, *Łódź Ghetto*, xxxvii.

13. Dobroszycki, *Łódź Ghetto*, xxxix.

14. Gutman, "Introduction: Distinctiveness," xxxi; Dobroszycki, *Łódź Ghetto*, xxv.

15. Gutman, "Introduction: Distinctiveness," xxxi–xxxii, lvi; Dobroszycki, *Łódź Ghetto*, xxv.

16. Gutman, "Introduction: Distinctiveness," xxxiii; Dobroszycki, *Łódź Ghetto*, ix, xxvi.

17. Gutman, "Introduction: Distinctiveness," xxxvi; Dobroszycki, *Łódź Ghetto*, lii.

18. Dobroszycki, *Łódź Ghetto*, xlviii, xliv, xlii–xlvii. See also Gutman, "Introduction: Distinctiveness," xxxiv, lv.

19. Ruben, *Żydzi w Łodzi pod niemiecką okupacją 1939–1945*. For further discussion, see Shapiro, "Translator-Editor's Introduction"; Gutman, "Introduction: Distinctiveness," xxxiii, xxxvi, xxxl.

20. Gutman, "Introduction: Distinctiveness," xxxix; Dobroszycki, *Łódź Ghetto*, l.

21. Dobroszycki, *Łódź Ghetto*, l.

22. Gutman, "Introduction: Distinctiveness," xli. See also "Lodz," in *Pinkas Hakehillot Polin* (Jerusalem: Yad Vashem, 1976), translated in *Encyclopedia of Jewish*

Communities of Poland, vol. 1, JewishGen, https://www.jewishgen.org/yizkor/pinkas_poland/pol1_00005.html#6d, chapter 9d.

23. Miron, *Yad Vashem Encyclopedia of Ghettos*, s.v. "Łódź." See also Gutman, "Introduction: Distinctiveness," xli; Dobroszycki, *Łódź Ghetto*, lx.

24. Wachsmann, KL: *A History of the Nazi*, 46; Dobroszycki, *Łódź Ghetto*, lxi. Gutman, "Introduction: Distinctiveness," xlv.

25. Gutman, "Introduction: Distinctiveness," xliv.

26. Gutman, "Introduction: Distinctiveness," xlv.

27. Gutman, "Introduction: Distinctiveness," xl.

28. Gutman, "Introduction: Distinctiveness," xliii; Dobroszycki, *Łódź Ghetto*, lin135.

29. Gutman, "Introduction: Distinctiveness," xliii; Dobroszycki, *Łódź Ghetto*, li.

30. Jackel, "Forever in the Shadow of Hitler?," 115–22.

31. Dobroszycki, *Łódź Ghetto*, li.

32. Dobroszycki, *Łódź Ghetto*, lii.

33. Dobroszycki, *Łódź Ghetto*, lii.

34. Dobroszycki, *Łódź Ghetto*, xxxvii.

35. Dobroszycki, *Łódź Ghetto*, 250–55.

36. Gutman, "Introduction: Distinctiveness," li; Dobroszycki, *Łódź Ghetto*, l, xxvii.

37. Lisciotto, "Chaim Mordechai Rumkowski."

38. Dobroszycki, *Łódź Ghetto*, 63; Gutman, "Introduction: Distinctiveness," xli–xlii, liii.

39. Roth, *Professor of Desire*, 175–76. The wording of the quote has been partly reordered from the original. Cf. Friedrich Nietzsche, who wrote "He who has a why to look for can bear almost any how." Nietzsche, *Twilight of the Idols*.

40. Dobroszycki, *Łódź Ghetto*, lx.

41. Dobroszycki, *Łódź Ghetto*, lxi. Longerich, *Himmler*, 665.

42. Longerich, *Himmler*, 665–68.

43. Dobroszycki, *Łódź Ghetto*, lx–lxi, lxiii. Breitman, *Architect of Genocide*, 202.

44. Dobroszycki, *Łódź Ghetto*, lx--xi, lxiii.

45. Fest, *Inside Hitler's Bunker*, 94.

46. Speer, *Infiltration*, 10.

47. Breitman, *Architect of Genocide*, 221.

48. Longerich, *Himmler*, 696, 702. The evidence suggests, for example, that it was Himmler who arranged the massive destruction of the city of Warsaw in 1944. Longerich, *Himmler*, 705.

49. Breitman, *Architect of Genocide*, 221.

50. Dobroszycki, *Łódź Ghetto*, lxiv–lxv. See also Gutman, "Introduction: Distinctiveness," xl.

51. Dobroszycki, *Łódź Ghetto*, lxv.

52. Friedman, "Pseudo-Saviors," 333–34; Gutman, "Introduction: Distinctiveness," xl; Dobroszycki, *Łódź Ghetto*, lxv.

53. Dobroszycki, *Łódź Ghetto*, lxvin68.

54. Dobroszycki, *Łódź Ghetto*, lxvi.

55. Dobroszycki, *Łódź Ghetto*, xxxix, lvii; Shapiro, "Translator-Editor's Introduction," xi.

56. Dobroszycki, *Łódź Ghetto*, lxvi.

3. A MINOR CLERICAL ERROR

1. Rosenberg, *Brief Stop*, 99.

2. This is a paraphrase of Charlotte Delbo, quoted in Kittel, "Liberation—Survival—Freedom,243.

3. Wiesel, *Night*, 6–7.

4. Neumann, "National Socialist Weltanschauung," 367.

5. Frankl, *Man's Search for Meaning*, 9.

6. Breitman, *Architect of Genocide*, 233.

7. Hayes, *From Cooperation to Complicity*, 244, 264, 271.

8. Hayes, *From Cooperation to Complicity*, 245.

9. Hayes, *From Cooperation to Complicity*, 241, 245.

10. Hayes, *From Cooperation to Complicity*, 241; Breitman, *Architect of Genocide*, 233.

11. Breitman, *Architect of Genocide*, 233–34.

12. Agassi, *Jewish Women Prisoners*, 158–15; Breitman, *Architect of Genocide*, 233–34.

13. Rosenberg, *Brief Stop*, 115. A group of seven thousand of the women (that did not include my mother) were temporarily spared when they were transported from Auschwitz to Stutthof, a concentration camp near Danzig on the Baltic. Almost all of them would die in the next few months from either starvation or sickness, or by being murdered in railroad cars or in Stutthof's primitive gas chamber. Rosenberg, *Brief Stop*, 203.

14. Rosenberg, *Brief Stop*, 122.

15. Agassi, *Jewish Women Prisoners*, 158–59; Saidel, *Jewish Women*, 133.

16. Holocaust Encyclopedia, "Genocide of European Roma." In 2018 there were estimates that over 100,000 Germans who were still fearful of lingering racism might have been hiding that they were of Romany heritage. Heike Klovert, "Alles ist besser, al 'Zigeuner' zu sein," *Der Spiegel*, February 24, 2018, www.spiegel.de/karrieve /sintiund-roma-allesist-berre-als-ciu-zigeuner-zu-sein-a-1193918-html&prev=search.

17. Testimony of Chana Gertles, Yad Vashem, O.3–9866, 1999.

18. Agassi, *Jewish Women Prisoners*, 158.

19. Agassi, *Jewish Women Prisoners*, 159.

20. Testimony of Dvora Lezerkeritz, Yad Vashem O.3–6889, 1996.

21. Ferencz, *Less Than Slaves*, 93.

22. Manchester, *Arms of Krupp*, 543.

23. Agassi, *Jewish Women Prisoners*, 159.

24. Agassi, *Jewish Women Prisoners*, 159.

1. Manchester, *Arms of Krupp*, 367–85.

2. Manchester, *Arms of Krupp*, 367.

3. Manchester, *Arms of Krupp*, 390.

4. Manchester, *Arms of Krupp*, 383, 411. While no single "weapon accounted for the stunning successes of the 1939 blitzkrieg invasion of Poland" or the 1940 conquests of France and Belgium, "Krupp factories had fashioned an arsenal of remarkably sophisticated" instruments of war that could not be matched in either proficiency or numbers by any military force in Europe. Manchester, *Arms of Krupp*, 411. Their tanks were unparalleled for their size and mobility, as well as their sheer speed and "striking power." William L. Shirer wrote that as the German assault began "lurching into the Ardennes Forest," their Krupp tanks "stretched in three columns back for 100 miles far beyond the Rhine." Shirer, *Rise and Fall of the Third Reich*, 723; Manchester, *Arms of Krupp*, 416. The company had become much more than just one of Nazi Germany's weapons suppliers. It was essential to the success of German aggression. As William Manchester notes: "'Krupp's assembly lines in his hundred factories turned out guns of all calibers—antiaircraft guns, antitank guns, and heavy naval guns—in addition to tank, submarine, and other warship and aircraft parts, and the steel used by other munitions producers.' . . . To an extent unprecedented in the history of industry, a corporation had become an integral part of a warlord's apparatus" Young, *Fall and Rise*, 54–55, quoted in Manchester, *Arms of Krupp*, 411.

5. Manchester, *Arms of Krupp*, 445–49; Ferencz, *Less Than Slaves*, 71.

6. Ferencz, *Less Than Slaves*, 71; Manchester, *Arms*, 631.

7. Manchester, *Arms of Krupp*, 397, 398.

8. Manchester, *Arms of Krupp*, 488, 11, 90, 492.

9. Manchester, *Arms of Krupp*, 494, 493, 490–92; Ferencz, *Less Than Slaves*, 88–90. In June 1943 Krupp had overcome opposition to his plan to build a plant producing automatic weapons parts within the camp itself and staffed it with Jewish slave laborers forced to produce weapons for their persecutors. The Auschwitz factory workers who managed to survive the war would later describe that from this Krupp plant they had been able to see the three big chimneys of the crematorium. Manchester, *Arms of Krupp*, 490–91.

10. Manchester, *Arms of Krupp*, 10.

11. Manchester, *Arms of Krupp*, 489; see also Ferencz, *Less Than Slaves*, 102–3.

12. Manchester, *Arms of Krupp*, 450.

13. Ferencz, *Less Than Slaves*, xviii; *see also* Bazyler, *Holocaust Justice*, 60.

14. Breitman, *Architect of Genocide*, 234.

15. Ferencz, *Less Than Slaves*, xvii.

16. As his family's workshops grew dependent on forced laborers, the number exploited by Krupp grew exponentially. It was Alfried who ran a corporation using the inmates of dozens of concentration camps "in nearly a hundred factories across Germany, Poland, Austria, France, and Czechoslovakia" in what was labeled *Arbeitseinsatz der Haftlinge* (prisoner's contribution). Working for him in these plants, as well as in the actual concentration camps themselves, were about 100,000 slaves made up of approximately 70,000 foreign civilians, more than 23,000 prisoners of war, and typically at any given moment about 5,000 Jewish workers. Manchester, *Arms of Krupp*, 11, 412, 492–93.

17. Manchester, *Arms of Krupp*, 453.

18. "Hitler's conquests made Krupp the greatest mogul in the chronicles of world trade before the Nazi tide: [He] ruled an economic colossus sprawling across 12 nations, from the Ukraine to the Atlantic, from the North Sea to the Mediterranean and owned factories everywhere, a complex of shipyards in the Netherlands, and ore mines in Greece, Russia, France, the Sudeten lands, Norway, and Yugoslavia." Manchester, *Arms of Krupp*, 429.

19. Manchester, *Arms of Krupp*, 495, 453.

20. Agassi, *Jewish Women Prisoners*, 159.

21. Agassi, *Jewish Women Prisoners*, 159–60. See also testimony of Bracha Fride and Malka Golir, Yad Vashem, O.3–5279, 1996.

22. Agassi, *Jewish Women Prisoners*, 159. See also testimony of Dvora Lezerkeritz, Yad Vashem, O.3–6889, 1996.

23. Agassi, *Jewish Women Prisoners*, 160.

24. Ferencz, *Less Than Slaves*, 93–94.

25. Manchester, *Arms of Krupp*, 559. See also Ferencz, *Less Than Slaves*, 94–95.

26. Manchester, *Arms of Krupp*, 554. At this stage of the war, given the lack of alternatives, it would have been logical to prevent the loss of even Jewish workers, lest the company risk being unable to satisfy its quotas. There must have been SS factory supervisors who recognized the significant downside that could result from a labor shortfall. This had long been understood by Krupp when it came to preserving the lives of Soviet prisoners of war. Herbert, *Foreign Workers*, 217, 159. Yet deeply rooted anti-Semitism, or perhaps the fear of upsetting the SS hierarchy, may have trumped production concerns of many of those tasked with supervising Jewish slave laborers.

27. Most of the Jewish women working under the direct supervision of this Lagerführer at Essen were between fourteen and twenty-five, but one was in her thirties. When she proved unable to keep up with her younger coworkers, the Lagerführer "whipped her to death." Manchester, *Arms of Krupp*, 554.

28. Agassi, *Jewish Women Prisoners*, 160.

29. Agassi, *Jewish Women Prisoners*, 161.

30. Testimony of Bracha Fride and Malka Golir, Yad Vashem, O.3–5279, 1996.

31. Agassi, *Jewish Women Prisoners*, 160–64; see also Manchester, *Arms of Krupp*, 555.

32. Testimony of Dvora Lezerkeritz, Yad Vashem, O.3–6889, 1996.

33. Agassi, *Jewish Women Prisoners*, 161.

34. Agassi, *Jewish Women Prisoners*, 161.

35. Agassi, *Jewish Women Prisoners*, 161.

36. Agassi, *Jewish Women Prisoners*, 161, 168.

37. Agassi, *Jewish Women Prisoners*, 161.

38. Agassi, *Jewish Women Prisoners*, 163.

39. Agassi, *Jewish Women Prisoners*, 163.

40. "When a woman became ill, she would be brought back to the main camp, usually murdered, and replaced." Saidel, *Jewish Women*, 95; see also Agassi, *Jewish Women Prisoners*, 162.

41. Agassi, *Jewish Women Prisoners*, 162.

42. Kittel, "Liberation—Survival—Freedom," 250. See also Viktor Frankl for a description of his experiences in the Holocaust: "In calories, it was absolutely inadequate, especially taking into consideration our heavy manual work and our constant exposure to the cold in inadequate clothing. . . . Because of the high degree of undernourishment which the prisoner suffered, it was natural that the desire for food is the major primitive instinct around which mental life centered." Frankl, *Man's Search*, 29, 28.

5. THE CHILDREN OF LUCK

1. Manchester, *Arms of Krupp*, 503, 505.

2. Richie, *Faust's Metropolis*, 573; Agassi, *Jewish Women Prisoners*, 160.

3. Agassi, *Jewish Women Prisoners*, 160.

4. Agassi, *Jewish Women Prisoners*, 160–61.

5. Breitman, *Architect of Genocide*, 159.

6. Agassi, *Jewish Women Prisoners*, 162.

7. Agassi, *Jewish Women Prisoners*, 162–63.

8. Agassi, *Jewish Women Prisoners*, 162–63.

9. Agassi, *Jewish Women Prisoners*, 163.

10. Agassi, *Jewish Women Prisoners*, 160.

11. Agassi, *Jewish Women Prisoners*, 163.

12. Kittel, "Liberation—Survival—Freedom," 245.

13. Ivor Markman, "Remembering the Holocaust," *Herald*LIVE, April 30, 2017, http://www.heraldlive.co.za/news/2017/04/30/remembering-the-holocaust/.

14. The war crimes trials of the SS members who had staffed Ravensbrück were held in Hamburg and Rastatt between 1946 and 1948, though police investigations continued into the 1970s. Bazyler and Tuerkheimer, *Forgotten Trials*, 140–44, 149 152–53, 155–56.

15. Agassi, *Jewish Women Prisoners*, 164.

16. Agassi, *Jewish Women Prisoners*, 164.

17. Tillion, *Ravensbrück*, 5; Agassi, *Jewish Women Prisoners*, 99.

18. Simone Gournay, quoted in Helm, *Ravensbrück*, 600.

6. THE LAST PARTY OF THE THIRD REICH

1. Beevor, *Fall of Berlin*, 249, 255; Richie, *Faust's Metropolis*, 573.

2. Kempowski, *Swansong 1945*, 10; Beevor, *Fall of Berlin*, 249, 255.

3. Lehmann and Carroll, *In Hitler's Bunker*, 75. "On the evening 19 April 1945 . . . the Hotel Adlon was still in operation, in spite of the bombs and grenades that were already landing in the street. In the brightly lit dining hall, waiters in tuxedos and maître d's in tailcoats went on solemnly and unflappably serving purple pieces of kohlrabi on silver trays meant for better days. Everything was orderly and smart, without an agitated word or sign of haste." Kempowski, *Swansong 1945*, 65–66, quoting Wolfen ss officer Leon Degrelle. See also Richie, *Faust's Metropolis*, 579–80.

4. Speer et al., *Inside the Third Reich*, 473.

5. Richie, *Faust's Metropolis*, 567; Kempowski, *Swansong 1945*, 33.

6. Fest, *Inside Hitler's Bunker*, 45. See also, Kempowski, *Swansong 1945*, 91.

7. Kempowski, *Swansong 1945*, 1.

8. Speer et al., *Inside the Third Reich*, 472. See also Beevor, *Fall of Berlin*, 250.

9. Fest, *Inside Hitler's Bunker*, 50–51; Beevor, *Fall of Berlin*, 251; Kempowski, *Swansong 1945*, 47.

10. Speer et al., *Inside the Third Reich*, 474.

11. "The event had the air of a visit to a terminally ill patient where the victim and the well-wishers skirt delicately around the sad reason for their presence." Lehmann and Carroll, *In Hitler's Bunker*, 76. See also Fest, *Inside Hitler's Bunker*, 48.

12. Fest, *Inside Hitler's Bunker*, 49. See also Beevor, *Fall of Berlin*, 261.

13. Fest, *Inside Hitler's Bunker*, 47, 46.

14. Helm, *Ravensbrück*, 585; Richie, *Faust's Metropolis*, 573.

15. Richie, *Faust's Metropolis*, 573. See also Fest, quoting the notes of Luftwaffe chief of staff, General Karl Koller, in *Inside Hitler's Bunker*, 52–53; Beevor, *Fall of Berlin*, 249; Kempowski, *Swansong 1945*, 3.

16. Richie, *Faust's Metropolis*, 573–74.

17. Beevor, *Fall of Berlin*, 262.

18. Richie, *Faust's Metropolis*, 574. Apparently, as far as Hitler was concerned, the citizenry of the capital, whom he suspected had never sufficiently appreciated their Führer's true greatness, had failed him, but the city could still "become a gigantic funeral pyre" for its leader. Richie, *Faust's Metropolis*, 566–67. Repeating again and again his determination to stay in Berlin, he would soon

proclaim, in the imagery of a failed art student, a never-to-be-fulfilled design to die in a grand theatrical gesture on the Chancellery's steps. Fest, *Inside Hitler's Bunker*, 63, 65–66.

19. Beevor, *Fall of Berlin*, 251. See also Wulff, *Zodiac and Swastika*, 164.

20. Speer et al., *Inside the Third Reich*, 474–75. See also Kempowski, *Swansong 1945*, 83. After Göring's departure, Hitler briefly walked into what was left of the Chancellery garden, accompanied by the so-called Gang of Four, whose loyalty the German leader could not doubt: Joseph Goebbels, Martin Bormann, Albert Speer, and Heinrich Himmler. Fest, *Inside Hitler's Bunker*, 48. See also Kempowski, *Swansong 1945*, 68. From their lofty positions within the Nazi hierarchy these four men had successfully persuaded Hitler to expand their domains by imposition of what they coined "Total War." To them "Total War" meant that as foreign troops crossed into the lands of the Third Reich, control of field operations was transferred from military commanders to these four political leaders. So long as they did nothing that could be perceived as a deviation from the orders of their Führer, and being careful not to give the appearance of challenging Göring's superficial authority, they exercised de facto power in the Reich land. Longerich, *Himmler*, 700.

21. On May 1, 1945, unable to bear the thought of a world without their Führer, Goebbels and his wife, Magda, not only took their own lives, but lethally poisoned their six young children, one of whom unsuccessfully fought back.

22. Goebbels and Himmler had often disagreed on policy. While Goebbels had inspired the November 1938 street riots known as Kristallnacht, which resulted in the murder of over 100 Jews and the destruction of 267 synagogues in Germany, Austria, and the Sudetenland, Himmler had felt that any such actions meted out against the Jews should be accomplished less publicly so as to protect Germany's international image. Breitman, *Architect of Genocide*, 5, 36, 52–53.

23. Breitman, *Architect of Genocide*, 12, 33, 245.

24. Breitman, *Architect of Genocide*, 245.

25. Breitman, *Architect of Genocide*, 17.

26. Breitman, *Architect of Genocide*, 34–35. Himmler issued an order that his officers "father as many children as possible so as to compensate for the loss of the best German blood in the war," specifically suggesting that Aryan men and women should be willing to produce children outside of marriage. Breitman, *Architect of Genocide*, 108–9.

27. Breitman, *Architect of Genocide*, 34.

28. Longerich, *Himmler*, 741. "Those who throng to the SS are men inclined to the authoritarian state, [and] wish to serve and obey, [said Hitler]." Wagener and Turner, *Hitler—Memoirs of a Confidant*, 19–21. Many of Himmler's recruits, like Himmler himself, were raised in Catholic families in the predominantly Catho-

lic areas of Germany, but they would find a new religion in the service of racial purity. Breitman, *Architect of Genocide*, 34.

29. See, generally, Wachsmann, *KL: A History*.

30. Kershaw, "Working towards the Fuhrer," 103–18.

31. Breitman, *Architect of Genocide*, 32, 124, 139, 206.

32. Breitman, *Architect of Genocide*, 198–200, 203, 88. "[Himmler] saw an opportunity of extending the Holocaust to more and more groups of Jewish victims. First the whole [of] occupied Poland . . . followed by . . . [t]he rest of the European countries." Longerich, *Himmler*, 744–45.

33. Breitman, *Architect of Genocide*, 144, 206, 210–11, 220.

34. Breitman, *Architect of Genocide*, 173–77, 189–96, 236. In Minsk Belorussia, Himmler ordered one hundred alleged partisans to be taken from jail and shot. There was a blonde, blue-eyed youth among the men. Before the shooting began,

> Himmler asked him: "Are you a Jew?
> Yes.
> Are both of your parents Jews?
> Yes.
> Do you have any ancestors who were not Jews?
> No.
> Then I can't help you!" (Breitman, *Architect of Genocide*, 195.)

35. Kessel, *The Man with the Miraculous Hands*, 228.

36. Breitman, *Architect of Genocide*, 29; Longerich, *Himmler*, 748.

37. Longerich, *Himmler*, 211, 206.

38. Longerich, *Himmler*, 648, 711–12, 746–47. See also Lehmann and Carroll, *In Hitler's Bunker*, 76. Himmler even had the power to reorganize the army if he felt it necessary. Longerich, *Himmler*, 746–47.

39. Masur, *My Meeting with Himmler*, para. 18.

40. Longerich, *Himmler*, 716, quoting 1st General Staff Officer Colonel Hans Georg Eismann.

41. Longerich, *Himmler*, 716.

42. Hitler also reduced Himmler's prior responsibilities for the nation's armaments manufacturing. Longerich, *Himmler*, 696, 702, 704, 717–18, 722–23.

43. Fest, *Inside Hitler's Bunker*, 95.

44. Longerich, *Himmler*, 734.

45. Persson, *Escape from the Third Reich*, 236.

7. MEETING HIMMLER

1. Breitman, *Architect of Genocide*, 44.

2. Allen, *Himmler's Secret War*, xvii.

3. Breitman, *Architect of Genocide*, 8.

4. Masur, *My Meeting with Himmler*, para. 15.

5. Allen, *Himmler's Secret War*, 260. See also Masur, *My Meeting with Himmler*, para. 14; Tillion, *Ravensbrück*, 110.

6. Masur, *My Meeting with Himmler*, paras. 4–7.

7. Masur, *My Meeting with Himmler*, paras. 14–15.

8. Einhorn, *Handelsresande I Liv*, 12–13.

9. Einhorn, *Handelsresande I Liv*, 27–29.

10. Einhorn, *Handelsresande I Liv*, 12–13.

11. Persson, *Escape from the Third Reich*, 28.

12. Even the leaders of the Swedish Jewish community, some of whose families had lived for generations in Sweden, preferred the admission into the country of only Jews who had the greatest likelihood of being able to provide for themselves. Einhorn, *Handelsresande I Liv*, 123.

13. Not only was Sweden's gentile population concerned about admitting Jews, there were some members of the Swedish Jewish community who feared that the wholesale introduction of large numbers of foreign-born Jews into their relatively stable society might have the result of increasing the already existing antisemitism in their homeland. Einhorn, *Handelsresande I Liv*, 124.

14. Einhorn, *Handelsresande I Liv*, 34.

15. Einhorn, *Handelsresande I Liv*, 167.

16. Einhorn, *Handelsresande I Liv*, 244–46.

17. Einhorn, *Handelsresande I Liv*, 164–65, 321–22, 244–46.

18. Einhorn, *Handelsresande I Liv*, 466. Rudberg, *Swedish Jews*, 205, 227, 239, 242.

19. Einhorn, *Handelsresande I Liv*, 155–56, 164–65. Storch's plan to ransom Baltic Jews failed, but he succeeded in possibly saving thousands of Jews when he managed to send nearly 100,000 parcels to Gothenburg concentration camp. Persson, *Escape from the Third Reich*, 29.

20. Einhorn, *Handelsresande I Liv*, 188.

21. Einhorn, *Handelsresande I Liv*, 201–2.

22. Jangfeldt, *Hero of Budapest*, 136, 153, 168; Carlberg, *Wallenberg*, 166, 193–94; Masur, *My Meeting with Himmler*, para. 3

23. What nations couldn't do might be performed by small organizations or individuals independent of state authority. Einhorn, *Handelsresande I Liv*, 466.

24. Einhorn, *Handelsresande I Liv*, chapter 45, in general, and 325, 379–82; see also Persson, *Escape from the Third Reich*, 157, 154–55, citing the research and conclusions reached by Israeli historian Dov Dinur, https://sok.riksarkivet.se/?postid =Arkisref SE/RA/730128/01/F/F 21&s=Balder.

25. Einhorn, *Handelsresande I Liv*, 380–82, 376–77. For a further discussion of Storch's involvement in attempts to rescue Jews, see Bauer, *Jews for Sale?*, 245.

26. Waller, *Devil's Doctor*, 7; Kessel, *Man with Miraculous Hands*, 9, 14.

27. In 1940, Himmler's search for relief from his stomach pains finally led him to Kersten, whom he summoned to his Gestapo headquarters for what was to be the first of many treatment sessions. Einhorn, *Handelsresande I Liv*, 38–42.

28. Trevor-Roper, "Strange Case of Himmler's Doctor." See also Waller, *Devil's Doctor*, 12–13; Longerich, *Himmler*, 381; Einhorn, *Handelsresande I Liv*, 38–49; Masur, *My Meeting with Himmler*, para. 1.

29. Wulff, *Zodiac and Swastika*, 124.

30. Masur, *My Meeting with Himmler*, paras. 1–3. See also Einhorn, *Menschenhandel*, 247; Bauer, *Jews for Sale?*, 248.

31. Waller, *Devil's Doctor*, 3; Porter, *Kasztner's Train*, 294. See also Kittel, "'White Bus' Operation," 225.

32. Wulff, *Zodiac and Swastika*, 172; Waller, *Devil's Doctor*, 143.

33. "There were times when Schellenberg found it both embarrassing and disagreeable to obtain the large sums of money from his foreign exchange accounts and from the Reichsbank which Himmler then gave to Kersten." Wulff, *Zodiac and Swastika*, 172.

34. Einhorn, *Handelsresande I Liv*, 321–22, 346–47.

35. "Storch and Masur gave passports to Jews being sent to Bergen-Belsen." Einhorn, *Menschenhandel*, 325; Wulff, *Zodiac and Swastika*, 144.

36. Einhorn, *Handelsresande I Liv*, 124, and see chapter 50 generally.

37. Einhorn, *Handelsresande I Liv*, 324.

38. Einhorn, *Handelsresande I Liv*, 124.

39. Kessel, *Man with Miraculous Hands*, 215, 218.

40. Waller, *Devil's Doctor*, 179–80; Persson, *Escape from the Third Reich*, 160.

41. Einhorn, *Handelsresande I Liv*, 396.

42. Einhorn, *Handelsresande I Liv*, 13–15.

43. Einhorn, *Handelsresande I Liv*, 244–46, 394–95.

44. Einhorn, *Handelsresande I Liv*, 428. See also Masur, *My Meeting with Himmler*, paras. 3–4; Kittel, "'White Bus' Operation," 224–25.

45. Einhorn, *Handelsresande I Liv*, 396–97.

46. Kittel, "'White Bus' Operation," 225.

47. Einhorn, *Handelsresande I Liv*, 164–65, 167. See also Masur, *My Meeting with Himmler*, para. 1.

48. Jangfeldt, *Hero of Budapest*, 131.

49. Waller, *Devil's Doctor*, 183; Breitman, *Architect of Genocide*, 6.

50. Kessel, *Miraculous Hands*, 219.

51. Waller, *Devil's Doctor*, 202–3.

52. Einhorn, *Handelsresande I Liv*, 445–46. "Gilel Storch had been a great resource as a negotiator," Einhorn, *Handelsresande I Liv*, 466, quoting Masur's and Storch's

contemporary Svante Hansson. Soon, Kersten, Masur, and Storch would be at "odds with each other on the question of credit for the result of the talks." Persson, *Escape from the Third Reich*, 100.

53. Masur, *My Meeting with Himmler*, paras. 5–7.

54. Masur, *My Meeting with Himmler*, paras. 4–6. See also Wistrich, *Hitler and the Holocaust*, xi.

55. Jangfeldt, *Hero of Budapest*, 131.

56. See Carlberg, *Raoul Wallenberg*, 212, citing Levai, *Raoul Wallenberg*.

57. Carlberg, *Wallenberg*, 592–94; Jangfeldt, *Hero of Budapest*, 349–57.

58. Masur, *My Meeting with Himmler*, para. 55.

59. Breitman, *Architect of Genocide*, 86, 107.

60. Masur, *My Meeting with Himmler*, paras. 5–7.

61. Masur, *My Meeting with Himmler*, para. 9.

62. Masur, *My Meeting with Himmler*, para. 7.

63. Kessel, *Miraculous Hands*, 220.

64. Kempowski, *Swansong 1945*, 31.

65. Neumann, "National Socialist Weltanschauung," 363. See also Kempowski, *Swansong 1945*, 6–7, 30–31.

66. Kessel, *Miraculous Hands*, 222, 220, 223.

67. Masur, *My Meeting with Himmler*, paras. 8–9, 14; Helm, *Ravensbrück*, 591.

68. Masur, *My Meeting with Himmler*, para. 9.

69. Wulff, *Zodiac and Swastika*, 166. See also Einhorn, *Handelsresande I Liv*, 400–402.

70. Masur, *My Meeting with Himmler*, para. 12; See also Wulff, *Zodiac and Swastika*, 166.

71. In 1942, in order to make use of the camp as a source of cheap labor, Siemens established a factory in Ravensbrück to construct parts for the V-1 and V-2 rockets. In the summer of that same year, medical experiments began being conducted on some of the women by infecting them first with diseases and then administering new drugs to determine whether they were effective in fighting bacteria. In April 1943 a crematorium was created in the camp.

By 1945, those Jewish women who had not yet died there were typically kept in Ravensbrück for less than a month before being sent to one of two large nearby external camps (Malchow or Neustadt-Glewe), which the Germans considered to be a part of Ravensbrück itself. See, generally, Agassi, *Jewish Women Prisoners*; see also Bazyler and Tuerkheimer, *Forgotten Trials*, 129–57.

72. Saidel, *Jewish Women of Ravensbrück*, 17–18.

73. Agassi, *Jewish Women Prisoners*, 19–20. "Women from twenty-three nations, including a Jewish woman from the United States, suffered the horrors of Ravensbrück concentration camp." Saidel, *Jewish Women of Ravensbrück*, 26.

74. Saidel, *Jewish Women of Ravensbrück*, 35–37; Kersten, *Memoirs*, 273; Waller, *Devil's Doctor*, 24–25. See also Einhorn, *Handelsresande I Liv*, 405.

75. Masur, *My Meeting with Himmler*, para. 13.

76. Kittel, "'White Bus' Operation," 235.

77. Rosenberg, *Brief Stop*, 136.

78. Kittel, "'White Bus' Operation," 244.

79. Masur, *My Meeting with Himmler*, para. 37.

80. Kittel, "White Bus Operation," 244; Richie, *Faust's Metropolis*, 577; Agassi, *Jewish Women Prisoners*, 145.

81. Agassi, *Jewish Women Prisoners*, 142–43.

82. Although no physical proof remains, and there was no mention of it to be found in the International Red Cross files, there is testimonial evidence that in early 1945 what was likely a wooden gas chamber had been built and began operation in Ravensbrück. Agassi, *Jewish Women Prisoners*, 38; Helm, *Ravensbrück*, 552, 554–55, 564.

83. Helm, *Ravensbrück*, 552.

84. Helm, *Ravensbrück*, 569, quoting a letter written by Sylvia Salvesen. Prior to the postwar war crimes trials beginning in Hamburg, an ss officer admitted to having conducted gassings at Ravensbrück and outlined what the chamber had looked like and how the killings had taken place. The camp commandant, Fritz Suhren, similarly confirmed the existence of such a death chamber. Survivors, who had for decades lived under communist regimes in postwar Eastern Europe, eventually came forward and described having been assigned the duties of removing the bodies from the gas chamber. Helm, *Ravensbrück*, 553.

85. Tillion, *Ravensbrück*, 108.

86. Helm, *Ravensbrück*, 613.

87. Helm, *Ravensbrück*, 575–76.

88. Kittel, "White Bus Operation," 227; Helm, *Ravensbrück*, 587.

89. Breitman, *Architect of Genocide*, 241.

90. See Bazyler and Tuerkheimer, *Forgotten Trials*, 136.

91. Longerich, *Himmler*, 724; Kittel, "White Bus Operation," 226.

92. Longerich, *Himmler*, 709–10.

93. Richie, *Faust's Metropolis*, 578.

94. Longerich, *Himmler*, 709–10. On April 30, "2775 Jews from Rehmsdorf were being marched to Theresienstadt; only 500 reached their destination alive." Richie, *Faust's Metropolis*, 579. See also Broszat, "Concentration Camps," 504. "On April 6, 1945, the evacuation of the main Buchenwald camp commenced. 3,100 Jewish prisoners were marched off, of whom 1,400 were murdered en route. Over the next four days, another 40,000 prisoners were evacuated from the camp, of which 13,500 were killed." Thus, the ss brutally removed over half of Buchenwald's Jewish prisoners by death marches and transports. "On April 11, 1945, in expectation of liberation, starved and emaciated prisoners stormed

the watchtowers, seizing control of the camp. Later that afternoon, U.S. forces entered Buchenwald." Holocaust Encyclopedia, "Buchenwald."

It was in mid-March 1945 that Himmler told Felix Kersten that he would agree not to blow up the concentration camps as the Allies advanced upon them and would forbid further killings of the inmates. Longerich, *Himmler*, 724.

95. Longerich, *Himmler*, 711.

96. Kittel, "'White Bus' Operation," 227, 252.

8. APPOINTMENT WITH THE EXECUTIONER

1. Wulff, *Zodiac and Swastika*, 166.

2. Wulff, *Zodiac and Swastika*, 166.

3. Wulff, *Zodiac and Swastika*, 170.

4. Masur, *My Meeting with Himmler*, para. 15.

5. Einhorn, *Handelsresande I Liv*, 405.

6. McNally, "Walter Schellenberg."

7. Breitman, *Architect of Genocide*, 117, 159, 150. The hierarchy of the German army, perhaps more concerned about avoiding responsibility for the crimes than they were about preventing the killing of Jews, had first objected to the SS Einsatzgruppen's murdering entire communities of Polish Jews. Some generals argued that it "created a problem of discipline within the Army and a danger to security within Poland." Breitman, *Architect of Genocide*, 105, 107, 150. See also Longerich, *Himmler*, 433–34.

8. McNally, "Walter Schellenberg"; Schellenberg, *Labyrinth*.

9. Masur, *My Meeting with Himmler*, para. 16.

10. Einhorn, *Handelsresande I Liv*, 406.

11. Kessel, *Miraculous Hands*, 224. See also Beevor, *Fall of Berlin 1945*, 249.

12. Masur, *My Meeting with Himmler*, para.19.

13. Einhorn, *Handelsresande I Liv*, 393; Schellenberg, *Labyrinth*, 392. See also Kempowski, *Swansong 1945*, 64.

14. Kessel, *Miraculous Hands*, 225. Einhorn, *Handelsresande I Liv*, 406–12.

15. Longerich, *Himmler*, 717.

16. Breitman, *Architect of Genocide*, 4.

17. Masur, *My Meeting with Himmler*, para. 20; Kittel, "Liberation—Survival—Freedom," 223. See also Lehmann and Carroll, *Eyewitness Account*, 83.

18. Masur, *My Meeting with Himmler*, para. 20.

19. Breitman, *Architect of Genocide*, 250.

20. "The Remains of Jewish Victims Killed for Skeleton Collection of Nazi Anatomy Professor Buried," Telegraph, Sept. 6, 2015, https://www.telegraph.co.uk/news/worldnews/europe/france/11847483/Remains-of-Jewish-victims-killed-for-skeleton-collection-of-Nazi-anatomy-professor-buried.html. Memorandum

and Report for Rudolf Brandt Concerning the Jewish Skeleton Collection, http://nuremberg.law.harvard.edu/documents/150-memorandum-and-report -for-rudolf?q=evidence:no*#p.1.

21. Einhorn, *Handelsresande I Liv*, 406–12.

22. Einhorn, *Handelsresande I Liv*, 407–12; Kessel, *Miraculous Hands*, 226.

23. Kessel, *Miraculous Hands*, 225; Helm, *Ravensbrück*, 591.

24. Breitman, *Architect of Genocide*, 242.

25. Kessel, *Miraculous Hands*, 226.

26. Schellenberg, *Labyrinth*, 391. See also Einhorn, *Handelsresande I Liv*, 402.

27. Schellenberg, *Labyrinth*, 393.

28. Masur, *My Meeting with Himmler*, para. 21.

29. Masur, *My Meeting with Himmler*, paras. 20, 25.

30. Kessel, *Miraculous Hands*, 226.

31. Masur, *My Meeting with Himmler*, para. 22.

32. Masur, *My Meeting with Himmler*, paras. 20, 27.

33. Masur, *My Meeting with Himmler*, paras. 20, 53.

34. Masur, *My Meeting with Himmler*, paras. 20, 28–29.

35. Masur, *My Meeting with Himmler*, paras. 20, 26.

36. Breitman, *Architect of Genocide*, 242.

37. Longerich, *Himmler*, 689.

38. Breitman, *Architect of Genocide*, 243.

39. Masur, *My Meeting with Himmler*, para. 24.

40. "I constantly had to keep my goal of liberation for Jews and other prisoners in my mind, and to choose my words carefully." Masur, *My Meeting with Himmler*, paras. 20, 28.

41. Masur, *My Meeting with Himmler*, para. 20.

42. Einhorn, *Handelsresande I Liv*, chap. 20. See also Masur, *My Meeting with Himmler*, para. 52.

43. The young Himmler had lacked "an emotional core and possess[ed] a weak ego that allowed him to identify with whomever he was with." Breitman, *Architect of Genocide*, 10–11, paraphrasing the thoughts of Peter Loewenberg, "Unsuccessful Adolescence of Heinrich Himmler," 616–18.

44. Masur, *My Meeting with Himmler*, para. 25.

45. Masur, *My Meeting with Himmler*, paras. 33–34.

9. TRADING FOR JEWISH LIVES

1. Breitman, *Architect of Genocide*, 49.

2. Breitman, *Architect of Genocide*, 60.

3. Breitman, *Architect of Genocide*, 101.

4. Breitman, *Architect of Genocide*, 60, 121–22, 119–21, 125–27, 130, 139, 152,155.

5. Breitman, *Architect of Genocide*, 59, 63.

6. Breitman, *Architect of Genocide*, 63; Domarus, *Hitler*, 1058.

7. Breitman, *Architect of Genocide*, 155.

8. Breitman, *Architect of Genocide*, 63.

9. Among Kasztner's many works was providing some of the funds needed to feed and clothe the Jews on Oskar Schindler's list. He traveled to neutral Switzerland to attend the negotiations he had helped organize, and then voluntarily returned to occupied Budapest to continue his efforts to forestall the killing of as many Jews as he could. Porter, *Kasztner's Train*, 4, 261.

10. Porter, *Kasztner's Train*, 143–44.

11. Weitz, *Man Who Was Murdered Twice*, 21. Although there is also evidence that the offer discussed 100,000 Jews. Porter, *Kasztner's Train*, 175.

12. Porter, *Kasztner's Train*, 143–44. Although Churchill had expressed his sympathy for the Jews of Europe, he would never agree to give any equipment to Germany that might prove useful against his own soldiers. Porter, *Kasztner's Train*, 212. Weitz, *Man Who Was Murdered Twice*, 22.

13. Bauer, *Jews for Sale?*, 40, 80; Porter, *Kasztner's Train*, 225–26, 234–35.

14. Porter, *Kasztner's Train*, 137, 141, 160, 164, 170.

15. Porter, *Kasztner's Train*, 154.

16. Porter, *Kasztner's Train*, 215.

17. Eichmann was already involved in a different attempted deception of Kasztner. The head of the ss Jewish Section told Kasztner that he could promise tens of thousands of Jews would not be deported to Auschwitz but would be sent to a place where their lives might be spared. The Nazi referred to this as putting "Jews on ice." In exchange, Kasztner would be expected to pay for them, preferably with the delivery of a significant number of trucks. In reality, at this point in the war, demands were being made by short-staffed German companies as well as the nation's allies for Jewish laborers. Eichmann would soon be required to send several thousand Jews to work in places like Austria. He was thus attempting to charge the Jews, through Kasztner, for something he was already being ordered to do. At first, he promised that thirty thousand Jews would be "put on ice." When the time came to actually ship Jews to labor in Austria, the number had been reduced by Eichmann to fifteen thousand. Thanks to a clerical error, however, twenty thousand ended up being shipped to forced labor in Strasshof, Austria. Porter, *Kasztner's Train*, 180–81, 205; Jangfeldt, *Hero of Budapest*, 199.

18. Porter, *Kasztner's Train*, 180, 213. When Kasztner asked Becher whether he would fulfill an earlier agreement to allow some of these Hungarian Jewish prisoners, who had been kept in a somewhat more protected environment in Bergen-Belsen, to be taken to the Swiss border and released, the German lieutenant colonel responded that the money he had previously been provided was not enough because the "exchange rate for the dollar had changed considerably."

Since the arrangement had been based upon the old conversion rate, Becher would need more money before he would cooperate. Kasztner charged some of the well-to-do riders between $1,500 and $5,000 so as to cover the $1,000 ticket price of those who did not have the money. Additionally, Becher insisted that he be given fifty seats to sell. Kasztner would still be responsible for providing the Germans $1,000 for each of these fifty passengers, but the wealthy Hungarian Jews to whom Becher sold his allotment of seats (and who likely compensated the rapacious SS economic advisor with other gifts and favors) would discreetly pay him $25,000. Porter, *Kasztner's Train*, 180, 243.

19. Porter, *Kasztner's Train*, 204.

20. Porter, *Kasztner's Train*, 216.

21. Porter, *Kasztner's Train*, 269.

22. Einhorn, *Handelsresande I Liv*, chapter 45 in general, 325, 379–82; see also Persson, *Escape from the Third Reich*, 157, 154–55, citing the research and conclusions reached by Israeli historian Dov Dinur, https://sok.riksarkivet.se/?postid= Arkisref SE/RA/730128/01/F/F 21&s=Balder.

23. Porter, *Kasztner's Train*, 289; Longerich, *Himmler*, 728.

24. Bauer, *Jews for Sale?*, 249. Becher was not, however, similarly successful with respect to the camp at Neuengamme, where he obtained no cooperation from the commandant. Porter, *Kasztner's Train*, 290.

25. Porter, *Kasztner's Train*, 289.

26. Though raising large sums from even Jewish sources for the purpose of bribing Nazis had been made difficult because prior attempts had too often failed to prevent the ransomed Jewish captives from being killed, there was still more chance of discreetly obtaining capital from the Jewish sources than directly from Allied governments. Porter, *Kasztner's Train*, 175, 226; see also Porat, *Blue and the Yellow Stars of David*.

27. Porter, *Kasztner's Train*, 261.

28. Porter, *Kasztner's Train*, 262. As an additional incentive, and without authorization to make any such payment, McClelland offered twenty million Swiss francs in return for the immediate cessation of deportations of Jews to the camps and a guarantee of safety for all inmates. The American Quaker told the thirty-four-year-old Kurt Becher that the funds could be used for whatever the Germans wanted except to acquire war materials. Becher, who similarly had no authorization to make or fulfill any such promise, agreed.

Lieutenant Colonel Becher had arrived in Budapest in March 1944, almost immediately after his nation's army first marched into the capital of its wavering ally. He had a broad mandate from the Gestapo leader to economically exploit (loot) Hungarian assets, but it may have been even more important to Himmler that his representative successfully open a direct line of communication to an agent of the American government. Becher, who was afraid of his Reichsführer, was eager to please him. Porter, *Kasztner's Train,* 132 262, 265, 267–68.

29. The next morning Kurt Becher went shopping in Zürich for a present for his mistress and to purchase a particular Swiss remedy to treat the interior minister's kidney problem. In reality, McClelland's offer of twenty million Swiss francs in return for Himmler's ending the deportation of Jews to the camps and guaranteeing their safety was without authorization and had therefore been a bluff to stall for time. The War Refugee Board had concluded that so long as the ss believed Jewish lives had value, they would have incentive to keep some of them alive. Though the entire twenty million would never be delivered, on December 8, five million Swiss francs were deposited in an appropriate account. The five million, accompanied by a never-fulfilled pledge that an additional fifteen million would soon follow, did temporarily satisfy Becher, and seemingly Himmler as well. Porter, *Kasztner's Train,* 262–63.

30. Walter Rapp, assistant to the chief U.S. Prosecutor at Nuremberg, recalled that Kurt Becher, who had been "taken into custody by the Americans on May 24, 1945 . . . was merely one of many suspects" until Kasztner's arrival. Porter, *Kasztner's Train,* 310.

Having been the ss official whom Himmler himself had placed in charge of economically exploiting the Jews of Hungary, Becher would undoubtedly have been put on trial and convicted of war crimes. "He has Kasztner to thank for his freedom," said Rapp. Porter, *Kasztner's Train,* 310; see also Bauer, *Jews for Sale?,* 164. According to eyewitness accounts, Kasztner emphatically coached Becher to "remember" how he had persuaded Himmler to allow those Jews still remaining in Budapest to be rescued rather than killed. Porter, *Kasztner's Train,* 307–10.

While Jewish testimonials on behalf of suspected war criminals were rare, the sworn affidavit former Lieutenant Colonel Becher was able to procure from Rezso Kasztner is arguably the most famous. Kasztner told prosecutors at Nuremberg that "there can be no doubt that Becher belongs to the very few [ss] leaders having the courage to oppose the program of annihilation of the Jews and trying to rescue human lives." Porter, *Kasztner's Train,* 310.

31. Porter, *Kasztner's Train,* 131.
32. Porter, *Kasztner's Train,* 130.
33. Bauer, *Jews for Sale?,* 250; Porter, *Kasztner's Train,* 322.
34. Porter, *Kasztner's Train,* 354–55, 57.

10. A TRUE BELIEVER

1. Masur, *My Meeting with Himmler,* para. 42. See also Kempowski, *Swansong 1945,* 80.
2. Masur, *My Meeting with Himmler,* para. 42. See, generally, Einhorn, *Handelsresande I Liv;* "Himmler's Masseur und Schwedens Extratour," *Fenster zur*

Welt, aired January 18, 1999 (ARTE Deustchland); see also Kittel, "'White Bus' Operation," 225.

3. Longerich, *Himmler*, 726, 725; Richie, *Faust's Metropolis*, 598. Himmler likely hoped that, in spite of his having been in charge of the death camps and the Einsatzgruppen mobile mass-murder squads, the Allies would never learn of his involvement. See also Holocaust Encyclopedia, "Einsatzgruppen (Mobile Killing Units)"; and Breitman, *Architect of Genocide*, 173–77, 189–96, 236. Toward this end, in late April 1945, Himmler dispatched his longtime secretary on an unsuccessful mission to find and destroy all records detailing his involvement in the killing of civilians. He also appears to have speculated that even if the Allies did uncover these crimes, Western governments would understand that since the Jews were Germany's mortal enemy, the Reich's actions against them had been a legitimate defensive wartime measure. From his distorted perspective, everything he and his fatherland had done had been in self-defense. Breitman, *Architect of Genocide*, 189, 177.

4. See Richie, *Faust's Metropolis*, 579; Goldhagen, *Hitler's Willing Executioners*, 356.

5. Longerich, *Himmler*, 719.

6. Masur, *My Meeting with Himmler*, paras. 46–48.

7. Allen, *Himmler's Secret War*, 193–95; Breitman, *Architect of Genocide*, 189.

8. Breitman, *Architect of Genocide*, 48. Sometime between July 13 and July 15, 1941, Himmler had told Auschwitz commandant Rudolf Hoess, "The Jews are the sworn enemies of the German people and must be eradicated." Breitman, *Architect of Genocide*, 189; Hoess, *Commandant of Auschwitz*, 173; Gilbert, *Nuremberg Diary*, 149–50. To Himmler, the Jews would remain "the most important target, the arch-enemy throughout the war." Breitman, *Architect of Genocide*, 181, 183.

9. Breitman, *Architect of Genocide*, 74.

10. Breitman, *Architect of Genocide*, 224.

11. Goldhagen, *Hitler's Willing Executioners*, 42.

12. Goldhagen, *Hitler's Willing Executioners*, 41–42.

13. Fox, "A Jew Talks to Himmler," para. 7; see also Waller, *Devil's Doctor*, 180–81.

14. Even in the United States, where Roosevelt received more than 80 percent of the Jewish vote in each of his four successful presidential campaigns, the State Department, until overruled by the president himself, not only made it difficult for Jews to obtain visas but also suppressed evidence of the existence of a Holocaust and even interfered with potential rescue efforts. Zuckerman, "FDR's Jewish Problem." See also Wyman, *Abandonment of the Jews*, 205; and, generally, Breitman and Lichtman, *FDR and the Jews*. Additionally, even the limited late-war creation of the War Refugee Board by the United States appears to have been done without much cooperation from Britain's leadership. A July 11, 1944, note sent from Churchill to British foreign secretary Anthony Eden set forth his

position that there should "be no negotiations of any kind" with Germany on the question of releasing Jewish captives. Porter, *Kasztner's Train*, 212.

15. Kempowski, *Swansong 1945*, 2.

16. In 1941 Martin Heidegger wrote in private notes, as revealed in 2014, that the "empty rationality and incalculable ability [of] World Jewry is ungraspable everywhere. [They do not] need to get involved in military action, while continuing to . . . influence, whereas we are left to sacrifice the best blood of the best of our people." Jennifer Schuessler, "Heidegger's Notes Renew Focus on Anti-Semitism," *New York Times*, March 31, 2014.

17. Masur, *My Meeting with Himmler*, para. 33.

18. Beevor, *Fall of Berlin 1945*, 293; Longerich, *Himmler*, 719; Allen, *Himmler's Secret War*, 270–71.

19. Masur, *My Meeting with Himmler*, paras. 37–40.

20. Masur, *My Meeting with Himmler*, paras. 32, 39. According to Masur, Himmler also promised the release of other prisoners:

> The freeing of a number of French women, in accordance with the list of the Swedish Foreign Ministry is also approved. About 50 Norwegian Jews in camps will be freed and brought to the Swedish border. The cases of the 20 Swedish prisoners in Grini, who were convicted by German courts, will be reexamined favorably and, if at all possible, they will be freed. The cases of the liberation of the Norwegian hostages will also be reexamined favorably. A larger number of mostly Dutch prisoners, who were listed by name in Theresienstadt will be freed, as long as the Red Cross can pick them up. (Masur, *My Meeting with Himmler*, para. 39.)

> It is a matter of some controversy as to whether these releases took place as promised.

21. Persson, *Escape from the Third Reich*, 155.

22. Longerich, *Himmler*, 730–31.

23. Porter, *Kasztner's Train*, 292.

24. "The main contribution and the crucial goal was to save the camps and the inmates, 300,000–400,000 persons. And we managed to do that, in my opinion, partly through my efforts to make the International Red Cross president intervene with the German leaders and partly through the talks that Storch, Kersten, Masur, and Bernadotte conducted directly with Nazi leaders." Gerhart Riegner, quoted in Einhorn, *Handelsresande I Liv*, 467.

25. Breitman, *Architect of Genocide*, 6.

26. Masur, *My Meeting with Himmler*, para. 37.

27. Longerich, *Himmler*, 707, 709, 734–35.

28. Masur, *My Meeting with Himmler*, para. 34.

29. Schellenberg, *Labyrinth*, 393.

30. Masur, *My Meeting with Himmler*, para. 39.

31. Masur, *My Meeting with Himmler*, paras. 39–40, 55. See also Bauer, *Jews for Sale?*, 246.

32. Wulff, *Zodiac and Swastika*, 171.

33. Bergen, *War and Genocide*, 164, 232.

34. Louise Ridley, "The Holocaust's Forgotten Victims: The 5 Million Non-Jewish People Killed By the Nazis." *HuffPost UK*, January 27, 2015. http://www .huffingtonpost.com/2015/01/27/holocaust-non-jewish-victims_n_ 6555604 .html.

35. "At least a million prisoners were thought to be still alive in Hitler's concentration camps in April 1945, all threatened with massacre in the last days, and most dying the same horrible deaths already exposed in Belsen and Buchenwald." Helm, *Ravensbrück*, 588.

36. Einhorn, *Handelsresande I Liv*, 467.

11. THE COUNT OF THE RED CROSS

1. Einhorn, *Handelsresande I Liv*, 266.

2. Einhorn, *Handelsresande I Liv*, 157. See also Masur, *My Meeting with Himmler*, para. 65.

3. Bernadette was not only a member of the Swedish Royal family, he was also married to an American, and while recently in Paris he had met with General Eisenhower. Helm, *Ravensbrück*, 539–40. See also Persson, *Escape from the Third Reich*, 9; Helm, "The Swedish Schindler."

4. Bauer, *Jews for Sale?*, 248–49.

5. Kittel, "White Bus Operation," 225.

6. Longerich, *Himmler*, 728; Beevor, *Fall of Berlin 1945*, 294; Wulff, *Zodiac and Swastika*, 174. In gratitude, or perhaps as a form of payment, Count Bernadotte would soon provide Schellenberg temporary postwar refuge in Sweden.

7. See Bauer, *Jews for Sale*, 246; Hewins, *Count Folke Bernadotte*, 141; Kittel, "White Bus Operation," 226; Persson, *Escape from the Third Reich*, 200; Longerich, *Himmler*, 728.

8. Persson, *Escape from the Third Reich*, 102, 200; Longerich, *Himmler*, 729; Hewins, *Count Folke Bernadotte*, 141.

9. Waller, *Devil's Doctor*, 186. On April 28, in fulfillment of this understanding with the count, it appears that a total of perhaps as many as 7,500 camp inmates may have been released. While Count Bernadotte later described the rescuing of an additional 3,000 Jewish women, the total number of Jewish women seems to have been closer to another 1,000 Jews in addition to my mother's previously released group of 1,000. There is, however, evidence that on April 27, 1945, a number of the remaining prisoners in Ravensbrück were "evacuated" by death march. Kittel, "'White Bus' Operation," 252. See also Masur, *My Meeting with Himmler*, paras. 53, 55, 63; Agassi, *Jewish Women Pris-*

oners, 180; Lehmann and Carroll, *In Hitler's Bunker*, 83; Longerich, *Himmler*, 728. When Soviet troops eventually arrived at the camp, a few days after April 28, there were only a few remaining prisoners, who had been too sick to travel. Kittel, "'White Bus' Operation," 252.

10. The second group of prisoners released as the result of the Bernadotte-Himmler agreement began their trip, as did the Jewish women before them, by land with Denmark and then with Sweden as their planned destination. Kittel, "'White Bus' Operation," 252. A few days after my mother's group left Ravensbrück, perhaps as many as 4,000 additional women prisoners of the camp were packed aboard a train with 50 freight cars bound for Hamburg. Lost in the fog of war, the train finally reached the outskirts of Lübeck, where its engine broke down. Four of the already weakened women died on the arduous journey, while others needed hospitalization. The remaining 3,989 survivors were finally able to reach the Danish border. Rosenberg, *Brief Stop*, 141.

11. Agassi, *Jewish Women Prisoners*, 181.

12. Bernadotte would present himself as the "sole planner and executor of the [entire] mission." Kittel, "'White Bus' Operation," 233.

13. Persson, *Escape from the Third Reich*, 72, 71; Kittel, "White Bus' Operation," 232–33; see also Urquhart, "Introduction," xii.

14. "Masur's comments are contained in a report of his meeting with Himmler that he wrote for the Swedish government the very next day, and which is therefore remarkably fresh and almost contemporaneous." Helm, *Ravensbrück*, 591.

15. Persson, *Escape from the Third Reich*, 72, 71.

16. Palmer, "Felix Kersten and Count Bernadotte"; Kittel, "White Bus' Operation," 233.

17. See Persson, *Escape from the Third Reich*, 200. See also Waller, *Devil's Doctor*, 208; Kittel, "White Bus' Operation," 233.

18. Masur, *My Meeting with Himmler*, paras. 39–40, 55; Rudberg, *Swedish Jews*, 244. See also Bauer, *Jews for Sale?*, 246.

19. "All the Ravensbrück survivors in Israel who had been evacuated to Sweden and were later interviewed by us reported that they considered Bernadotte their Savior and a hero." Agassi, *Jewish Woman Prisoners*, 15. See also Kittel, "White Bus' Operation," 230.

20. Kittel, "'White Bus' Operation," 232–33. Once the war was nearing its end, Jewish refugees who actually arrived in Sweden were often treated with great kindness and generosity, yet even after the war there were some Swedish workers who openly expressed their unwillingness to work with Jews and feared they might lose their jobs to the new arrivals. Those Jewish survivors who chose to settle in Sweden often had to wait until the mid-1950s before being allowed citizenship. Rosenberg, *Brief Stop*, 169–72, 275.

21. Helm, *Ravensbrück*, 565; Persson, *Escape from the Third Reich*, 20, 36.

22. Persson, *Escape from the Third Reich*, 8; Waller, *Devil's Doctor*, 172. There are reports that Count Bernadotte had previously attempted to secure the release of Jews, but that prior to meeting with Norbert Masur, Himmler had been unwilling to discuss the subject. Helm, "Swedish Schindler," 3.

23. Waller, *Devil's Doctor*, 216. See also Trevor-Roper, "Strange Case of Himmler's Doctor," n11.

24. Persson, *Escape from the Third Reich*, 141.

25. Persson, *Escape from the Third Reich*, 159; Kittel, "White Bus' Operation," 234.

26. After the war Felix Kersten claimed that the count "had advised him in somewhat threatening tones to omit Jews" from their discussions as to who was to be released from the German camps. Waller, *Devil's Doctor*, 216; Kittel, "White Bus' Operation," 232.

27. "Bernadotte had given up on the transport of Danish Jews . . . from Theresienstadt [because it] could very well jeopardize further transport operations involving Scandinavian prisoners." Persson, *Escape from the Third Reich*, 175. Eventually, however, with the aid of Bernadotte, 423 Danish Jews were in fact rescued from Theresienstadt. Persson, *Escape from the Third Reich*, 249.

28. Waller, *Devil's Doctor*, 216.

29. See Trevor-Roper, "Strange Case of Himmler's Doctor," 361. See also Waller, *Devil's Doctor*, 213–14.

30. Though after so long a period of time it is difficult to be certain how widespread Swedish anti-Semitism was in the period between the wars, one news story seems to demonstrate how outlandish were the claims of those who fell prey to its hysteria: "[It is an] incontrovertible fact that the fate of today's world lies largely in the hands of the Jewish people, which directs and controls all capital and financial activity, whilst at the same time visibly leading political and social, even purely revolutionary and anti-capitalist movements among the people." *Sodertalje Tidning*, September 15, 1924. Quoted in Rosenberg, *Brief Stop*, 85.

31. Einhorn, *Handelsresande I Liv*, 30. In 1942 Jewish entry into Sweden had basically been stopped. Rudberg, *Swedish Jews*, 186.

32. Eidum, *Blodsporet*. "The . . . limited extent of [Sweden's] aid during the different phases of the Nazi era are ultimately attributable more to rigid governmental policies . . . than to lack of will on the part of Swedish Jews." Rudberg, *Swedish Jews*, 259.

33. Rudberg, *Swedish Jews*, 215–16; Carlberg, *Wallenberg*, 208–9.

34. Rudberg, *Swedish Jews*, 216.

35. Hungary's leader may have grown personally uncomfortable with German liquidation of his country's Jewish population once he became convinced of the fate of those delivered to Auschwitz. With Allied victory becoming more inevitable, there also first appeared a palpable international willingness to intervene on behalf of the Jews. Beevor, *Fall of Berlin 1945*, 201. In June 1944, the same month as the Swedish

king's appeal to Admiral Horthy, Pope Pius XII (though specifically emphasizing Christians of Jewish ancestry) also urged the already wavering Horthy to "put a stop to the suffering and torments that countless people are being subjected to simply on the grounds of their nationality or race." Porter, *Kasztner's Train*, 183. It has been reported that when President Roosevelt's seeming ultimatum to end the monstrous treatment of Jews did not result in an immediate answer, Roosevelt is believed to have responded by ordering an intense American bombing raid against Budapest. If true, it does seem likely that the implied threat of other such attacks may have most influenced Horthy's eventual decision to stop the shipments of Hungary's Jews to the death camps. The deportations halted by the Hungarian government in early July 1944, however, began again three months later, when in October Horthy was removed from power by the Germans, allowing Adolf Eichmann to supervise renewed shipments to Auschwitz. Jangfeldt, *Hero of Budapest*, 149. See also Rudberg, *Swedish Jews*, 217; Carlberg, *Wallenberg*, 209.

36. The king had previously offered Wallenberg's position to Bernadotte, who turned it down. Jangfeldt, *Hero of Budapest*, 150.

37. Carlberg, *Wallenberg*, 236, 238, 251, 260, 265, 290-291, 298, 313, 310, 332, 327, 403.

38. Carlberg, *Wallenberg*, 309–11.

39. Carlberg, *Wallenberg*, 176, 267, 308, 310, 403. Jangfeldt, *Hero of Budapest*, 170–74, 187.

40. Carlberg, *Wallenberg*, 316; See also, Metzler, "Raoul Wallenberg."

41. "In total, 120,000 Jews survived the Nazi extermination in Hungary. According to Per Anger, Wallenberg's friend and colleague, Wallenberg must be honored with saving at least 100,000 Jews." Metzler, "Raoul Wallenberg," www .jewishvirtuallibrary.org/raoul-wallenberg-3. Carlberg, *Wallenberg*, 310–11.

42. Carlberg, *Wallenberg*, 207–8, 252.

43. Carlberg, *Wallenberg*, 207–8, 227, 252.

44. Carlberg, *Wallenberg*, 256.

45. Carlberg, *Wallenberg*, 208, 252.

46. Carlberg, *Wallenberg*, 221–22, 246. Rudberg, *Swedish Jews*, 217.

47. Jangfeldt, *Hero of Budapest*, 131.

48. Jangfeldt, *Hero of Budapest*, 131.

49. Jangfeldt, *Hero of Budapest*, 132.

50. Jangfeldt, *Hero of Budapest*, 146.

51. Porter, *Kasztner's Train*, 226.

52. Jangfeldt, *Hero of Budapest*, 136.

53. See Persson, *Escape from the Third Reich*. In Sune Persson's spirited and scholarly advocacy of what he asserts to have been Sweden's significant success in saving Jews, the author comments on three other books (Paul A. Levine, *From Indifference to Activism: Swedish Diplomacy and the Holocaust; 1938–44;* Monty Penkower, *The Jews Were Expendable: Free World Diplomacy and the Holocaust;* Steven Koblik, *The Stones*

Cry Out: Sweden's Response to the Persecution of the Jews; 1933–1945), which are less complimentary of Sweden's efforts. In his critique of their coverage and conclusions, Persson maintains that the first of these books failed to discuss the critical last year of the war, while the other two were unfortunately superficial. He then also notes, for what purpose one can only speculate, that "it is interesting, and significant to Swedish research scholars, that all three authors were American Jews." Persson, *Escape from the Third Reich*, 62–63. Persson suggests that one of the reasons for there actually being insufficient acknowledgment of Count Bernadotte's accomplishments in saving Jews may be "that after 1948 an anti-Bernadotte campaign blossomed from the Jewish side." Persson, *Escape from the Third Reich*, 72. Though apparently encumbered by nationality and ethnicity, I do feel it necessary to offer a brief comment. I would have thought that anyone who has spent significant time studying the Holocaust would have resisted the urge to reduce the Jewish members of a group to a single identity; and then, because of that identity, minimize their contribution.

54. Hewins, *Count Folke Bernadotte*, 141n1; See also Sterebe, "Ravensbrück," 215–58; Agassi, *Jewish Women Prisoners*, 3; Kittel, "White Bus Operation," 223, 234, 234n90, 237n5; Helm, "Swedish Schindler"; and Persson, *Escape from the Third Reich*.

55. Jona Malleyron, "Negotiated with Himmler," *Jerusalem Post*, August 8, 1971.

56. Agassi, *Jewish Women Prisoners*, 15; Helm, "Swedish Schindler," 5.

57. Kittel, "White Bus Operation," 239n72; Helm, "Swedish Schindler," 5. See also Persson, *Mediation and Assassination*.

12. THE BUSES WERE WHITE

1. As was typical within the hierarchy of the SS, those in charge of Ravensbrück were men. Bazyler and Truckheimer, *Forgotten Trials*, 134.

2. Saidel, *Jewish Women of Ravensbrück*, 9, 12, 19–20; Bazyler and Tuerkheimer, *Forgotten Trials*, 140–48.

3. Bazyler and Tuerkheimer, *Forgotten Trials*, 130.

4. Helm, *Ravensbrück*, 594.

5. Einhorn, *Handelsresande I Liv*, 422–26; Helm, *Ravensbrück*, 594.

6. "Suhren had the gas chambers destroyed on 23 April." Persson, *Escape from the Third Reich*, 207. Compare, "The precise date of the final gassing at Ravensbrück is not known, but Adolf Winklemann told the Hamburg court that he had gone on selecting for gassing until 24 or 25 April." Helm, *Ravensbrück*, 604.

7. Helm, "Swedish Schindler," 4.

8. Kittel, "'White Bus' Operation," 229. Most of the Jewish women prisoners finally agreed to cooperate, though a few women who were not part of my mother's group refused to reveal themselves to be Jews and were not considered as potential candidates to be among the thousand to board the white buses. Some of those women who did not cooperate were eventually liberated from the camp,

but there is no complete record as to how many died before they could later be liberated. Kittel, "'White Bus' Operation," 239n58.

9. Agassi, *Jewish Women Prisoners*, 164.

10. Kittel, "'White Bus' Operation," 235.

11. Agassi, *Jewish Women Prisoners*, 164.

12. Agassi, *Jewish Women Prisoners*, 164.

13. After a little less than two weeks in Ravensbrück, the women's hunger was unbearable, and the Red Cross sent food parcels and had them distributed to the prisoners. (Some of these may possibly have been part or all of the cargo brought to Germany in the small plane that had ferried Norbert Masur into the country.) This proved to be as much of a curse as it was a blessing as the canned meats made some of the prisoners ill. Agassi, *Jewish Women Prisoners*,164.

14. Judith Buber Agassi, the granddaughter of the world-renowned Jewish philosopher Martin Buber and the daughter of author Margarete Buber-Neumann, a gentile who had endured four years as a political prisoner in Ravensbrück, devoted years to meticulously interviewing women who had survived the camp. The following description of the Red Cross transport appears in her book, *The Jewish Women Prisoners of Ravensbrück*: "Two groups of Jewish prisoners, the smaller one made up of women who had worked at Siemens, and the larger one, with 450–490 nearly all Polish Jewish women and girls from Łódź, Auschwitz, and Krupp-Neukölln, who had arrived in Ravensbrück about 8 or 12 days before, must have been among the evacuees of 25 and 26 April" (181).

15. Helm, *Ravensbrück*, 606.

16. Agassi, *Jewish Women Prisoners*, 164–65, 14. Persson, *Escape from the Third Reich*, 182; Saidel, *Jewish Women*, 181; Kittel, "'White Bus' Operation," 228–29.

17. Agassi, *Jewish Women Prisoners*, 164.

18. Kittel, "White Bus Operation," 230; Agassi, *Jewish Women Prisoners*, 165.

19. Wulff, *Zodiac and Swastika*, 177; Helm, *Ravensbrück*, 604; Agassi, *Jewish Women Prisoners*, 165.

20. Agassi, *Jewish Women Prisoners*, 165.

21. Richie, *Faust's Metropolis*, 579; Broszat, "Concentration Camps," 248.

22. Broszat, "Concentration Camps," 157.

23. Kittel, "'White Bus' Operation," 229; Agassi, *Jewish Women Prisoners*, 165.

24. Helm, "Swedish Schindler," 4. See also Agassi, *Jewish Women Prisoners*, 165; Kittel, "'White Bus' Operation," 230; 165; Helm, *Ravensbrück*, 604.

25. Agassi, *Jewish Women Prisoners*, 181.

26. Saidel, *Jewish Women*, 181; Agassi, *Jewish Women Prisoners*, 165.

27. Himmler's fall from power came too late to affect the freedom already reached by the women whose release from Ravensbrück he had authorized. Nor did it prevent the last group of released Ravensbrück inmates from eventually reaching Sweden on May 2. Kittel, "'White Bus' Operation," 228.

28. Kittel, "'White Bus' Operation," 228; see also Helm, "Swedish Schindler," 1.

1. Longerich, *Himmler*, 734.
2. Longerich, *Himmler*, 734–35.
3. Richie, *Faust's Metropolis*, 598.
4. Longerich, *Himmler*, 734–35; see also John Waller, who sets the date of Himmler leaving Bavaria as May 10. Waller, *Devil's Doctor*, 202. Himmler began his attempted escape with Rudolf Brandt, Otto Ohlendorf, Professor Karl Gebhardt, Heinz Macher, and military aide Werner Grothmann. Longerich, *Himmler*, 35.
5. Breitman, *Architect of Genocide*, 8; Longerich, *Himmler*, 736.
6. Breitman, *Architect of Genocide*, 8; Masur, *My Meeting with Himmler*, para. 20.
7. Longerich, *Himmler*, 736.
8. As part of what we now understand to have been a hoax, the documents included an alleged departmental memorandum credited to John Wheeler-Bennett of the British Foreign Office. This memo was said to include the following passage: "We cannot allow Himmler to take the stand in any prospective prosecution, or indeed allow him to be interrogated by the Americans. Steps will therefore have to be taken to eliminate him as soon as he falls into our hands." Allen, *Himmler's Secret War*, 289.

   It was also claimed that there was a telegram in the National Archives dated May 24, 1945, supposedly sent just a few hours after Himmler's reported suicide, stating: "We successfully intercepted HH last night at Luneberg [*sic*] before he could be interrogated. As instructed, action was taken to silence him permanently." Allen, *Himmler's Secret War*, 290.

   Additionally, there was a letter purportedly written by Brandon Bracken, minister for political warfare, a few days after Himmler's death, in which he is supposed to have said: "I am sure that if it were to become public knowledge that we had a hand in this man's demise, it would have devastating repercussions for this country's standing. I am also sure that this incident would complicate our relations with our American brethren; under no circumstances must they discover that we eradicated 'Little H.'" Allen, *Himmler's Secret War*, 291.
9. Paul Lewis, "The 29 Fakes behind the Rewriting of History," *The Guardian*, May 4, 2008; see also Ben Fenton, "Historian Calls for an Inquiry over Fake Himmler Documents," *The Telegraph*, July 4, 2005. "When I first examined the documents in the autumn of 2003, there was nothing about them to indicate that they were anything but genuine letters and memoranda. There seemed to be no purpose in 'seeding' the British National Archive with inauthentic documents. Given the evidence, I have to say that I accept that certain documents now held by the National Archives and proclaimed as fake are likely to be inauthentic." Allen, *Himmler's Secret War*, 291.

10. Lisciotto, "Heinrich Himmler: 'Treue Heinrich'"; Breitman, *Architect of Genocide*, 244.

11. Manchester, *Arms of Krupp*, 11, 597, 605–6; Ferencz, *Less Than Slaves*, 70.

12. Manchester, *Arms of Krupp*, 606, 608.

13. Manchester, *Arms of Krupp*, 486, 649–50.

14. Manchester, *Arms of Krupp*, 649–50. Saur, who would be ostracized in postwar West Germany for his candor, which many Germans considered as tantamount to treason, testified that "[he had] not been able to find a single case, nor [had he] heard of a single one, in which someone was sent to a concentration camp because he failed to fulfill his production quota." Manchester, *Arms of Krupp*, 486. In addition, he noted that, given his long and early ties as a member of the National Socialist hierarchy, "the relationship between Krupp and ourselves was different from our relationship with other firms." Since no one else had ever suffered physical punishment for not meeting expectations, the powerful Krupp would have understood that he would certainly not have been singled out for such grim sanction. Manchester, *Arms of Krupp*, 486, 650, 662.

15. Manchester, *Arms of Krupp*, 657; U.S. Military Tribunal, Nuremberg, United States v. Alfried Krupp et al., 13231–13402, July 31, 1948. See also Ferencz, *Less Than Slaves*, 71.

16. Manchester, *Arms of Krupp*, 657.

17. James, *Krupp*, 229.

18. Hoffman, *After Such Knowledge*, 85.

19. Hoffman, *After Such Knowledge*, 84, 168, 85.

20. Manchester, *Arms of Krupp*, 671. Even some American newspapers, like the *New York Herald Tribune*, questioned whether it was irresponsible to continue punishing an industrialist like Alfried Krupp at a time when America should be rebuilding its newly democratic ally as a bulwark against Communist aggression. Manchester, *Arms of Krupp*, 642. Some in the U.S. government were eager to see various convicted Nazi war criminals completely pardoned so that their prior crimes would no longer follow them. This, to his credit, appears to have been a bridge too far even for the U.S. High Commissioner for Occupied Germany, John J. McCloy. However, though McCloy was not willing to support exoneration, he was prepared to accelerate prisoners' releases. Manchester, *Arms of Krupp*, 13, 669–71, 7.

21. Manchester, *Arms of Krupp*, 671, 13.
A former Wall Street attorney and named partner in the powerful firm of Milbank, Tweed, Hadley and McCloy, the American high commissioner, who had agonized over his involvement in the eventual early release of Nazis convicted of having been members of mass-murdering squads, appears to have been somewhat sympathetic to the plight of the businessmen who had been the

beneficiaries of Nazi slave labor. Ferencz, *Less Than Slaves*, 73. He considered them as having been in a category quite separate from the others convicted at Nuremberg. Ignoring that those found guilty had requested concentration camp inmates as forced workers, McCloy's clemency board blithely and erroneously declared that the slaves had been assigned to the companies by the Nazi government and that such laborers had always remained under strict Gestapo and not corporate control. Ferencz, *Less Than Slaves*, 74.

This was not the first time that John J. McCloy had made a controversial decision as a member of the executive branch. When, in the second half of 1944, the War Department was considering various proposals to either bomb Auschwitz or the railway lines leading to it, it was Assistant Secretary of War McCloy who officially rejected all such ideas. Geoffrey Ward, "Roosevelt in Auschwitz," review of *1944: FDR and the Year that Changed History*, by Jay Winik, *Wall Street Journal*, September 19–20, 2015. Concluding that such an operation could be performed only by diverting "considerable air support" and would still be of such "doubtful efficacy" as to not "warrant the use of our resources," McCloy then added that "even if practicable, it might provoke even more vindictive action by the Germans." Tatz and Higgins, *Magnitude of the Genocide*, 148. What form this feared heightened Nazi vindictiveness would or could have taken was never made clear.

Nor was this the only time McCloy was accused of having acted out of apparent expediency and with seeming indifference to the plight of those involuntarily confined by reason of their ethnicity or national origin. As the wartime official most responsible for the treatment of Japanese Americans, he had been a strong proponent of internment as a military necessity. Irons, *Justice at War*, 15, 195. It was McCloy who successfully held off Interior Secretary Ickes and others in the administration who wanted to concede the absence of any evidence of American-Japanese espionage. Irons, *Justice at War*, 209, 344, 302. As the U.S. Supreme Court prepared to hear arguments in the case of *Korematsu v. United States*, 323 U.S. 214 (1944) that would eventually and controversially uphold the constitutionality of interning even American citizens if they were of Japanese ancestry, McCloy allegedly buried a report contradicting the factual basis for his hard-liner position. Irons, *Justice at War*, 209, 344, 302.

22. Manchester, *Arms of Krupp*, 674–76.

23. Such leniency was not universally cheered. One Krupp biographer noted that "no single act of the occupation created a greater emotional shock than did McCloy's rejection of the Krupp verdict." Manchester, *Arms of Krupp*, 680. See also Ferencz, *Less Than Slaves*, 75. The 1951 French and British press vilified the premature freeing of these industrialists from prison and the return of the Krupp fortune. Manchester, *Arms of Krupp*, 681. New York liberal Republican congress-

man Jacob Javits unsuccessfully protested to the new U.S. secretary of state, Dean Acheson. On the other hand, virulently anti-Communist Republican senator Joseph McCarthy called it an "extremely wise" decision in the ongoing war against the expansionist Soviet Union. Manchester, *Arms of Krupp*, 673, 680–82.

24. Business Abroad: "The House of Krupp Rebuilt," *Time*, August, 19, 1957. See also Ferencz, *Less Than Slaves*, 76.

25. Manchester, *Arms of Krupp*, 790–93.

26. Quoted in Manchester, *Arms of Krupp*, 790.

27. Manchester, *Arms of Krupp*, 790.

28. Bazyler, *Holocaust Justice*, 60.

29. Ferencz, *Less Than Slaves*, 87–88.

30. Batty, *House of Krupp*, 224.

31. Manchester, *Arms of Krupp*, 790, 793.

32. Manchester, *Arms of Krupp*, 871.

33. Manchester, *Arms of Krupp*, 871.

34. As settlement discussions dragged on, plaintiffs were considering the unprecedented step of filing suit in a New York court, where they would seek $100,000 on behalf of each of the forced laborers. Even John J. McCloy, to whom Krupp owed his early release and the return of his fortune, suggested to Krupp that a settlement would be a wise business decision. Ferencz, *Less Than Slaves*, 81–85. See also James, *Krupp*, 244. The former American high commissioner and Krupp had remained in close contact, with Alfried apparently having grown to view the older American as something of a mentor. Manchester, *Arms of Krupp*, 791, 834.

   Yet even this counsel, as well as the prospect of a lawsuit filed in American courts, was not enough to persuade Europe's richest industrialist to settle. Ferencz, *Less Than Slaves*, 84. There was at that moment, however, one additional bit of outside pressure that would lead Krupp to finally compromise with his Jewish adversaries. In spite of it having been one of the brokered conditions for his original prison release and the return of his property, Alfried still hoped to avoid having to divest his corporation of its Nazi-sanctioned monopolistic holdings. Dredging up his past crimes might delay or even interfere with what would eventually prove to be his successful campaign to maintain his existing industrial monopolies. Ferencz, *Less Than Slaves*, 85.

35. Manchester, *Arms of Krupp*, 12.

36. Ferencz, *Less Than Slaves*, 79–80.

37. John J. McCloy arranged a meeting between the parties in the midtown New York offices of Chase Manhattan Bank. As a product of those talks a settlement was finally reached. Ferencz, *Less Than Slaves*, 81, 85.

38. Manchester, *Arms of Krupp*, 791.

39. Ferencz, *Less Than Slaves*, 86.

40. Jewish Telegraphic Agency Bulletin, December 28, 1959, and February 3, 1960, quoted in Ferencz, *Less Than Slaves*, 86. Insightful members of the news media were not persuaded by the settlement's rejection of legal responsibility or the company's press releases, which alleged the payment was a voluntary contribution made in order to "heal the wounds suffered during World War II." The *London Sunday Dispatch* found this claim to be "mean-spirited and tawdry." Jewish Telegraphic Agency Bulletin, December 28, 1959, and February 3, 1960, quoted in Ferencz, *Less Than Slaves*, 86. For Krupp's refusal to agree to a larger payout, a Labour Party member of Britain's Parliament called Alfried a "rascal [who] got away with murder and is now getting away with the swag." However, when the meager extent of the final settlement was raised on the floor of the British Parliament, the undersecretary of state for foreign affairs explained that while his government was sympathetic to the ill treatment of the survivors who had not been compensated, Britain would not become involved. *Jewish Chronicle*, February 17, 1961, quoted in Ferencz, *Less Than Slaves*, 88.

41. "Everyone had assumed that . . . all . . . inmates had been gassed and cremated at Buchenwald. The truth was that the SS Commandant had rejected them, explaining to their distraught guards that the war was going to end at any moment and that he had his hands full trying to murder the Jews he already had." "To the astonishment of Krupp, actual, breathing Jews with unimpeachable qualifications were popping up everywhere." Manchester, *Arms of Krupp*, 792.

In addition to fewer Jews having died in the camps than Krupp had perhaps assumed, there is also a possibility he may have failed to consider the nearly five hundred women in my mother's group. Mistakenly sent from Auschwitz to Neukölln instead of the non-Jewish workers requested (and having been beneficiaries of the agreement struck between Norbert Masur and Heinrich Himmler), a high percentage of these women were alive and now filing claims for reparations. It would ironically turn out that the man who had built a wartime fortune on a business plan in part dependent on working Jewish slaves to death would eventually be outlived by most of the Jewish women who had toiled at his munitions factory near Berlin.

Furthermore, though Krupp would have been correct if he believed that systematic wartime deprivations would have likely shortened the longevity of many survivors, he overestimated the numbers of those who had already succumbed. When interviewed by Ferencz at his New York office, Jewish former slave workers all described suffering from chronic insomnia, and would often "burst into tears" when describing their lives under Krupp. Manchester, *Arms of Krupp*, 865. The Jewish claimants from Krupp's factory at Essen, who were almost all in their late thirties and early forties at the time of the settlement, prematurely suffered from ailments that would normally have not appeared until old age. One report concluded that by the 1970s nearly two-thirds of the Jewish survivors of the nightmarish conditions of slave labor at the Essen factory had passed away; but in 1960, most of even these former slaves were still alive and eager to file for even a minimal amount of their long overdue compensation.

42. Ferencz, *Less Than Slaves*, 96.

43. Ferencz, *Less Than Slaves*, 96–97, 100.

44. Ferencz, *Less Than Slaves*, 97, 100–101.

45. Ferencz, *Less Than Slaves*, 97; Manchester, *Arms of Krupp*, 792.

46. Manchester, *Arms of Krupp*, 792.

47. Ferencz, *Less Than Slaves*, 97.

48. Ferencz, *Less Than Slaves*, 98.

49. Manchester, *Arms of Krupp*, 791.

50. Manchester, *Arms of Krupp*, 794.

51. Manchester, *Arms of Krupp*, 793, 794.

52. Ferencz, *Less Than Slaves*, 88.

53. Ferencz, *Less Than Slaves*, 87.

54. Ferencz, *Less Than Slaves*, 87. Though, of course, no longer ignited by reparations payments to survivors, anti-Jewish incidents are still taking place in Germany at the time of the writing of this book. See Haaretz, DPA, and The Associated Press, April 18, 2018, "'Jewish Man' Attacked in Berlin Admits He's an Israeli-Arab Who Didn't Believe Germany Was Anti-Semitic." https://www.haaretz.com/world-news /europe/jewish-man-attacked-in-germany-admits-he-s-an-israeli-arab-1.6012220.

55. James, *Krupp*, 255.

56. Krupp's financial success had been dependent upon financing from a Frankfurt firm owned by a large group of German banks. James, *Krupp*, 257–59.

57. Funding education, science, healthcare, sports, and culture, rather than producing profits, would become the Krupp foundation's claimed mission. Ironically, one of the men who would play a key role in arranging the transformation of the Krupp industries was Berthold Beitz, to whom Krupp had turned over much of the operations of his empire in 1953. Manchester, *Arms of Krupp*, 855–56, 859. Alfried Krupp had wanted someone who "was 100% his man," and he had found him in Beitz. James, *Krupp*, 240. One of the arguably less than noble things Beitz had done for his employer had been negotiating the meager slave labor reparations settlement in 1959. Ferencz, *Less Than Slaves*, 75. However, Beitz was also acclaimed for having protected several hundred Jewish workers and their families from deportation between 1941 and 1944 in the Boryslav region of what is now Ukraine. As a result of these humanitarian acts, World Jewish Congress president Ronald S. Lauder praised him, and in 1973 Israel's official Holocaust remembrance organization, Yad Vashem, added his name to the Righteous Among the Nations, a list of gentiles who are so honored for having saved Jewish

lives during the Holocaust. Beitz would run the reorganized Alfried Krupp Foundation until his death at age ninety-nine in September 2013. After reorganizations and mergers, the company's early twenty-first-century iteration and descendent corporation of the Krupp industrial conglomerate was known as ThyssenKrupp AG. Melissa Eddy, "Berthold Beitz: German Steel Industrialist Who Saved Jews," August 1, 2013, http://www.nytimes.com/2013/08/02/business/berthold-beitz-german-steel-industrialist-who-saved-jews-dies-at-99.html.

58. Reuters, "Secrets Stolen in Cyber Attack on German Firm Making Israeli Subs," *Jerusalem Post*, December 8, 2016, http://m.jpost.com/International/Secrets-stolen-from-German-firm-building-Israeli-subs-in-massive-cyber-attack-474805#article=6017QUJCOTc3OTdERThBRkI2RDZCQUU0NkI3QTNCRDM0Q0M=. See also Anna Ahronheim, "Germany Approves Sale of Three Submarines to Israel," *Jerusalem Post*, July 2, 2017. "Israel will receive three more Dolphin submarines in a €1.5 billion deal with German conglomerate Thyssen-Krupp, in addition to the one already being built under the shadow of corruption allegations." Raoul Wootliff, "Former Netanyahu Bureau Chief Named as Aid Arrested in Submarine Probe," *Times of Israel*, September 3, 2017, https://www.timesofisrael.com/ex-netanyahu-chief-of-staff-named-as-aide-arrested-in-submarine-probe/. For more on what Thyssenkrupp manufactures today, see https://www.thyssenkrupp.com/en/products/.

59. Yaniv Kubovich, "Submarine Affair: Circle of Suspects Grows as Former Intel Minister's Aides Questioned," *Haaretz*, September 12, 2017, https://www.haaretz.com/israel-news/.premium-1.811890; "The Israeli Submarine Scandal: What We Know," *Haaretz*, November 6, 2017, https://www.haaretz.com/israel-news/LIVE-the-israeli-submarine-scandal-what-we-know-1.5626626.

60. Apologies to William Shakespeare's character, Feste: "And thus the whirligig of time brings in his revenges." Shakespeare, "Twelfth Night," 376–77.

61. Manchester, *Arms of Krupp*, 827, 845, 858.

14. THERE WAS NO RETURNING

1. Saidel, *Jewish Women*, 181; Kittel, "White Bus Operation," 255–56; Agassi, *Jewish Women Prisoners*, 166.

2. Agassi, *Jewish Women Prisoners*, 157–58, 167.

3. Masur, *My Meeting with Himmler*, para. 66; Kittel, "White Bus' Operation," 235.

4. Agassi, *Jewish Women Prisoners*, 167.

5. Kittel, "White Bus Operation," 261n32.

6. Hoffman, *After Such Knowledge*, 19; Epstein, *Children of the Holocaust*, 94–95. "By April 1945, 'a dozen Polish towns were named as places where Jews had been killed, allegedly by members of the Polish Home Guard (Armia Krajowa), the armed force formed by and loyal to the Government-in-Exile.'" Tamara Zieve, "Document Reveals Poles Treated Jews as Badly as Germans Did," *Jerusalem*

Post, March 1, 2018, http://www.jpost.com/Diaspora/1946-US-document
-reveals-Poles-treated-Jews-as-badly-as-Germans-did-543940.

7. Hoffman, *After Such Knowledge*, 19.

8. Hoffman, *After Such Knowledge*, 137–38, 141–42.

9. Zieve, "Document Reveals Poles Treated Jews as Badly as Germans Did." See
also Isabel Kershner and Joanna Berendt, "Poland and Israel in Tense Talks over
Law Likened to Holocaust Denial," *New York Times*, March 1, 2018, https://www
.nytimes.com/2018/03/01/world/europe/poland-israel-holocaust.html.

10. Agassi, *Jewish Women Prisoners*, 166.

11. Agassi, *Jewish Women Prisoners*, 167.

12. Agassi, *Jewish Women Prisoners*, 167.

13. Hoffman, *After Such Knowledge*, 81.

14. Hoffman, *After Such Knowledge*, 82.

15. MEMORY

1. Hoffman, *After Such Knowledge*, 37.

2. Hoffman, *After Such Knowledge*, 99; Rosenberg, *Brief Stop*, 277, 283.

3. Hoffman, *After Such Knowledge*, 37–38, 40, 42–43, 46–47; Rosenberg, *Brief Stop*, 44. See
also Catherine Porter, "Canada Struggles as It Opens Its Arms to Victims of ISIS, March
16, 2018, www.nytimes.com/2018/03/16/world/canada/canada-refugees-yazidi.html.

4. Mary Rourke and Valerie J. Nelson, "Holocaust Memory Keeper," *Los Angeles
Times*, July 3, 2016.

5. Singer, "The Cafeteria," 27. The order of the sentences in this quote has been
changed from the original.

6. Hoffman, *After Such Knowledge*, 56, 60, 63–64, 69.

7. Children of survivors tended to report greater feelings of alienation than the
children in the control group. Survivors perceived their children as being more
disturbed than parents of the control group perceived their children. Children
of survivors appeared to be more dependent on their parents than members of
the control group, and also had more difficulty coping with problems. Epstein,
Children of the Holocaust, 182.

8. Shulevitz, "Science of Suffering"; see also Ian Brown, "The Holocaust's Long
Reach: Trauma Is Passed on to Survivor's Children," *Globe and Mail*, April
3, 2015, https://beta.theglobeandmail.com/life/the-holocausts-long-reach
-trauma-is-passed-on-to-survivors-children/article23793425/?ref=http://www
.theglobeandmail.com.

9. Shulevitz, "Science of Suffering."

10. Helen Thompson, "Study of Holocaust Survivors Finds Trauma Passed on to
Children's Genes," *The Guardian*, August 21, 2015, https://www.theguardian.com
/science/2015/aug/21/study-of-holocaust-survivors-finds-trauma-passed-on

-to-childrens-genes. Judith Shulevitz also notes that "the children of survivors [of catastrophic experiences] often have unusual levels of cortisol, a hormone released in response to stress." Shulevitz, "Science of Suffering." For a contrary position to the conclusions reached by the studies finding a physiological as well as psychological consequence to parental trauma, see Seema Yasmin "No, Trauma Is Not Inherited," *Dallas Morning News*, May 30, 2017, https://www.dallasnews.com/news/debunked/2017/05/30/trauma-inherited; "Experts Debunk Study that Found Holocaust Trauma Is Inherited," *Chicago Tribune*, June 9, 2017, www.chicagotribune.com/ . . . /ct-holocaust-trauma-not-inherited-20170609-story.html; Josie Glausiusz, "Doubts Arising about Claimed Epigenetics of Holocaust Trauma," *Haaretz*, April 30, 2017, https://www.haaretz.com/science-and-health/.premium-doubts-arising-about-claimed-epigenetics-of-holocaust-trauma-1.5466710.

11. Hoffman, *After Such Knowledge*, 189.
12. Hoffman, *After Such Knowledge*, 193.
13. Epstein, *Children of the Holocaust*; Hoffman, *After Such Knowledge*, 69, 62–63, 70-71.
14. Hoffman, *After Such Knowledge*, 63.
15. Hoffman, *After Such Knowledge*, 63, 89.
16. Hoffman, *After Such Knowledge*, 70–71; see also Hare, *Knuckle*, 53.

16. THE LAST CHAPTER

1. Hoffman, *After Such Knowledge*, 69.
2. Dostoyevsky, *House of the Dead*, chap. 1.
3. "Drop by drop, in sleep upon the heart, fall the laborious memories of pain; against one's will comes wisdom." Aeschylus, *Agamemnon*, 176–80.
4. Bazyler, *Holocaust Justice*, 64.
5. Bazyler, *Holocaust Justice*, 59–60; Rosenberg, *Brief Stop*, 104.
6. Bazyler, *Holocaust Justice*, 60, 64.
7. Bazyler, *Holocaust Justice*, 59.
8. Bazyler, *Holocaust Justice*, 66–69.
9. For a somewhat different account of the events surrounding the Krupp corporation's payments to former slave laborers, compare a book written with the financial support of the Alfried Krupp Foundation: James, *Krupp*, "Acknowledgments," 244.
10. Manchester, *Arms of Krupp*, 5.
11. The same evidence also revealed that the majority of companies had shown "little hesitation about making use of the system of slave labor." Hayes, *From Cooperation to Complicity*, 271. See also Herbert, *Hitler's Foreign Workers*, 154. They eagerly took full advantage of the grotesque opportunity by accepting cheap and plentiful forced workers of all ages. Manchester, *Arms of Krupp*, 5.
12. Bazyler, *Holocaust Justice*, 62.

13. Bazyler, *Holocaust Justice*, 78.

14. Longerich, *Himmler*, 729. See also Wulff, *Zodiac and Swastika*, 176; Persson, *Escape from the Third Reich*, 231–33.

15. Fest, *Inside Hitler's Bunker*, 94.

16. Fest, *Inside Hitler's Bunker*, 94; Longerich, *Himmler*, 729; Waller, *Devil's Doctor*, 188.

17. Fest, *Inside Hitler's Bunker*, 95. See also Richie, *Faust's Metropolis*, 596–98; Porter, *Kasztner's Train*, 294.

18. Fest, *Inside Hitler's Bunker*, 85–86, 95, based on a description by Hanna Reitsch, the companion of the Sixth Air Fleet General Ritter von Greim.

19. Waller, *Devil's Doctor*, 188; Fest, *Inside Hitler's Bunker*, 95.

20. Fest, *Inside Hitler's Bunker*, 94–95.

21. Richie, *Faust's Metropolis*, 599.

22. Longerich, *Himmler*, 730. See also Richie, *Faust's Metropolis*, 599.

23. Richie, *Faust's Metropolis*, 599–600.

24. Hitler's bunker had already become the setting for extraordinary scenes of surreal melodrama. As the military position became more and more dire, the nation's leader eerily issued impossible orders for the movement of nonexistent troops and tanks. As the head of state descended even deeper into discernible madness, "his face so distorted that it was barely recognizable," he blamed everyone else for his nation's military position. Ohler, *Blitzed*, 271.

25. Richie, *Faust's Metropolis*, 596, 598.

POSTSCRIPT

1. Powers, *Problem from Hell*, 52.

2. Convention on the Prevention and Punishment of the Crime of Genocide, art. 6, December 9, 1948, S. Treaty Doc., no. 81–15, 78 U.N.T.S. 277.

3. Powers, *Problem from Hell*, 55, 479–80; A. M. Rosenthal, "ON MY MIND; A Man Called Lemkin," *New York Times*, October 18, 1988, https://www.nytimes.com /1988/10/18/opinion/on-my-mind-a-man-called-lemkin.html; Goldman, "Man Who Made Genocide a Crime," 299. "If there is no judge and no judgement, then everything is arbitrary and Hitler, may his name perish, was right: force is the only law. Then it is normal to play with the skulls of small children and to order a father to dig a grave for himself and his family." Isaac Bashevis Singer, *Shadows on the Hudson*, 50.

4. Goldman, "Jew Who Met Himmler."

5. Hoffman, *After Such Knowledge*, 181.

BIBLIOGRAPHY

Aeschylus. *The Aeschylus of Agamemnon.* Translated by Louis MacNeice. New York: Harcourt, Brace, 1937.

Agassi, Judith Buber. *Jewish Women Prisoners of Ravensbrück.* Lubbock: Texas Tech University Press, 2014.

Allen, Martin. *Himmler's Secret War: The Covert Peace Negotiations of Heinrich Himmler.* New York: Carroll and Graf, 2005.

Batty, Peter. *The House of Krupp: The Steel Dynasty That Armed the Nazis.* New York: Cooper Square, 1969.

Bauer, Yehuda. *Jews for Sale? Nazi-Jewish Negotiations, 1933–1945.* New Haven CT: Yale University Press, 1994.

Bazyler, Michael J. *Holocaust Justice: The Battle for Restitution in America's Courts.* New York: New York University Press, 2003.

Bazyler, Michael J., and Frank M. Tuerkheimer. *Forgotten Trials of the Holocaust.* New York: New York University Press, 2014.

Beevor, Antony. *The Fall of Berlin 1945.* New York: Viking Penguin, 2002.

Bergen, Doris L. *War and Genocide: A Concise History of the Holocaust.* 2nd ed. Lanham MD: Rowman & Littlefield, 2009.

Blanket-Sulkowicz, Abraham. "Destruction of Brzezin." In *Brzeziny Memorial Book,* 140–43.

Breitman, Richard. *The Architect of Genocide: Himmler and the Final Solution.* New York: Random House, 1991.

Breitman, Richard, and Alan J. Lichtman. *FDR and the Jews.* Cambridge MA: Belknap Press of Harvard University Press, 2013.

Broszat, Martin. "The Concentration Camps." In *Anatomy of the ss State,* edited by Helmut Krausnick, 397–504. London: Collins, 1968.

Brzeziny Memorial Book. Edited by A. Alperin and N. Summer. New York: Brzeziner Book Committee, 1961. Online English edition translated by Renee Miller, edited by Fay Bussgang. https://www.jewishgen.org/yizkor/brzeziny/brz135.html.

Carlberg, Ingrid. *Raoul Wallenberg: The Heroic Life and Mysterious Disappearance of the Man Who Saved Thousands of Hungarian Jews from the Holocaust*. London: MacLehose Press, 2015.

Degrelle, Leon. *The Eastern Front: Memoirs of a Waffen SS Volunteer, 1941–1945*. Newport Beach CA: Institute for Historical Review, 2015.

Dobroszycki, Lucjan. *The Chronicle of the Lodz Ghetto*. New Haven CT: Yale University Press, 1984.

Domarus, Max. *Hitler, Reden und Proklamationen, 1932–1945*. Munich: Bolchazy-Carducci, 1998.

Dostoevsky, Fyodor. *The House of the Dead*. Translated by David McDuff. London: Penguin Books, 2003.

Dublon-Knebel, Irith, ed. *A Holocaust Crossroads: Jewish Women and Children in Ravensbrück*. London: Vallentine Mitchell, 2010.

Eidum, Epsen. *Blodsporet*. Oslo: Forlaget Kristiansen, 2012.

Einhorn, Lena. *Handelsresande I Liv: Om Vilja Och Vankelmod I Krigets*. Stockholm: Prisma, 1999.

———. *Menschenhandel Unterm Hakenkreuz*. Translated by Wolfgang Butt. Stuttgart: Klett-Cotta, 2002.

Epstein, Helen. *Children of the Holocaust: Conversations with Sons and Daughters of Survivors*. New York: G. P. Putnam's Sons, 1979.

Ferencz, Benjamin B., and Telford Taylor. *Less Than Slaves: Jewish Forced Labor and the Quest for Compensation*. Bloomington: Indiana University Press, 2002.

Fest, Joachim. *Inside Hitler's Bunker: The Last Days of the Third Reich*. Translated by Margot Dembo. New York: Farrar, Straus and Giroux 2004.

Fox, Frank. "A Jew Talks to Himmler." *St. Croix Review* 5 (October 2003): 29–37. http://www.stcroixreview.com/archives_nopass/2003-10/Fox.html. See also *Zwoje* [The Scrolls]. 2004. http://www.zwoje-scrolls.com/zwoje38/text18p.htm.

Frankl, Viktor E. *Man's Search for Meaning: An Introduction to Logotherapy*. New York: Pocket Books, 1963.

Friedman, Philip, and Ada June Friedman. "Pseudo-Saviors in the Polish Ghettos: Mordechai Chaim Rumkowski of Lodz." In *Roads to Extinction: Essays on the Holocaust*, 333–52. New York: Conference on Jewish Social Studies, Jewish Publication Society of America, 1980.

Gilbert, G. M. *Nuremberg Diary*. New York: Da Capo Press, 1947.

Goldhagen, Daniel Jonah. *Hitler's Willing Executioners: Ordinary Germans and the Holocaust*. New York: Random House, 1996.

Goldman, Stanley A. "The Jew Who Met Himmler, and Other Stories." *Loyola of Los Angeles International and Comparative Law Review* 32, no. 1 (Winter 2010): 1–18.

———. "The Man Who Made Genocide a Crime: The Legacy of Raphael Lemkin." *Loyola of Los Angeles International and Comparative Law Review* 34, no. 3 (Spring 2012): 295–300.

Gutman, Israel. "Introduction: The Distinctiveness of the Łódź Ghetto." In *Łódź Ghetto: A History*, by Isaiah Trunk. Translated and edited by Robert Moses Shapiro, xxix–lvii. Bloomington: Indiana University Press, 2006.

Hare, David. *Knuckle.* London: Samuel French, 1970.

Hayes, Peter. *From Cooperation to Complicity: Degussa in the Third Reich.* Cambridge: Cambridge University Press, 2005.

Helm, Sarah. *Ravensbrück: Life and Death in Hitler's Concentration Camp for Women.* New York: Nan A. Talese/Doubleday, 2014.

———. "The Swedish Schindler: How Count Bernadotte Saved Thousands of Jews from Death." *Newsweek,* May 14, 2015. http://www.newsweek.com/swedish-schindler-how-count-bernadotte-saved-thousands-jews-death-331778.

Hendler-Gocial, Rebecca. "The Brzeziner Jewish Community during the Time of the Ghetto." In *Brzeziny Memorial Book,* 156. https://www.jewishgen.org/yizkor/brzeziny/brz003.html.

Herbert, Urlich. *Hitler's Foreign Workers: Enforced Foreign Labor in Germany under the Third Reich.* Cambridge: Cambridge University Press, 1997.

Hewins, Ralph. *Count Folke Bernadotte: His Life and Work.* Chicago: T. S. Denison, 1950.

Hoess, Rudolf. *Commandant of Auschwitz: The Autobiography of Rudolf Hoess.* London: Phoenix Press, 2000.

Hoffman, Eva. *After Such Knowledge: Memory, History, and the Legacy of the Holocaust.* New York: Public Affairs, 2004.

Holocaust Encyclopedia. "Buchenwald." https://www.ushmm.org/wlc/en/article.php?ModuleId=10005198.

———. "Einsatzgruppen (Mobile Killing Units)." http://www.ushmm.org/wlc/article.php?lang=en&ModuleId=10005130.

———. "Genocide of European Roma (Gypsies), 1939–1945." https://www.ushmm.org/wlc/en/article.php?ModuleId=10005219.

Irons, Peter. *Justice at War: The Story of the American Japanese Internment Cases.* Oakland: University of California Press, 1983.

Jackel, Eberhard. "Forever in the Shadow of Hitler?" Translated by James Knowlton and Truett Cates. Atlantic Highlands NJ: Humanities Press, 1993. Originally published as "Die elende Praxis der Untersteller." In *Historikerstreit,* edited by Rudolf Augstein et al. München: Piper Verlag, 1987.

James, Harold. *Krupp: A History of the Legendary German Firm.* Princeton NJ: Princeton University Press, 2012.

Jangfeldt, Bengt. *The Hero of Budapest: The Triumph and Tragedy of Raoul Wallenberg.* Translated by Harry Watson. London: Palgrave MacMillan, 2014.

Kempowski, Walter. *Swansong 1945: A Collective Diary of the Last Days of the Third Reich.* Translated by Shaun Whiteside. New York: W.W. Norton, 2015.

Kershaw, Ian. "'Working towards the Fuhrer': Reflections on the Nature of the Hitler Dictatorship." *Contemporary European History* 2, no. 2 (July 1993): 103–18.

Kersten, Felix. *Memoirs of Doctor Felix Kersten.* New York: Doubleday, 1947.

Kessel, Joseph. *The Man with the Miraculous Hands.* New York: Farrar, Straus and Giroux, 1961.

Kittel, Sabine. "History and Politics of the Rescue of Jewish Prisoners by the Swedish Red Cross in the 'White Bus' Operation." In *A Holocaust Crossroads: Jewish Women and Children in Ravensbrück,* edited by Irith Dublon-Knebel, 221–40. London: Vallentine Mitchell, 2010.

———. "Liberation—Survival—Freedom: Jewish Prisoners of Ravensbrück Concentration Camp Recall Their Liberation." In *A Holocaust Crossroads: Jewish Women and Children in Ravensbrück,* edited by Irith Dublon-Knebel. London: Vallentine Mitchell, 2010.

Krausnick, Helmut, Martin Broszat, and Hans-Adolf Jacobsen. *Anatomy of the ss State.* London: Collins, 1968.

Lehmann, Armin D., and Tim Carroll. *In Hitler's Bunker: A Boy Soldier's Eyewitness Account of the Führer's Last Days.* Edinburgh: Mainstream, 2003.

Levai, Jeno. *Raoul Wallenberg: His Remarkable Life, His Heroic Battles and the Secret of His Mysterious Disappearance.* Melbourne: White Ant, 1989.

Lipson, Alfred, ed. *The Book of Radom: The Story of a Jewish Community in Poland Destroyed by the Nazis.* Yizkor Book Project and JewishGen, https://www.jewishgen.org/yizkor/radom/Radom.html#TOC20. Originally published as *Sefer Radom.* Edited by Y. Perlow and Alfred Lipson [English section]. Tel Aviv, 1961.

Lisciotto, Carmelo. "Chaim Mordechai Rumkowski." Holocaust Education & Archive Research Team, 2007. http://www.holocaustresearchproject.org/ghettos/rumkowski.html.

———. "Heinrich Himmler: 'Treue Heinrich.'" Holocaust Education & Archive Research Team, 2007. http://www.holocaustresearchproject.org/holoprelude/himmler.html.

Loewenberg, Peter. "The Unsuccessful Adolescence of Heinrich Himmler." *American Historical Review* 76, no. 3 (June 1971): 612–41.

Longerich, Peter. *Heinrich Himmler.* Translated by Jeremy Noakes and Leslie Sharpe. Oxford: Oxford University Press, 2012.

Manchester, William. *The Arms of Krupp: The Rise and Fall of the Industrial Dynasty That Armed Germany at War.* Boston: Little, Brown, 1968.

Masur, Norbert. *My Meeting with Himmler.* Stockholm: World Jewish Congress, 1945. https://ia801600.us.archive.org/23/items/NorbertMasurMyMeetingWithHeinrichHimmler/Norbert%20Masur%20My%20Meeting%20with%20Heinrich%20Himmler.pdf.

McNally, Brendan. "Walter Schellenberg: ss Spymaster Genius or Total Putz." *Nazis and Dinosaurs* (blog), November 26, 2012. http://brendanmcnallynazisanddinosaurs.blogspot.com/2012/11/walter-schellenberg-ss-spymaster-genius.html.

Melville, Herman. *Moby Dick*. Chicago: Encyclopedia Britannica, 1982.

Metzler, David. "Raoul Wallenberg." *Jewish Virtual Library*. http://www.jewishvirtuallibrary.org/raoul-wallenberg-3.

Miron, Guy. *The Yad Vashem Encyclopedia of Ghettos During the Holocaust*. Jerusalem: Yad Vashem, 2009.

Morag, Dvora Kovalsky, and Hadar Morag. "Thou Shalt Tell Your Daughter." https://www.youtube.com/watch?v=2RiYohnADlc.

Neumann, Boaz. *The National Socialist Weltanschauung: Space, Body, Language*. Tel Aviv: Haifa University Publishing House and Sifriat Ma'ariv, 2002 [Hebrew].

Nietzsche, Friedrich. *Twilight of the Idols*. Edited by Michael Tanner. Translated by R. J. Hollingdale. Westminster: Penguin Classics, 1990.

Ohler, Norman. *Blitzed: Drugs in Nazi Germany*. London: Penguin Random House UK, 2016.

Palmer, Raymond. "Felix Kersten and Count Bernadotte: A Question of Rescue." *Journal of Contemporary History* 29 (1994): 39–46.

Persson, Sune. *Escape from the Third Reich*. Barnsley UK: Frontline Books, 2009.

———. *Mediation and Assassination: Count Bernadotte's Mission to Palestine in 1948*. Berkshire UK: Ithaca Press, 1979.

Porat, Dina, and Saul Friedlander. *The Blue and the Yellow Stars of David: The Zionist Leadership in Palestine and the Holocaust, 1939–1945*. Cambridge MA: Harvard University Press, 1990.

Porter, Anna. *Kasztner's Train: The True Story of an Unknown Hero of the Holocaust*. London: Macmillan, 2008.

Powers, Samantha. *A Problem from Hell: America and the Age of Genocide*. New York: HarperCollins, 2002.

Richie, Alexandra. *Faust's Metropolis: A History of Berlin*. New York: Carroll and Graf, 1998.

Rosenberg, Göran. *A Brief Stop on the Road from Auschwitz*. Translated by Sarah Death. London: Granta, 2015.

Roth, Philip. *The Professor of Desire*. New York: Farrar, Straus and Giroux, 1977.

Ruben, Icchak-Henryk. *Żydzi w Łodzi pod niemiecką okupacją 1939–1945*. London: Kontra, 1988.

Rudberg, Pontus. *The Swedish Jews and the Holocaust*. Abingdon: Routledge, 2017.

Saidel, Rochelle. *The Jewish Women of Ravensbrück Concentration Camp*. Madison: University of Wisconsin Press, 2004.

Schellenberg, Walter. *The Labyrinth: Memoirs of Walter Schellenberg, Hitler's Chief of Counter Intelligence*. New York: Harper and Brothers, 1956.

Shaibowicz, Joseph. "Brzeziny in History." In *Brzeziny Memorial Book*, 3–20. https://www.jewishgen.org/yizkor/brzeziny/brz003.html.

Shakespeare, William. *The Complete Works of William Shakespeare,* 6th ed. Edited by David Bevington. Chicago: Pearson, 2009.

Shapiro, Robert Moses. "Translator-Editor's Introduction." In *Łódź Ghetto: A History,* by Isaiah Trunk, translated by Robert Moses Shapiro, xi–xx. Bloomington: Indiana University Press, 2006.

Shirer, William L. *The Rise and Fall of the Third Reich.* New York: Simon and Schuster, 1960.

Shulevitz, Judith. "The Science of Suffering." *New Republic,* November 16, 2014. https://newrepublic.com/article/120144/trauma-genetic-scientists-say-parents-are-passing-ptsd-kids.

Singer, Isaac Bashevis. "The Cafeteria," *New Yorker,* December 28, 1968, 27.

———. *The Family Moscat.* Translated by A. H. Gross. New York: Farrar, Straus and Giroux, 1978.

———. *Shadows on the Hudson.* New York: Farrar, Straus and Grioux, 1998.

Speer, Albert. *Infiltration: The SS and German Armament.* Translated by Joachim Neugroschel. London: Macmillan, 1981.

Speer, Albert, Richard Winston, Clara Winston, and Eugene Davidson. *Inside the Third Reich: Memoirs.* London: Macmillan, 1970.

Sterebe, Bernhard. "Ravensbrück—dos zentrale Frauenkonzentrationslager." In *Die Nationalsozialistichen Konzentrutionslager,* Entwicklung und Strucktur, edited by Ulrich Herber, Karin Orth, and Christoph Dieckmann. Gottinger: Wallstein, 1998.

Tatz, Colin, and Winston Higgins. *The Magnitude of the Genocide.* Santa Barbara CA: Praeger, 2016.

Tillion, Germaine. *Ravensbrück.* New York: Anchor Press, 1975.

Trevor-Roper, H. R. "The Strange Case of Himmler's Doctor Felix Kersten and Count Bernadotte." *Commentary,* April 1, 1957, 356–64. https://www.commentarymagazine.com/articles/the-strange-case-of-himmlers-doctorfelix-kersten-and-count-bernadotte/.

Twain, Mark. *Personal Recollections of Joan of Arc.* San Francisco: Ignatius, 1989.

Urquhart, Brian. "Introduction." In *Escape from the Third Reich,* by Sune Persson. Barnsley UK: Frontline Books, 2009.

Wachsmann, Nikolaus. *KL: A History of the Nazi Concentration Camps.* New York: Farrar, Straus and Giroux, 2015.

Wagener, Otto, and Henry Ashby Turner. *Hitler—Memoirs of a Confidant.* New Haven CT: Yale University Press, 1985.

Waller, John H. *The Devil's Doctor: Felix Kersten and the Secret Plot to Turn Himmler against Hitler.* Hoboken NJ: Wiley, 2002.

Warhaft, Dr. S. "I Saw the Destruction of Our Shtetl." In *Brzeziny Memorial Book*, 135–39. https://www.jewishgen.org/yizkor/brzeziny/brz003.html.

Weitz, Yechiam. *The Man Who Was Murdered Twice: The Life, Trial and Death of Israel Kasztner*. Translated by Chaya Naor. 1995. Reprint, Jerusalem: Yad Vashem, 2011.

Wiesel, Elie. *Night*. New York: Hill and Wang, 2006.

Wistrich, Robert S. *Hitler and the Holocaust*. New York: Modern Library, 2003.

Wulff, Wilhelm. *Zodiac and Swastika: How Astrology Guided Hitler's Germany*. New York: Coward, McCann & Geoghegan, 1973.

Wyman, David S. *The Abandonment of the Jews*. New York: Pantheon, 1984.

Yad Vashem Collection of Testimonies. Holocaust Resource Center. Yad Vashem, Jerusalem.

Young, Gordon. *The Fall and Rise of Alfried Krupp*. London: Cassell, 1960.

Zagon-Winer, Dora. "I Saw the Destruction." In *Brzeziny Memorial Book*, 147–48.

Zuckerman, Lawrence. "FDR's Jewish Problem." *The Nation*, August 5–12, 2013. https://www.thenation.com/article/fdrs-jewish-problem/.